Building Anti-Fragile Organisations

This book is dedicated to Charmaine,
who taught me the true need to be Anti-Fragile.

Building Anti-Fragile Organisations

Risk, Opportunity and Governance in a Turbulent World

TONY BENDELL
Services Limited and The Anti-Fragility Academy

Routledge
Taylor & Francis Group

LONDON AND NEW YORK

First published 2014 by Gower Publishing

2 Park Square, Milton Park, Abingdon, Oxon OX14 4RN
711 Third Avenue, New York, NY 10017, USA

Routledge is an imprint of the Taylor & Francis Group, an informa business

First issued in paperback 2016

Gower Applied Business Research
Our programme provides leaders, practitioners, scholars and researchers with thought provoking, cutting edge books that combine conceptual insights, interdisciplinary rigour and practical relevance in key areas of business and management.

British Library Cataloguing in Publication Data
A catalogue record for this book is available from the British Library

ISBN 978-1-4724-1388-8 (hbk)
ISBN 978-1-138-27277-4 (pbk)

Library of Congress Cataloging-in-Publication Data
Bendell, A.
  Building anti-fragile organisations : risk, opportunity and governance in a turbulent world / by Tony Bendell.
    pages cm
  Includes bibliographical references and index.
  ISBN 978-1-4724-1388-8 (hardback)
1. Organizational change. 2. Organizational behavior. 3. Management. 4. Risk management. I. Title.

  HD58.8.B4585 2014
  658.4'06--dc23
                                                    2013048215

Contents

List of Figures

List of Tables

About the Author

Professor Tony Bendell is committed to making organisations less fragile and more anti-fragile. This was the rationale behind his establishment of The Anti-Fragility Academy in 2012, for whom he acts as Lead Trainer. He is distinguished for, amongst other qualities, an incisive intellect that draws him to innovative thinking and its application to his field, an infectious passion about business improvement, and an idiosyncratic sense of humor. These are all qualities that lie behind his quest to bring Anti fragility into the practical domain of business and entrepreneurship. He is also an international expert speaker, consultant and trainer with extensive experience in the fields of Quality Management, Organisational Excellence, Lean Operations and Six Sigma, sharing views that are always stimulating, challenging and of practical importance, making him a well-known invited keynote speaker at conferences and events worldwide.

A respected academic, he has visiting remits at the BPP Business School and Middlesex and Coventry universities. Formerly he has held posts as the Rolls-Royce funded Professor of Quality and Reliability Management at the University of Leicester, UK, and previously the East Midlands Electricity Professor of Quality. Tony has had both an outstanding academic career and an extensive professional consultancy role at the highest level within both manufacturing and service organisations and the public sector. Clients have included the UK Ministry of Justice, Edexcel, the BBC, Citibank, the UAE Oil and Gas industry and numerous Local Government, police and related bodies. He is a leading figure in the UK and internationally in quality and productivity improvement, and in the excellence and public sector transformation movements. In this arena he has fought for the implementation of Lean as an alternative to the current climate of 'slash and burn' in public services. He has published extensively and is principal author of the best-selling *Financial Times* book *Benchmarking for Competitive Advantage*, which is available in six languages.

Tony has always been at the forefront of business and public sector innovation and practice. He was a major contributor to the UK National Quality Campaign and the Managing in the 90s programmes. He currently chairs the MS6 Technical Committee of BSI, which did most of the development work on the creation of the ISO 13053 international Six Sigma standard and is working on a new ISO auditable international standard for Six Sigma and Lean. He also chairs the Royal Statistical Society Quality Improvement Section. He has experience in advising and mentoring senior managers and board members to the highest level.

He is married and lives and works from his home in rural Nottinghamshire, where his consultancy company Services Limited is based.

Foreword

Anti-fragility has always engrossed and enthralled the human race. The perpetual quest for agelessness and immortality is witness to this. Individuals, corporates, societies and nations have all been looking to mitigate the risks of the unpredictable, even as randomness is becoming increasingly prevalent in the scheme of most of the things we do and we get.

Peter L. Bernstein, in his remarkable book on the story of risk, *Against the Gods*, writes that there is a persistent tension between those who assert that the best decisions are based on quantification and numbers drawn from past data, and those who base their decisions on more subjective degrees of belief about the uncertain future. As Bernstein rightly wrote, we cannot quantify the future because it is unknown. Mathematical models fail when ambiguity of facts obliterate them.

Risk Management in banking is a great case study of shifting models, experimentations and failures. With the possible exception of the postulation of Markowitz, which brought to the fore concentration risk, and which most banks have successfully implemented in order to avoid massive losses, most of the theories and models have shown cracks and demise. Nonetheless, the banking sector and the theorists have not given up the research on finding more and better ways of managing unpredictability. As the world of banking has become multidimensional, multivariate and multidisciplinary with interplays defying predictable patterns and transmissions, anti-fragility as a discipline is taking roots, competing, complementing and at times replacing traditional Risk Management. Like any evolving subject, it began as a philosophical postulation. However, practitioners have quickly stepped in and academics have started exploring the subject, mapping the branches of anti-fragility with traditional Risk Management ideas and finding practical ways of implementing this evolving subject and discipline. Professor Tony Bendell's book is a creditable step in this direction.

Before I deal with anti-fragility, and the possibilities that the book in your hand offers, let me remind all readers that, as leaders, our constant goal is: 'How to make smarter decisions.' All of us take bets as we decide.

When it comes to strategic decisions, these are generally high-risk bets because they affect the organisation financially, affect the morale of people and the interest of shareholders. Increasingly, the vast majority of our decisions are being taken in situations where a clear causal model is not available. In other words, we may know what the critical success factors are but, in nearly all cases, we do not have the complete picture. If a bank is introducing a new retail product, its effect on competition, the reaction of the competition and emergence of new factors and their causal relationships are often not predictable, creating fragility. Operational excellence and operational Risk Management, study of multiple tools, decongesting organisational processes and removing cognitive biases are all part of the anti-fragility discipline and this book deals with them in various chapters. Often, delaying a decision could be the best anti-fragility measure and not to take any decision at all could be the best decision.

A foreword to a book on anti-fragility would not be complete without a reference to the work of Nassim Nicholas Taleb. The subtitle of his book *Antifragile* is 'How to live in a world we don't understand'. Many times, reading a book backwards aids one's understanding of it. Taleb's book ends with chapters on the ethical aspects of anti-fragility. He summarises, 'Everything gains or loses from volatility. Fragility is what loses from volatility and uncertainty.' He goes on to argue that fragility is good for life and absorbing the true import of it. In his words, 'The best way to verify that you are alive is by checking if you like variations. Remember that food would not have a taste if it weren't for hunger; results are meaningless without effort, joy without sadness, convictions without uncertainty, and an ethical like isn't so when stripped of personal risks.'

In the world of banking (and for most of the other fields) there are too many uncertainties. Whether banking as we know it will survive is being debated because the measures of volatility and uncertainty have failed to hold. Capital as the omnibus prescription of anti-fragility is either untenable or unsustainable because of its limited supply or because no one knows how much is enough. In such a circumstance, an investment in knowing anti-fragility is probably the best bet. At the end of everything, we have to decide and make judgements. Warren Bennis writes, 'Judgement is the core, and judgement regularly trumps experience.' Judgement requires a simultaneous view of the recorded past and randomly happening future. In business, as in managing fragility, organisation, structure, procedures and machinery are all important but at the end of it everything is judged on the end call. That end call, for most of us, cannot be guaranteed to succeed every time. However, knowledge of anti-fragility, knowledge that things defy linear thinking, knowledge that despite all modern tools we may not succeed with predicting stuff, will be of help.

I congratulate Professor Tony Bendell on this work.

Mrutyunjay Mahapatra
Regional Head
State Bank of India
London

Preface

This book aims to change how you think about management and organisations. No longer will you think primarily about *efficiency* and *effectiveness*, instead you will focus on the *fragility* of organisations, and how we can design and manage them to build in the ability for them to get stronger over time, as they are subject to stress. Anti-fragility is a major paradigm shift, and as such hard to accomplish, but necessary as the pursuit of efficiency itself often causes fragility.

The failure of our organisations has a high human cost, in terms of wasting money, resources, and human ability, motivation and optimism. It also, on occasion, causes trauma. The Darwinists argue that such failures are necessary to allow natural selection to identify the strong, the successful business models that will grow and prosper. It also helps to develop our entrepreneurs, but at what cost? But what if we can strengthen from birth the whole population of organisations, not just this generation, but all future generations? Wouldn't it be worth doing it? More importantly, wouldn't you want to do it to your organisations, organisations which, in one way or another, you have a stake? By doing so we would be helping your organisations to succeed and, if all organisations did it, we'd be ensuring that the future organisations as a whole will be stronger than those in the past.

Would this change our competitive business model, based on survival of the fittest? It would. Just as public hygiene and basic healthcare have increased all our life expectancies and given some of the weak a chance to live, participate and contribute, so too would this approach to organisational hygiene and healthcare increase the life length of our organisations, and reduce the waste of resources. As with us, however, all organisations are different, and will continue to vary in strength, potential and longevity.

Is it possible to achieve this, to reduce the fragility of our organisations, increase their robustness and even make our organisations anti-fragile? The answer is yes. This book explores how to do this, to think out of the box, outside of the limitations of current paradigms. It explores all aspects of the organisational changes necessary. But fundamental change has a prerequisite of belief; you have to believe in the goal, the vision, you have to believe it possible, you have to convince others, you have to see it through. Then you have to learn, and keep learning, as you implement.

Good luck on your journey.

Tony Bendell
September 2013

Acknowledgements

This book would not have been possible without the support of my colleagues, Charmaine Roche and Jenny Levers, both of whom I owe a great thank you. Thank you too to the small emerging group of Anti-fragility practitioners and theorists who have looked at Anti-fragility from different perspectives and added to my thoughts. Thank you in advance for reading this book and propagating its messages.

Chapter 1
Developing an Anti-Fragile Organisation

How Fragility Hurts Organisations of All Types and How it Can be Avoided, Managed and Reduced

Human organisations are fragile. And to some extent rightly so; such micro-level fragility reflects an underlying diversity of approaches, forms and business models that enables the natural selection of successful organisations through a Darwinian process. As such it contributes to the common good, the overall success of the economy and the society. But fragility comes at a price. At the macro-level it clearly wastes resources, whilst at the micro-level it represents major cost and loss to the stakeholders. In addition, fragility does not always kill the organisation outright; it may leave a human organisation struggling on with inherent weakness, a chronically ill sufferer, implying ongoing pain and waste of further resources and human energy, before the inevitable end. It may also endanger other human organisations, and even on occasion the whole macro-system.

It is without doubt also true that some organisations are more fragile than others. In retrospect, we can identify the points of fragility, the dimensions of weakness that underlie the inevitable failure and demise of the losers. We may predict the likelihood of such unfortunate fates, but typically without certainty. Fate is fickle, and human organisations, like humans themselves, are surprisingly resilient and adaptive. This is their intrinsic anti-fragility, but recent history has reflected what we have long known, that reliance on such inherent strength alone is not enough.

Further, in this Darwinian world, just because a human organisation was appropriate for survival yesterday, alas does not mean that its intrinsic features are appropriate for survival today. Changes in the external or internal environment may well mean that its suitability, its adaption to purpose, is short lived. The magnitude and frequency of such changes may be said to have increased dramatically in recent decades, and are showing no signs of diminishing.

A Google of the phrase 'list of high profile organisational failures' yields about 52,300,000 results and, as we know well, the resultant articles yield some very well-known names... The Equitable Life Assurance Society, Trans World Airlines, Enron, Home Base, One Tel, Polaroid Corporation, Sabena, Bethlehem Steel, World Championship Wrestling, Arthur Anderson, Claims Direct, Jensen Motors, Railtrack, Swissair, Alders, West Coast Computers, Unwins, Golden Wonder, Tower Records, Scarborough Football Club, Terra Securities, Sentinel Management Group, Dolcis Shoes, Lehman Brothers, Sterling Airlines, The Officers Club, Woolworth Group, Crabtree and Evelyn, Land of Leather, Viyella, Waterford Wedgewood, Habitat, Comet Group, JJB Sports PLC and Jessops.

This is not just a new phenomenon, although it may be seen to be accelerating; Laker Airways, Triumph Engineering, Sinclair Vehicles, Jet Records, American Saving and Loan Association, British Satellite Broadcasting, Eastern Airlines, Polly Peck International, Pan American World Airways, State Bank of Victoria, Aldershot Football Club, Norton Motorcycle Company, Maxwell Communications Corporation, Windsor Safari Park, Ferranti, Athena, Commodore International, Barings Bank, Fokker, the Theatre Royal Henley, F.W. Woolworth Company, and of course many more, all evidence this. Some evidence for the acceleration is provided by Professor Richard Foster from Yale University who states that the average lifespan of a company listed in the Standard and Poor's 500 index (S&P) of leading US companies has decreased by more than 50 years in the last century, from 67 years in the 1920s to just 15 years today. Professor Foster estimates that by 2020, more than three-quarters of the S&P 500 will be companies that we have not heard of yet. Indeed, there is no real proof that age makes a company any more profitable than younger companies; evidence from the stockmarket suggests that age could be a hindrance. If the S&P 500 were made up of only the companies that were part of the index in 1957, overall performance would be some 20 per cent worse. The immediate causes of failure are numerous; changing markets, simple insolvency, corporate crime, inability to adapt.

And yet, as we partially know from the emergent concept of High Reliability Organisations (HROs), this fragility can be tamed (see for example, LaPorte, 1996). Whilst there have been numerous recent failures of ostentatiously iconically secure human organisations (see for example Hubbard, 2009) we still have some apparently secure, unassailable, entities (see for example, Joyce, Nitin and Robertson, 2003 and Kanda, 2012). These include the HROs – defined as organisations that have succeeded in avoiding catastrophes in environments where normally high-impact incidents can be expected due to risk factors and complexity. The origins of the HRO concept were developed by a group of researchers at the University of California, Berkeley who examined aircraft carriers, the Federal Aviation Administration's Air Traffic Control system and nuclear power operations. An initial conference at the University of Texas in April 1987 brought researchers together to focus attention on HROs. Further research has examined the fire incident command system, Loma Linda Hospital's Paediatric Intensive Care Unit and the California Independent System Operator.

Whilst diverse, these organisations have similarities. They operate in demanding social and political environments, their technologies are risky and have potential for error, and the scale of possible consequences from errors or mistakes precludes learning through experimentation. To avoid failures, these organisations use complex processes to manage complex technologies and work. HROs also share many characteristics with other high-performing organisations including highly skilled and trained employees, continuous training, effective reward systems, frequent process audits and Continuous Improvement activities. Other characteristics may be more distinctive; an organisation-wide sense of vulnerability, a widely distributed sense of responsibility and accountability for reliability, widespread concern about misperception, misconception and misunderstanding, pessimism about possible failures, redundancy in operational safeguards and a variety of checks and counter checks as a precaution against potential mistakes. Such organisations appear to have many characteristics of anti-fragility. These are:

- the ability to learn fast in an emergency, to contain it, and apply their learning;

- preoccupation with failure;

- reluctance to simplify interpretations;

- sensitivity to operations;

- commitment to resilience;

- deference to expertise.

Further evidence that fragility can be beaten is available from Japan. According to the credit rating agency Tokyo Shoko Research, there are more than 20,000 companies in Japan that are more than 100 years old, with a handful that are more than 1,000 years old. There is even a specific word for long-lived companies in

Japanese: *shinise*. Professor Makoto Kanda, who has studied *shinise* for decades, argues that Japanese companies can survive so long because they are small, mostly family-run, and because they focus on a central belief or credo that is not solely tied to making profit. He argues that the *shinise* focus primarily on the Japanese market, from Kikkoman's products to small sake manufacturers, and that they benefit from a corporate culture that has long avoided the mergers and acquisitions that are common among their western counterparts.

Despite this, do we really believe that, regardless of all the organisational failures, we still have some apparently secure, unassailable, entities? We now doubt even this. But, our most successful human organisations do appear, at least in part, to somehow, to some extent, know the secret, so why can't others? How can we avoid, manage and reduce the slings and arrows of outrageous fortune for our organisational and common good? This is not just about being robust against unexpected occurrences, but also to systematically learn and grow in strength from them.

The concept of *double loop learning*, due to Chris Argyris, gives us some insight into this ability to learn demonstrated by successful organisations. By using double loop learning, an individual or organisation is able, having attempted to achieve a goal on previous occasions, to modify the goal in the light of experience, or possibly even reject the goal. This should be contrasted with single loop learning, which is the repeated attempt at the same problem, often with no variation of method and without ever questioning the goal. Double loop learning is part of an anti-fragile organisation.

So it is, that this book is dedicated to the study of the development of anti-fragility in organisations, and how to build anti-fragile organisations.

The Concept of Anti-Fragility

I have always known about the concept of anti-fragility, but did not know it. Anti-fragility is more than robustness, since the robust purely waits for a big enough tide to overcome it. In contrast, the anti-fragile grows stronger with each tide, each challenge and each threat. The same latent familiarity with this idea is undoubtedly also true for you.

My revelation came at the Hay on Wye Book Festival in 2012, when Nassim Taleb spoke remotely about the concept from a New York coffee bar. Taleb's discussion, and his subsequent fat, insightful but puzzling book was primarily macro. Through storytelling, analogy and metaphor, it focused on the big ideas, the big global systems, like the financial markets, that determine all our fates. This was not primarily my world, although I have, and do, delve into it. My world is primarily focused at the level of the firm, of the human organisation, private sector, public sector or voluntary, that may or may not recognise that it lives in troubling times, and may be in need of help. How should such a human organisation equip itself, manage itself and conduct itself to survive and thrive?

According to Taleb, organisations and systems may be Fragile, Robust or Anti-Fragile:

- *Fragile* refers to systems and organisations that can be easily damaged by changes or shocks in the external or internal environment.

- *Robust* refers to systems and organisations that are able to withstand such adverse conditions.

- *Anti-Fragile* refers to systems and organisations that, like biological systems, are more than just robust and within limits actually improve their resilience through being stressed.

In considering these definitions for an organisation, we must see them in the context of the achievement of the organisation's objectives.

My particular interest in the micro-level of activity is threefold. In recent years, as a business school academic, I have long been disappointed at the lack of a coherent theory of, and approach to, the organisation. No current business school discipline, whether it is Strategy, Operations Management, Human Resource Management, Financial Management, or more recently Enterprise Risk Management (ERM), fully provides an unification to describe or study the human organisation as a whole, with all the ramifications and complexities that will determine its success or failure, life or death. The potential of anti-fragility is that it can provide just that; a unification of governance, human, resource and system infrastructure within an organisation-wide wrapper of development and survivability. Hence we can now meaningfully think of an anti-fragile theory of the firm to unify our hitherto disparate functional approaches to the human organisation.

The second new perspective that anti-fragility offers to me is linked to my now predominate role as an expert, trainer and consultant in Organisational

Change, Quality Management, Improvement, Leanness, Six Sigma and Excellence. In this regard, it is absolutely apparent that the approaches to improvement that the management of change community have been using up to this point in time are, at best, partial solutions to what is in essence an unified issue; how to ensure the continued and continuing anti-fragility of the human organisation. This is something that we all sensed and recognised, but until the emergence of anti-fragility did not have a language for. Whist anti-fragility is not the highest-level objective conceivable for the firm, it is higher than profitability, waste minimisation, customer satisfaction, variation reduction or a weighted sum of criteria scores in one of the popular models of excellence. Such models, such as the EFQM Excellence Model, for which the European Foundation for Quality Management (EQFM) is the guardian and I am a licensed trainer, have much resonance with the anti-fragility concept, but lack both the explicit minimal governance safeguards and the justification of weighting to be seen currently as universal models of anti-fragility.

The third new perspective is linked to the previous two. Initially trained as a business statistician, whilst teaching at university I spent a large part of my early career doing research using often complex stochastic models to describe, study and optimise real world phenomena, such as equipment usage, reliability and preventive replacement. As is typically the case, optimisation was based upon maximising usage, loading or efficiency. Anti-fragility calls to our attention the unwelcome truth that local optimisation often causes problems, and optimised systems are often fragile; for example Taleb uses examples of Heathrow Airport or New York traffic. By being heavily laden up to capacity, the chances are that the system will fail more frequently and dramatically than if it contains some slack. Thus we are optimising the wrong objective function; it should not be efficiency, but anti-fragility, with a side constraint of a minimum efficiency level, that we optimise. Optimising efficiency alone will give the wrong answer. For example, if we apply Lean Operations approaches to our processes to remove non-value adding activities or minimise throughput time or cost, or maximise utilisation, without fully considering the impact on system or organisational fragility, this may result in 'hard-wired' inflexible inagile systems, or optimally utilised heavily loaded systems that are so stretched to exploit their maximum capacity that they cannot cope with any disruptions or further load increases, and hence may fail catastrophically. In Chapter 4 we will develop the difference between the Fragile Lean and Anti-Fragile Lean models.

Each of the three new perspectives above represents a profound paradigm shift from current thinking and practice. Clearly, the concept of anti-fragility challenges our current thinking, analysis and interventions.

What We Can Learn from Nature

It is likely that the desire to see anti-fragility as a normal feature and objective of human organisations comes largely from the analogue of nature. Herbert Spencer's Darwinian ideas of survival of the fittest (Spencer, 1884) have long been used in the business world as an analogue for competitive markets, although with considerable debate. With anti-fragility, we can see something of the mechanism whereby the fittest get fitter, and hence survive and dominate. By exercising, by stressing my system, I can get stronger; but it all depends on how and when I do this in relation to my current physical and mental state. Too much exercise, or too severe, will harm me rather than help me. Too little will not be enough to adequately develop me for what's to come. Thus improving resilience through being stressed requires an innate or conscious mechanism whereby proportionality to the Current State is identified and exercised, and updated as the Current State accordingly develops. Within this range of proportionality, we can move at a faster speed by optimising the exercise regime within the practical constraints. Of course, we cannot optimise the uncontrollable natural environment.

But is it the right kind of exercise? Nature provides further guidance. As the environment changes, adaptability, possibility through a population whose members have collective strength through diversity, will depend upon which characteristics are important to survival in the particular realised circumstances and whether these exist within the population. This multiple dimensional requirement, possibly with very high dimensionality, may mean that the exercise turns out retrospectively to be of the wrong sort; something that we cannot eliminate with any certainty, but we can establish precautionary principles to try and protect ourselves against. A range of exercises, exercising most parts of the body and designed to meet the needs of a wide range of foreseeable threats, is to be preferred to a rigid one-dimensional programme.

But we are forgetting chance. Unpopular as it is to include an element of randomness in our model of survivability, the reality is that circumstances ('events, dear boy, events' to quote Harold MacMillan) will have a profound influence on organisational survivability. The model works in expectation only, not in relation to every member of the population, so we can spread our risk by deliberate duplication as well as diversity. In nature, redundancy, in the form of a duplicated organ, often appears as a form of robustness, if not anti-fragility. For human organisations, the scale of duplication and diversity should be determined by the risks. We shall discuss risk in Chapter 2.

There is learning in nature too. In addition to adaptability through natural selection across diversity, adaptability is created through individual entities learning to do, not do, or do differently things that have gone well or badly for them before. The spreading of the learning by communication across family members, or natural groups, adds to this process. Learning is a key to anti-fragility.

The Relationship to Current Holistic Organisational Models and Analysis Methods

As indicated above, in the university business schools there has been an absence of coherent holistic theories for human organisations. Rather, the emphasis has been on functional management, with Strategy, Finance, Human Resource Management or even ERM claiming the overall organisational unification.

Nevertheless, there are a number alternative holistic organisational models and analysis methods in professional use, with varying coverage, content and usage. The most popular of these are probably:

- ISO 9001;

- Excellence Models:
  - EFQM Excellence Model;
  - Malcolm Baldrige National Quality Award Model;
  - Deming Prize Model;

- The McKinsey 7 S Model;

- The Deloitte's Layer Model;

- Soft Systems Thinking.

In this and the following section of this chapter we shall discuss these from an anti-fragile perspective.

Generally, the so-called Excellence Models represent more anti-fragile aspirations for human organisations than does the international Quality Management standard, ISO 9001, and its related international standards. Of these, there are three models which have some real level of global recognition; the EFQM Excellence Model based in Europe, the Malcolm Baldrige National Quality Award Model based in the US, and the Deming Prize Model of Japan.

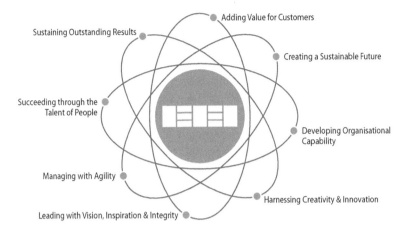

The EFQM Fundamental Concepts of Excellence

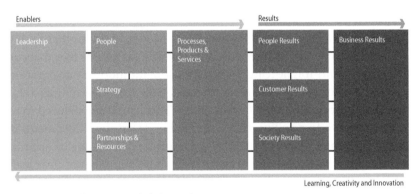

The EFQM Excellence Model Criteria

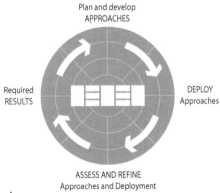

The RADAR mechanism

Figure 1.1   The EFQM Excellence Model

Source: www.efqm.org.

Each of these models, and the various alternatives and hybrids around the world, attempts to capture the essence of the human organisation in a coherent assessment framework based on clearly defined criteria covering the organisations' approaches, their deployment, and their assessment and refinement, as well as the adequacy of the results so achieved.

The EFQM Excellence Model depicted in Figure 1.1 is typical, and may be used as an illustration. Owned by the European Foundation for Quality Management based in Brussels, and with partner organisations across Europe and further afield, this has nine criteria, and 32 sub-criteria, and is based on eight fundamental concepts, as well the so-called RADAR mechanism. This stands for Results, Approach, Deployment, Assessment and Refinement; representing the stages of identifying targeted results to be achieved, developing approaches to deliver these, deploying these, and assessing and refining them as necessary.

It can be argued that the EFQM Excellence Model, and the other Excellence Models referred to, are fundamentally anti-fragile in nature, as they incorporate a number of key anti-fragile features. Firstly, use of the model by an organisation is typically based on self-assessment principles, to facilitate learning and change, hence increasing organisational anti-fragility. This has been enhanced in recent years by the move to a rolling easily updatable description document, based on so-called Enabler Maps, so that the organisation can update its approaches coherently in real time. The model also incorporates a number of clear learning loops, achieved through the application of the RADAR mechanism across the criteria. The model shows explicit consideration and balance across the stakeholder groups, has clear measurement, ideally on a frequent basis, and this covers the quality and deployment of the Leadership, Strategy, People, Partnership and Resources, and Processes, Products and Services provided, as well as the Results achieved for all stakeholder groups. The whole model is also reviewed and improved on a two-year cycle, using learning obtained from users. When the model was revised in 2013, the need to transition from a disciplined to an agile corporate culture was identified, with a view to spur organisations to build more flexible corporate structures.

However, the model unfortunately does not specify any explicit minimal governance safeguards for recognition, rather than working on an aggregate score. This is a significant disadvantage from an anti-fragile perspective, as it means high-scoring organisations can have major fragility in particular areas, but be 'all right on average'. Clearly, they would still then be fragile. Further, the model uses a consensus set of weightings across criteria, which is not based on anti-fragility considerations.

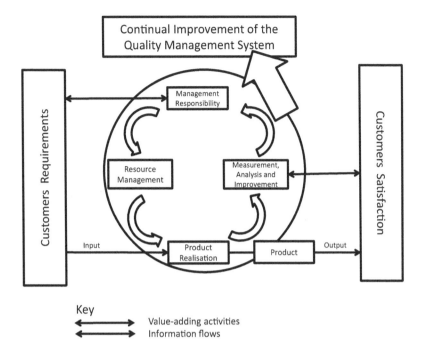

Key
⟷ Value-adding activities
⟷ Information flows

Figure 1.2   The ISO 9001 Process Model
Source: Based on ISO 9001 (2008).

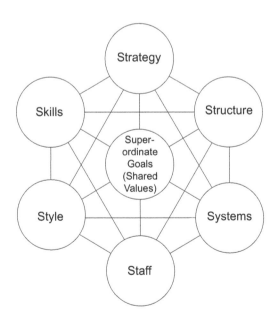

Figure 1.3   The 7 S Model
Source: Peters (2011).

Similar to the models of excellence, the international Quality Management system standard ISO 9001, and the analogous international environmental management, and occupational health and safety management, system standards ISO 14001 and OHSAS18001, incorporate formalised learning and improvement loops, which are by definition an anti-fragile feature (see Figure 1.2). They also involve organisational self-audit by independent personnel, leading to management review and action. The management representative for quality, typically the quality manager, also has a line of reporting to top management, to facilitate executive action when needed. However, in these standards more emphasis is placed on rule-based compliance, so that potentially they are more fragile systems, although this is to some extent mitigated by the extent of interpretation of rules possible.

Like the above models, the McKinsey 7 S Model depicted in Figure 1.3 has reached the business schools and, although it does not provide a coherent holistic theory for the human organisation, it does provide insight into linkages sufficient to assist the organisation to:

- improve performance;

- examine the likely effects of possible changes;

- align departments and processes during a merger or acquisition;

- determine how best to implement a proposed strategy.

The model was developed by Robert Waterman and Tom Peters, and is inherently robust if not anti-fragile in that it is based on a theory that recognises that for a human organisation to perform well, the seven named elements need to be aligned and mutually reinforcing.

The Deloitte's Layer Model (as show in Figure 1.4) is to an extent similar, in that it provides a unified representation of the human organisation to assist selection of strategic choices. Again, the linkages imply that it is robust though not necessarily anti-fragile.

Like the McKinsey 7 S Model, this depends on how it is used. If either model is used in a repeated learning and improvement cycle, it is anti-fragile, whilst if it is used only for a one-off analysis and improvement it is at best a robust feature.

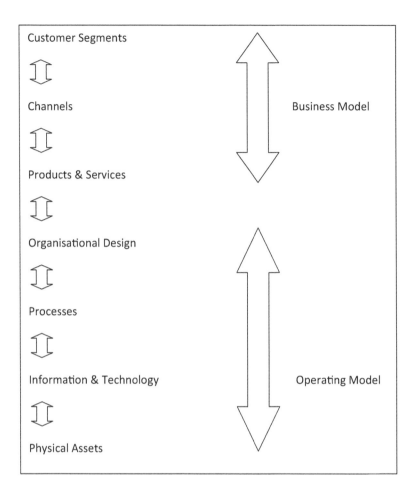

Figure 1.4   Deloitte's Layer Model
Source: Deloitte (2014).

In reality, all of the above holistic organisational models and analysis methods may, in practice, be subject to additional practical dangers of fragility than the above discussion suggests, as it is in their implementation within a human organisation that further fragility is introduced. For example, whilst it is not a feature of the ISO 9001 standard itself, there are many poor implementations within human organisations in which the system as implemented has little to do with the organisation's activities and processes, having been imported and imposed. This will create fragility, as will bureaucratic systems, largely delegated to middle and lower management with little executive management ownership, awareness and participation, and non-involvement of operational personnel.

The Place of Soft Systems Thinking

Of all the holistic organisational models and analysis methods in current use, Soft Systems Thinking is probably of greatest importance in the consideration of anti-fragility. This is because Soft Systems Thinking can provide considerable insight into the working of anti-fragile mechanisms within human organisations.

Typically, Soft Systems Thinking is useful in the context of systems involving human beings, where often we cannot even easily agree what the optimisation issue is, but instead need to consider conflicting stakeholder perspectives, or holons. It is focused on the complexity, causality and mutual dependence that exists amongst many variables. Rather than postulating structure and dissecting the elements of the organisation (methods which themselves imply some fragility) as in the previously described organisational models and analysis methods, instead Soft Systems Thinking focuses on the total linked systems and takes a universal view.

To understand the anti-fragile nature of Soft Systems Thinking, one needs to understand its partial origins from within the Hard Systems Thinking world. This is the world of Systems Analysis, Management Science, Structured Methods and Operations Research. Typically, such Hard Systems approaches assume that the problems associated with systems are well defined and have a single optimum solution, and that a scientific approach to problem solving will work well, and technical factors will tend to predominate.

During the 1970s, the effectiveness of the Hard Approaches was seriously challenged. The failure of Management Science and Operations Research was strongly debated by various authors including Churchman and Ackoff in the US, and Checkland in the UK (Ackoff and Emery, 1972; Churchman, 1982; Berente, 2007; Triarchy Press, 2014; Lancaster University Management School, 2014). The basis of the argument was that in situations in which the problem is not well defined, the Hard Approaches did not offer a suitable methodology. The Hard Approach works well when the problem and objectives we want to achieve were well defined but in situations when the 'problem' itself is not clear, the Hard Approaches fail to give useful insights. Peter Checkland argues that this is mainly because these approaches see the situation as an engineering problem; looking at 'how to do things' when 'what to do' is already defined (Checkland, 2010; Checkland and Haynes, 2006). Thus, when these methods were applied in social systems, for example to the public sector in California State in the early 1960s, the results were disappointing.

Thus, the Soft Systems Methodology (SSM) was developed in England by academics at the University of Lancaster Systems Department led by Professor Checkland, through a ten-year action research programme through the late 1960s. It is an approach to organisational process modelling or business process modelling that can be used both for general problem solving and in the management of change.

A particular consideration in our context of developing anti-fragile organisations is the distinction commonly made between the characteristics of human-made systems and natural systems. Natural systems, such as a living body or an ecosystem such as a meadow, have an enormous number and complexity of components and interactions, with virtually an infinite number of connections to all systems around them. In contrast, human-made systems, such as motor cars, can still be quite complex, but typically not quite as much, and are not as intricately linked to the systems around them. Thus, human-made systems are more self-contained and less open than natural systems.

But what about human organisations? It is reasonable to argue that human organisations exhibit something of a mixture between the characteristics of human-made and natural systems; the formal or 'hard' part of the organisation – the organisational structure, governance rules, management, skills, processes, procedures and technology-based systems – behaving in isolation like human-made systems; but the informal or 'soft' aspect of the organisation – the culture, leadership, team working, employee motivation and ownership – being like natural systems. When combined holistically within the human organisation, the resulting complexity means that any attempt to analyse the organisation's behaviour and performance on a 'hard' basis is only, at best, naïve and likely to lead to very wrong outcomes. It also means that the sources of fragility and anti-fragility within the organisation arise both within, and between, the 'hard' and 'soft' areas. This fits with the practical experience that the people aspects of organisations can be both their greatest strengths and their greatest weaknesses, and that in implementing organisational change we need to work holistically on both process and cultural aspects. Being a toolhead alone is not enough!

A further key to understanding the mechanisms of anti-fragility is to consider the generally agreed defining characteristics of systems. These are:

- for a system to carry out its purpose optimally, all the system's parts must be present;

- these parts must be arranged in a specific way for the system to carry out its purpose;

- all systems have specific purposes within larger systems;

- systems maintain their own stability through fluctuations and adjustments;

- systems have feedback.

Apart from loss of optimal functionality, at the most basic, something missing in a human organisation typically may cause fragility. This is because if we can take away parts of the system or organisation without affecting functioning and relationships, then there are few interrelationships between components, so it is more of a collection of parts rather than an organisation or system. Such missing components may include leadership, key personnel, skills, motivation, a positive culture, job descriptions, planning or control processes, work instructions and procedures. However, as part of the use of feedback to maintain the system's or organisation's stability, the system or organisation may restructure itself to compensate for the missing parts. Frequently, this will be through compensatory arrangements put in place and undertaken by humans, rather than through prior defined systems, governance rules or processes.

In a similar way, adding components to an organisation, patching in additional resources or changing the roles of specific components, will not necessarily solve a resource fragility issue, unless the interrelationships between the newcomer or reassigned resources and the other components are simultaneously put in place. Again, this may be achieved through 'soft' human interventions, rather than through prior defined systems, governance rules or processes.

A system or human organisation in which the parts are not properly arranged for the intended purposes will, if it functions satisfactorily at all, typically exhibit fragility, as parts and linkages will be compensating for the misalignment and this may break down over time.

Similarly, since all systems have specific purposes within the larger systems in which they are embedded, in trying to force two systems or organisations together to become a larger organisation, for example, following a merger or acquisition, even if we achieve functionality against purpose, we may create fragility. Equivalently, subdividing an organisation or system does not typically deliver two identical functioning systems, and, if it does, they may well be fragile. Clearly, dividing an elephant in half does not normally give you two identical but smaller elephants, and unfortunately they are likely to die.

In all of these cases concerned with arrangement of parts, or meeting the system's specific purpose, the human role in compensating in real time for the fragility created is again paramount, and, typically at a level of sophistication above that which can be achieved through the 'hard' aspects of the organisations. There are various levels of contribution within this role, from operational managers making day-to-day decisions as change occurs, to executives and specialist change managers who plan and control both day-to-day operations and transitions.

Anyone who has ever been involved in the change process within organisations is aware that whatever positive changes you attempt to make to the organisation to make it more fit for the future, typically the organisation itself in some way appears to resist the changes. This is often blamed on the people, but it is in reality more complicated than that. Left to themselves, systems maintain their stability, for example your body seeks to maintain your body temperature around 98.6 degrees Fahrenheit, or a company's infrastructure attempts to maintain its designated profit margin. This tendency for the system or organisation to hold steady overall arises because other parts of the system are designed to resist the change you are attempting to make, and bring the system's performance back to where it was designed to be. It is achieved through continual interactions, feedback and adjustments within the system and between it and its environment. One may be put in mind of the role of the Oracle in *The Matrix* films.

This phenomenon can be both a source of fragility and anti-fragility within an organisation, depending upon the circumstances. For example, this stabilising effect can restore business as usual after a major system disruption (clearly anti-fragile), or it can prevent needed improvement actions from becoming effective by, for example, preventing implementation in relation to process change (hence a fragile organisational feature). We shall look at this phenomenon and it's opposite, the tendency for virtuous or vicious circles to reinforce changes in performance and their impact on fragility and anti-fragility, in more detail below.

Before we do so, and in preparation for it, let us discuss the fifth and last defining characteristic of a system; that systems have feedback. In a system, information is transmitted through the system, and returned, acting as a catalyst for a change in system behaviour. There is both internal feedback and feedback between the system itself and larger systems. This may be slow or quick, and go by multiple varying routings. The availability of appropriate and correct timely information, speed of information flow and the ability to properly utilise the information for decision making, are all key aspects to help define the level of fragility within the organisation. The feedback loops represent robust and anti-fragile features, since they provide the basis for short-term decision making (robust), and longer-term adaption and learning (anti-fragile).

It is generally argued that there are a number of ways to look at Soft Systems Thinking. It can be thought of as set of tools, a framework for looking at issues as systemic wholes, possibly as a way of life, or as a language to communicate dynamic complexities and interdependencies. The reason for the latter is because English, like most western languages, is linear in its sentence construction; based on noun–verb–noun, which encourages us to think of causality in terms of 'x causes y'. The consequence is that our language tends to get us to focus on linear causal relationships, rather than circular or mutually causative ones, and this may cause us to miss key understanding of how things really work within our organisations and in their interfaces with broader systems. This is bad in itself and is likely to mitigate against our achievement of organisational objectives. Secondly, it will cause organisational fragility, since we do not have the basis for effective control if we do not understand the actual mechanisms, and may make things worse.

However, if we are able to properly capture and describe the causative behaviour through using Soft Systems Thinking approaches and tools, then this is the basis for anti-fragility within the organisation, since it then has a basis to adjust correctly to its current internal and external circumstances. Since real managerial problems within organisations are typically caused by a web of interconnected circular relationships, Soft Systems Thinking gives us a better language to understand and communicate these problems.

So, what are the principals of Soft Systems Thinking? In general, the approach considers the *Big Picture* rather than the single occurrence or local pattern, it balances the short-term and long-term perspectives, recognises the dynamic, complex and interdependent nature of systems, takes into account both measurable and non-measurable factors, and recognises that we are part of the systems in which we function and that we each influence the systems, as well as being influenced by them. Considering the Big Picture asks the questions:

- Apart from the obvious explanation for the problem, what other causal explanations could there be?

- Who are the actors in the story?

- What are the linkages between variables?

- How can we expand the picture to include more actors, variables and linkages?

The need to consider the Big Picture arises because, under stress, organisational executives and managers naturally focus on the immediate, most pressing problem. The implication of this is that they are likely to miss key characteristics of the typically complex problem that really underlies the situation, and are therefore likely to make incorrect decisions. This source of organisational fragility arises from management's emphasis on decomposition and narrow focus, so that they only see the effects of changes elsewhere in system, without appreciating real causes. In reality, today's problem is part of the bigger picture and we need to widen the focus to find the source of the problem. By doing this we are more likely to find more effective robust solutions, and by doing it routinely when such problems arise, we create an anti-fragile organisational management problem-solving approach.

We said above that we would look at the system stabilisation phenomenon, and it's opposite, the tendency for virtuous or vicious circles to reinforce changes in performance, together with their impact on organisational fragility and anti-fragility, in more detail. This we shall now do.

In a very real sense, the engines of system or organisational stability, growth or decline can all be described and modelled through the use of Reinforcing and Balancing Feedback Loops. These are closed circuits of interconnection between variables, which give sequences of mutual cause and effect. Every feedback loop depicts either a *reinforcing process* or a *balancing process*, which are the building blocks of any dynamic system structure. These can be combined in an infinite variety of ways to produce the complex systems that we find around us in practice. Reinforcing and Balancing Loops can be designed into organisations and systems to provide anti-fragile mechanisms. Conversely, if not properly understood, identified and managed, Reinforcing and Balancing Loops can represent the biggest sources of fragility within the organisation or system. This is true even if they were designed in for good purposes in the first place, but the assumptions on which they were based are no longer valid.

Figure 1.5
A simple Reinforcing Loop
Source: The Anti-Fragility Academy.

Figure 1.6
A simple Balancing Loop
Source: The Anti-Fragility Academy.

The Causal Loop Diagram in Figure 1.5 illustrates the simplest possible Reinforcing Loop; one with just two variables. Here, these are predefined as Sales and the Marketing Budget. The 'R' indicates that it is a Reinforcing Loop, and the 'Ss' indicate that both of these relationships have been assumed to work in the same direction; that is, that as sales goes up (or down), the marketing budget goes up or down with it. The relationship between the two variables works the other way round too; as the marketing budget goes up (or down), sales goes up or down with it. This clearly forms the basis for a virtuous or vicious circle, the choice depending only on whether either variable independently starts to get better or worse. Clearly here then, the same postulated relationship between Marketing Budget and Sales within this firm could be either a fragile feature, if we are spiralling downwards, or might be seen an anti-fragile feature, if we are spiralling up. In the former case, we can reduce fragility by intervention in the system to break the link between Marketing Budget and Sales, maybe investing more in Marketing Budget to stop the descent, and to start to spiral up. In the latter case, when we are spiralling up, this is typically at best only an anti-fragile feature within a limited parameter range, as an unexpected reversal in Sales, or in Marketing Budget, could cause decline and with it fragility.

In a similar way, the following Causal Loop Diagram in Figure 1.6 represents the simplest possible Balancing Loop; again one with just two variables, Price and Sales. Here the 'B' indicates it is a Balancing Loop, and this is achieved by the combination of one 'S' link and one 'O' link, the latter indicating an opposite

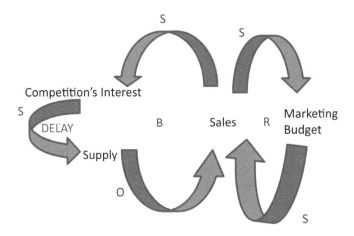

Figure 1.7   Sales–Marketing Reinforcing and Balancing Loops
Source: The Anti-Fragility Academy.

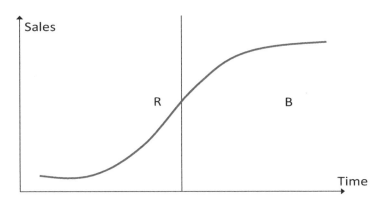

Figure 1.8   Sales performance over time

direction relationship, so that Sales decline as Price rise. In this case, we will approach stability, as any Price rise (or fall) will result in a fall in Sales (or rise) to compensate, which will then cause a corresponding fall (or rise) in Price, taking us back to where we were. This is an artificial example, but illustrates that again this Balancing Loop may represent either an anti-fragile feature, if we are concerned to protect the organisation from a sales and consequently revenue loss, or a fragile feature if the organisation does not have its costs under control, so that a price rise is needed to cover these. In the latter case, the price rise will not deliver the necessary revenue, as sales will drop to compensate.

As discussed above, we can combine such Reinforcing and Balancing Loops in an infinite variety of ways to model the complex systems that we find around us in practice. A simple example is shown in Figure 1.7. Starting with the initial Sales–Marketing Reinforcing Loop we had before, we have added a second, balancing, loop to illustrate the fact that as our organisation's sales rise, our competitor's interest in moving into this market rises also.

There will be a delay as they progressively ramp up Supply, but as this happens ours Sales will slow down and decline, as in the Behaviour Over Time (BOT) graph shown in Figure 1.8. Is this a representation of fragility or anti-fragility? Clearly fragility, as our virtuous circle is coming to an end, due to the shock of our competitor's intervention.

However, we should have anticipated this as a likely occurrence, and incorporated a further, third, Reinforcing Loop to provide some anti-fragility. What could this loop be? The introduction of new alternative lines? Diversification of markets? Differentiation or focus? All are possible anti-fragile strategies.

To summarise our discussion of Causal Loop Diagrams then: Reinforcing Loops are the engines of *growth* and *collapse*. They accelerate movement in given direction, and produce *virtuous* or *vicious* circles. Sometimes you can spot Reinforcing Loops are present because you can observe exponential growth or collapse, or from a BOT graph. If there is an even number of 'Os' in a Causal Loop Diagram (or none), then the loop is reinforcing.

In contrast, Balancing Loops are the great *stabilisers*, which are generally stabilising or goal seeking. They try to bring things to a desired state and keep them there. They resist change in one direction by producing change in the opposite direction. There is always an inherent visible or invisible goal in a balancing process, and a Balancing Loop driven by the gap between the goal or desired level and the actual level; as the discrepancy increases, this makes corrective action to reduce the gap.

Both types of loops may represent either fragile or anti-fragile features. To detect a Balancing Loop, we need to identify goal-seeking behaviour that characterises a balancing process. For these, conditions keep coming back to some sort of 'norm', no matter what anyone does, the conditions seem to resist change, growth falters or never quite starts, or unproductive behaviour never gets dropped. An even number of 'Os' indicates a Balancing Loop.

Reinforcing and Balancing Loops combined form the building blocks of complex behaviour; all dynamic behaviour is produced by a combination of Reinforcing and Balancing Loops. Behind any growth or collapse is at least one *Reinforcing Loop*. For every sign of goal-seeking there is a *Balancing Loop*. A period of rapid growth or collapse followed by a slowdown typically signals a shift in dominance from a Reinforcing Loop that is driving the structure, to a Balancing Loop.

Delays occurring in these loops, as in the example above, are neither good nor bad, fragile or anti-fragile, but it depends on how we design or treat them. Often there is a misconception, and we fail to take into account of them at all. Often also, it takes too long to perceive feedback, measure results, to decide how to respond and to implement solutions. This makes system's behaviour unpredictable and hard to control, hence typically fragile.

When dealing with real organisational systems, rather than our simplistic examples, these typically include many variables, with many factors at play, and many semi-independent but interlocking components. There is thus a vast number of Reinforcing and Balancing Loops and complicated interconnections. Over time the dominance of different feedback loops shifts, and timing and length of delays vary. Indeed, structures may even seem to be in conflict. Such complex systems:

- tend to be self-stabilising, hence to an extent potentially anti-fragile;

- are, or appear to be, purposeful, again implying some anti-fragility;

- like simple systems, are capable of using feedback to modify their behaviour, again an anti-fragile feature;

- can modify their environments;

- are capable of replicating, maintaining, repairing and reorganising themselves.

The self-stabilising phenomena arises since a complex system is likely to contain many Balancing Loops – these each keep some small component of the system in balance or functioning close to some desired level. This creates a *resistance to change*, for example, like cultural norms. Despite improvement campaigns or change programmes, progress falters and it eventually returns to the status quo – all the Balancing Loops are designed to keep things the way the system originally intended them to be. When viewed in this way, as typical, this feature produces fragility, as well as anti-fragility.

The apparent purposefulness occurs as the Balancing Loops seek to maintain the desired level of performance or goal, whilst the Reinforcing Loops seek to augment or diminish some phenomena in the system. In a complex system, such as an organisation, sometimes the goals of both growth and balancing processes are explicit and known. But often they are contradictory, ambiguous or implicit, and the system appears to function with a *mind of its own*.

Using feedback to self-modify behaviour is something all systems do. This provides *opportunity for change and growth* within the system, particularly if feedback is *explicit and accessible*. For example, an organisation has a better chance of improving performance if it collects data on problems such as delays and errors. A good understanding of the structure and workings of the system help us to take advantage of this to catalyse change within the system.

Since complex systems are *purposeful* and *can modify their behaviour*, it is not surprising that they can also modify their environments *to better achieve their goals*. Hence this is also potentially an anti-fragile feature. Such modifications may be subtle or bold, and legal or illegal. For example, a company may encourage an interest in employment within the local community. If the organisation or system wishes to change its environment, then identifying *links* between the organisation or system and its environment helps to *anticipate* how changes in the system will lead to changes in the environment.

Organisations can replicate themselves, for example through franchises. This can be an anti-fragile or fragile feature. However, as they also change in response to the environment, even apparent clone organisations are likely to contain some unique quirks or mutations. Organisations that are abruptly altered, for example, by a takeover or layoffs, often find ways to carry on essential functions or reorganise to continue pursuing goals. All natural systems can invent, reframe, learn and adjust to their environments, so can organisations.

As anti-fragile features, the inherent flexibility and looseness of large complex systems helps them to endure, although because of these features it may be hard to predict what they do next. The more complex a system is, the greater it's potential to process large amounts of information, learn quickly and act flexibly. This is again anti-fragile. However, such systems have many subsystems to coordinate, so there is a greater potential for things to go wrong, leading to fragility in human systems.

In practice, there are many common problems and sources of fragility with complex systems and organisations. These may develop internally conflicting goals, where the goals of subsystems conflict with system goals. For example, internal politics and empire-ism, and the centralisation/decentralisation dilemma. There may also be distorted feedback, as feedback from local to larger subsystems may be inaccurately conveyed or interpreted. Because of the complexity, there may also be a loss of predictability. For these reasons, many, including Taleb, argue against large entities, and for 'small is beautiful'.

In terms of developing anti-fragility within an existing system or organisation, Donella Meadows (2014) provided an insightful overall hierarchy of the effectiveness of the types of interventions we can make. This is shown in Table 1.1. It is a good guide on our path to developing an anti-fragile organisation.

Table 1.1   Donella Meadows's 12 leverage points for intervening in a system, in increasing order of effectiveness

12. Constants, parameters, numbers (such as subsidies, taxes, standards).
11. The size of buffers and other stabilising stocks, relative to their flows.
10. The structure of material stocks and flows (such as transport network, population age structures).
9. The length of delays, relative to the rate of system changes.
8. The strength of negative feedback loops, relative to the effect they are trying to correct against.
7. The gain around driving positive feedback loops.
6. The structure of information flow (who does and does not have access to what kinds of information).
5. The rules of the system (such as incentives, punishments, constraints).
4. The power to add, change, evolve or self-organise system structure.
3. The goal of the system.
2. The mindset or paradigm that the system – its goals, structure, rules, delays, parameters – arises out of.
1. The power to transcend paradigms.

Creating and Managing Anti-Fragile Organisations

As indicated at the start, the purpose of this book is to explore the methods, approaches and architecture to build anti-fragile organisations. The seminal book on anti-fragility by Nassim Taleb published at the end of November 2012 established his new concept of anti-fragility as a powerful alternative framework for the study of risk in the design and management of human systems. Anti-fragility is a new way of thinking about mitigating risk. With this view, we shall focus on the characteristics of biological systems that, being more than just robust, actually improve their resilience through being stressed.

In this book we shall apply this concept to the development and management of organisations, services and products, and identify the characteristics of these that will not only mitigate against the realisation of hazards, but will enable growth in protection, strength and anti-fragility over time. In this context, we can argue that anti-fragility also encompasses flexibility and agility. As we shall also argue, at the organisational level, anti-fragility (or not) is defined by the Organisational Strategy, Structure and Systems, its People, Relationships and its Culture. We can then build anti-fragility (or not) into our products, services, markets, use of information and technology base. This provides us with what, essentially, is a new model of the organisation, in which we can explore approaches to the development of anti-fragile strategy, structure and culture, and the construction and management of anti-fragile operations, supply chains, markets, and product and service portfolios.

Thus in this book we shall focus on establishing this Anti-Fragile Concept of the Firm, and explore its application for private, public and voluntary sector organisations of all types. Commencing from our brief exploration of anti-fragility in biological and ecological systems, we identify characteristics relevant to organisational survival in a turbulent world, and how our approach to risk needs to change in order to create and manage anti-fragile organisations. Applying this paradigm shift to organisational strategy and structure, and using the learning from our consideration of biological and ecological systems, we establish rules to enable exploitation of opportunities, whilst avoiding the fast tracks to extinction. The development of the corresponding Cultural Template at all levels of the organisation, and for all its stakeholder groups, is treated within the unified framework. The construction and management of anti-fragile processes, systems and use of information and technology, and the relationship to the existing approaches such as Six Sigma, Lean and Quality Management, forms the central part of our text, linking theory and practice. The penultimate two chapters discuss the meaning of anti-fragility in the context of developing and maintaining supply chains, markets, and product and service portfolios. In the final chapter, Local and Global Fragility and their interrelationship are discussed, and the implications for the organisation, individuals, government and global society reviewed. The development of organisational anti-fragility metrics, and the common pitfalls of fragile organisations, are discussed.

This Book's Objectives

The objectives of this book are to familiarise executives, managers, entrepreneurs and students with the concept, applicability and use of the concept of anti-fragility in designing, developing, optimising and managing organisations of all types, in all sectors:

- to connect and contrast anti-fragility thinking with conventional approaches;

- to develop an understanding of the mechanisms whereby business fragility is embedded within Organisational Strategy, Structure and Systems, People, Relationships and Culture, as well as products, services, markets, use of information and the technology base;

- to enable readers to take stock of fragility in relation to their own organisations and construct Action Plans to develop anti-fragility within them.

A Basic Fragility Test for Your Organisation

It's a good point to take stock now as to how the concept of anti-fragility applies to organisations in which you are a stakeholder. Is your organisation currently fragile? In what dimensions? There are no absolute answers to these questions, but their aim is to help to get you thinking about where your organisation is now, and where you would like it to go.

Try the short quiz below to help you to get thinking. Total your score and think about how you could increase it.

A Basic Fragility Test for Your Organisation (score out of 100):

- How good are our current approaches to managing the organisation? (0–10)

- Do we include deliberate diversity of approach and deployment? (0–10)

- How aware are we as an organisation of our environment? (0–10)

- Do we learn as an organisation? (0–10)

- Do we implement what we learn? (0–10)

- Do we learn fast? Fast enough? (0–10)

- Do we have the infrastructure to learn, and apply our learning? (0–10)

- Do we evolve? (0–10)

- Do we have the infrastructure to evolve? (0–10)

- How optimised are our processes? (0–10; 0 = maximum optimisation)

Chapter 2
Anti-Fragile Governance, Strategy and Risk

The Fragility of Governance, Enterprise Risk Management and the Desire for Anti-Fragility

In recent years the cases of spectacular failures of governance within iconic organisations have become apparently commonplace. Some of these have cost lives, livelihoods and global stability. So, it is no surprise that the phrase 'failure of governance' yields 37,500,000 results on a Google search.

The integrity of the governance of a human organisation contributes critically to determining the organisation's overall fragility, robustness or anti-fragility. Governance systems themselves may be fragile, robust or anti-fragile, and may have features of each. So what is anti-fragile governance? Given the definition of anti-fragility, the answer to this question needs to describe a form of governance that improves as the result of being stressed, not once but on an ongoing basis.

There is an argument to say that we have made major progress in the pursuit of anti-fragile organisational governance in recent years. As a result of the spectacular failures of governance, in general terms regulatory, professional and corporate governance has been strengthened and progressively improved across many sectors.

In another wider sense also, organisational governance has steadily improved in recent years, due to the application of specific learning at the macro-level to improvement at the micro-level. For example, sectors such as the airline industry have applied the lessons learnt from catastrophes to help prevent their reoccurrence in the future. In addition, bodies like the Health and Safety Executive and the Environment Agency have progressively applied their global learning in relation to their specialised areas of risk, to reduce individual organisations' risks through education and information.

Such ongoing improvements in governance are also nominally implied at the micro or organisational level by the utilisation of system standards like ISO 14001 for the environment, OHSAS18001 for occupational health and safety, as well as ISO 9001 for Quality Management. Within these, there is a requirement for ongoing risk reduction, as well as containment of issues, organisational learning and corrective and preventive action.

However, all is not well in the pursuit of anti-fragile organisational governance. There are, perhaps, two aspects to this:

Firstly, whilst attempts have been made to take a coherent holistic approach to risk across an organisation, there are a large number of practical difficulties in doing this, so that many organisations retain severe systemic weaknesses and fragility in their corporate governance systems. What is perhaps worse, is that we still regard this as normal and, by implication, acceptable.

Secondly, corporate governance systems rely critically for their efficacy on risk analysis, but there are fundamental flaws and weaknesses in our current approaches to do this.

We shall discuss each of these two issues in more detail; the first below, and the second in the next section of this chapter.

Over the last decade the desire for a coherent holistic approach to risk across an organisation has been the basis for the emergence of Enterprise Risk Management (ERM) as a new management discipline that calls for companies to identify all the risks they face, to decide which risks to manage actively, and then to make that plan of action available to all stakeholders, rather than just shareholders, as part of their annual reporting (see for example, Attalo-Hazel-Green, 2005). Risk is seen not just as upcoming threats, but also in terms of opportunities that may balance them. The release of the Committee of Sponsoring Organisations (COSO) ERM Integrated Framework in 2004 did much to establish ERM, and it has now become a business school discipline. ERM is generally seen to be a process, ongoing and flowing through an organisation and affected by people at every level within it, which is applied in strategy setting and across the enterprise at every level and unit, and includes taking an organisational-level portfolio view of risk. It is designed to identify potential events that, if they occur, will affect the organisation and to manage risk within its risk appetite, so as to be able to provide reasonable assurance to management and the board of directors, geared to the achievement of objectives.

Whilst ERM is, in theory at least, a robust feature in organisational governance, and an anti-fragile one if there is ongoing learning and improvements in governance based on experience, the practical difficulties in applying it do mean that in reality at present its application is limited to a relatively small number of organisations, with limited risk coverage, limited holistic formulation and limited effectiveness. For example, a Deloitte and Touche survey in 2005 found that 45 per cent of organisations had no formal ERM programme, whilst of the remainder, only 49 per cent had a programme in development and only 6 per cent considered ERM fully operational. At the simplest level, there is a general lack of consensus on the definition of risk in the management literature, and numerous definitions have been proposed. This reflects the fundamental underlying issues about current risk analysis, which we will address in the next section. Here, we shall focus on the particular nature of, and in consequence fragility issues with, ERM itself.

The elements of ERM are aligning risk appetite and strategy, enhancing risk response decisions, reducing operational surprises and losses, identifying and managing multiple and cross-enterprise risks, seizing opportunities and improving deployment of capital. Management considers the organisation's risk appetite in evaluating the strategic alternatives, setting related objectives and developing mechanisms to manage related risks. ERM provides the rigour to identify and select among alternative risk responses, such as risk avoidance, reduction, sharing and acceptance. Organisations using ERM enhance their capability to identify potential events and establish responses, aiming to reduce surprises, and the associated costs and losses. Every organisation faces countless risks affecting various parts of the organisation; ERM facilitates effective response to these interrelated impacts, and integrated responses to multiple risks. In addition, by considering a full range of potential events, the organisation's management is positioned to identify and proactively realise opportunities. Obtaining robust risk information also allows management to effectively assess overall capital needs and enhance capital allocation. In addition to all this, ERM can, in theory at least, help ensure effective reporting and compliance with law and regulations, help avoid damage to the organisation's reputation and the associated consequences, and help it get to where it wants to go, avoiding pitfalls and surprises along the way.

ERM objectives typically utilise the following distinct, but overlapping, categories:

- *strategic* high-level goals, aligned with and supporting organisational mission;

- *operations* – effective and efficient use of resources;

- *reporting* – reliability of reporting;

- *compliance* – compliance with applicable laws and regulations.

The judgement on effectiveness of an ERM implementation includes a reasonable assurance by the board of directors and management that they understand the extent to which the strategic and operations objectives are being achieved, that the reporting is reliable and that applicable laws and regulations are being complied with. Further, there must be no material weaknesses, and risk needs to have been brought within the risk appetite. The eight components below must also be present and functioning effectively:

- internal environment evaluation;

- objective setting;

- event identification;

- risk assessment;

- risk response;

- control activities;

- information and communication;

- monitoring.

ERM is undoubtedly useful on the journey towards anti-fragile organisations but, apart from the limited take up and practice of ERM to date, what are the other shortcomings in relation to its real contribution to developing an anti-fragile organisation? Unfortunately, there are numerous, and they are systemic and severe. It is commonly acknowledged that whilst ERM is conceptually relatively straightforward, its implementation is not. This may mean that an organisation's implementation in practice may have limited coverage of risks, particularly qualitative hard to measure ones, too much emphasis just on defensive regulatory compliance and rubberstamping, limited holistic bringing together of risks from the distinct risk silos and limited effectiveness. There may also be blame avoidance, an emphasis on time spent filling forms and ticking appropriate boxes, time spent maximising achievement of target metrics rather than progressing true objectives, and an emphasis on the wrong risks due to disproportionate regulator or stakeholder pressure.

Institutional concerns remain with the fragility of governance. The UK Corporate Governance Code 2012 update made two recommendations. These were that, firstly, much more attention needs to be paid to following the spirit of the Code as well as its letter. Secondly, that the impact of shareholders in monitoring the Code could and should be enhanced by better interaction between the boards of listed companies and their shareholders. To support this, the UK Stewardship Code, which provides guidance on good practice for investors, should be seen as a companion piece to this Code.

Similarly, the recent Roads to Ruin study report from the Cass Business School (Parsons, 2011) identified seven broad residual risk categories from study of crises affecting 21 organisations. These are:

1. Board skill and non-executive director control:
    – limitations in skills and competence to monitor and control the organisation;

2. Board risk blindness:
    – failure to recognise and engage with risks to the same degree that they engage with reward and opportunity;

3. Inadequate leadership on ethos and culture;

4. Defective internal communication:
    – important information not reaching appropriate staff;

5. Organisational complexity and change:
    – includes risks from acquisitions;

6. Incentives:
    – includes effects on behaviour that result from both explicit and implicit incentives;

7.   Risk 'glass ceiling':
         – inability of Risk Management and internal audit teams to report to, and discuss risks with, the top management team.

The report also identified problems in relation to *Groupthink*, and that there were more issues with *soft skills* than with technical know-how.

So, the desire for anti-fragile governance remains, but in general we have got a long way to go to approach achieving it. As we shall see elsewhere on our somewhat functional journey through this book, methods to achieve it exist but have weaknesses and limited adoption. We have much to do!

An Anti-Fragile Approach to Organisational Risk

Anti-fragility is potentially a new way of thinking about mitigating risk. This section reviews the arguments for and against an anti-fragile approach to Risk Management, explores the implications for system design and operation, and the place of Risk Management in system development, and identifies common shortfalls in current system architecture and management that leave them unnecessarily susceptible to risk.

Risk as a concept is a human construct; our way of coping with and trying to predict and manage the unknown. It reflects the fact that: 'Organisations of any kind face internal and external factors and influences that make it uncertain whether, when and the extent to which they will achieve or exceed their objectives.' *Risk* is then defined as the effect this uncertainty has on the organisation's objectives. This view of risk as a human construct is valid, whether or not one believes in a probabilistic, or a deterministic universe. And we may have got it wrong; for the contention of this book is that, despite good intents, much of Risk Analysis and Management as we know it today is part of the problem, not of the solution. The argument is that the way we conceive and approach risk and its management has led to increased exposure and fragility.

First, let us consider further the current conventional approach to Risk Analysis and Management. There are various methods used to assess or measure risk, or the extent to which potential events might impact objectives, in different application areas. Different disciplines, including Healthcare, Health and Safety, Finance, and Environmental Management, have established diverse, but related literature in this field. Underlying these, however, are general principles. According to the international standard ISO 31000: 2009 (International Organization for Standardization, 2009), all activities of an organisation involve risk, and organisations manage risk by anticipating, understanding and deciding whether to modify it. In this process, they communicate and consult with stakeholders and monitor and review the risk and the controls that are modifying the risk.

The standard claims that while all organisations manage risk to some degree, the ISO 31000 standard establishes a number of principles that need to be satisfied before Risk Management will be effective, and recommends that organisations should have a framework that integrates the process for managing risk into the organisation's overall governance, strategy and planning, management, reporting processes, policies, values and culture. It points out that Risk Management can be applied across an entire organisation, to its many areas and levels, as well as to specific functions, projects and activities.

Further, it argues that although Risk Management practice has been developed over time and within many sectors to meet diverse needs, the adoption of consistent processes within a comprehensive framework helps ensure that risk is managed effectively, efficiently and coherently across the organisation. It claims that the generic approach described in the standard provides the principles and guidelines for managing any form of risk in a systematic, transparent and credible manner and within any scope and context.

Whilst not everyone specifically follows this standard, generally the core of the underlying general approaches to, and principles of, Risk Analysis and Management appear common. That is, that Risk Assessment:

- allows an entity to understand the extent to which potential events might impact objectives;

- assesses risks from two perspectives:
  - likelihood;
  - impact;

- is used to assess risks and is normally also used to measure impact on the related objectives;

- employs a combination of both qualitative and quantitative risk assessment methodologies;

- relates time horizons to objective horizons;

- assesses risk on both an inherent and a residual basis.

Risk response then:

- identifies and evaluates possible responses to risk;

- evaluates options in relation to entity's risk appetite, cost versus benefit of potential risk responses and the degree to which a response will reduce impact and/or likelihood;

- selects and executes response based on evaluation of the portfolio of risks and responses.

Finally, Control Activities:

- are the policies and procedures that help ensure that the risk responses, as well as other entity directives, are carried out;

- occur throughout the organisation, at all levels and in all functions;

- include application and general information technology controls.

Now let us consider where and why the conventional approach to risk goes wrong, and the associated organisational fragility. There are numerous repeated and well-publicised failures of Risk Analysis and Management. Some authors discuss causes, with a view to future prevention. Our argument is that the focus of the current approach to Risk Analysis and Management itself encourages and facilitates much of this failure, by creating system fragility in the Risk Management system itself. What we are arguing is that Risk Management fails because it is not designed, nor conducted, to be anti-fragile, and that by so redesigning and conducting it, we can make our systems and organisations more than just robust.

The Risk Management process implicitly assumes:

- Our system or organisation is already designed, established and running, or it's on the drawing board, and that we are just considering potential risks in its operation with a view to reduction. *Is this the right emphasis? Would it not be better to design it to be anti-*

fragile; to enable it to continue to increase its resilience on an ongoing basis during operations through the process of being stressed, just as we do when we exercise?

- The formalised and standardised processes of risk identification and risk assessment take full account of all aspects of the internal and external conditions in the system or organisation, including its complexity and loading. *This is unlikely to be realistic, and the larger, more complex or optimally utilised (that is, heavily loaded) a system is, the more fragile it becomes.*

- That risks – in terms of occurrence, likelihood, severity and controllability – are in some sense stable; that they will remain proportionate, without newcomers, throughout the inter-assessment or review period. *Again, this is unlikely to be realistic in relation to the highly dynamic, complex non-linear system behaviour that is an increasing feature of our modern world, and complex organisations and systems.*

- That there will be no *Black Swans*; rare, non-predictable high-impact events. Clearly, this is again untrue. Many of the failures of Risk Analysis and Management have been associated with just such events; the exclusion from consideration is thus unrealistic.

- That the Risk Management process is carried out with full timely information and critical awareness, based on a holistic view, and in the spirit of continual improvement and risk reduction, with the full deployment of senior management attention, leadership and a fully committed Risk Management culture. *Clearly this is not, in general, the case. Frequently, Risk Management will be delegated to middle management, formalised and standardised, so it is in danger of becoming a compliance-driven ritual, with incomplete information; with most importance being given to the integrity of the paper trail for auditing purposes.*

All this implies, that our Risk Analysis and Management is at best incomplete, and based on unrealistic assumptions.

Our problem, however, is in a sense much bigger than this. The way we run our systems and organisations, and the associated Risk Management Processes, reflect the reactive management paradigm that itself causes fragility and is much in need of change. This is reflective of the human construct and definition of risk that we discussed above.

Our interest here is not in the philosophical basis of risk, and whether it is meaningful or not to link it to probabilities, as discussed by Taleb and others. Our concern is in practical basic risk minimisation in systems and organisations; and here the very definition of risk is getting in the way.

If, as defined above, *risk* is the effect of uncertainty on the achievement of the organisation's objectives, then Risk Management is perforce reactive to uncertainties, which gives an implied independent variable status for these uncertainties; that is, outside our control, so we can only react. That is the basis of conventional definitions of Risk Management, and also underlies the more recent concepts of Positive Risk Management and HROs. Such need for reactiveness to unforeseen uncertainties implies fragility, as it will generally require intervention for remedy after the realisation of an uncertain event to contain, mitigate or neutralise its effects. Such reaction may be inadequate, misconceived or too late. Anyway, it implies that we are just waiting for the bad things to happen.

But the Oxford English Dictionary also gives us a useful alternative definition of *risk*, as well as that of a situation involving exposure to danger and the possibility that something unpleasant or unwelcome will happen. This is taking responsibility for one's own safety or possessions, such as in the phrase: 'They undertook the adventure at their own risk.'

With this definition of risk, Risk Management can be much more concerned with proactivity, rather than reactivity, and becomes less a checking and controlling process and more a movement towards system design for prevention and anti-fragility.

Considering general organisations and systems, it is apparent that all organisational and system information gathering and feedback loops that potentially use current performance as the basis for control and/or change, potentially represent anti-fragility features. Included in this group are all Quality Control; Quality Assurance (QA); Budgetary Control; Developmental and Evaluative Performance Appraisals; Strategy Review; Health, Safety and Environment (HSE) Assurance; Continuous Improvement, Kaizan, Six Sigma, Lean Improvement, Agile Deployment, Organisational Assessment against the EFQM, Baldrige, or Deming Models (EQFM, 2013); and, of course, Risk Management activities. A key part of the anti-fragile mechanism in all these cases is the human role.

This is in line with the Soft Systems Thinking approach to anti-fragility in organisations and systems as discussed in Chapter 1.

In this sense then, Risk Management is an anti-fragility feature of our organisations and systems. But, as described in the previous section, this anti-fragility feature is often itself implemented in a fragile way. This second level fragility of our organisational architecture and management is reflective of the lack of a holistic approach to Fragility Minimisation and Management in current practice in organisational or system design and operation.

Holistic fragility is not an explicit consideration in relation to system architecture or management; rather attempted local optimisation is addressed in relation to specific aspects of system architecture and management against what are effectively partial optimisation criteria.

Accordingly, we may, for example, *Lean* our processes to remove *non-value adding* activities or minimise throughput time or cost, or maximise utilisation, without fully considering the impact on system or organisational fragility. This may result in *hard-wired* inflexible inagile systems, or *optimally utilised* heavily loaded systems that are so stretched to exploit their maximum capacity that they cannot cope with any disruptions or further load increases, and hence may fail catastrophically. Whilst the implementation of a Lean approach is itself an anti-fragile feature of a system or organisation, it can be implemented in a fragile or anti-fragile way. Again, this is a second-level fragility issue, which applies in a similar way to Six Sigma and all improvement or control applications.

In common with other partial optimisation methods, whether Lean is Fragile Lean or Anti-Fragile Lean depends on the same set of organisational characteristics – Organisational Strategy, Structure and Systems, People, Relationships and Culture, Products, Services, Markets, use of information and technology base – as we described for the organisation as a whole. Interestingly, often a practical approach to retaining anti-fragility in a Lean approach is to incorporate the development of the appropriate culture and multi-skilling; that is, an emphasis on People. In contrast, technology solutions to Lean, such as *hard-wiring* conveyor systems or reliance on restrictive standardised software system processing, are by definition inflexible and are typically fragile. People in systems are a major exploitable source of anti-fragility, whilst through, for example rigid control and bureaucracy, they can also be a major source of fragility too.

It can be argued that the above are common shortfalls in current system and organisational architecture and management that leave them unnecessarily susceptible to risk. However, we should also consider whether fragility alone is a sufficiently wide optimisation criterion for the architecture and management of such organisations and systems. According to our above definitions, and the biological systems analogue, it would appear that the answer should be 'yes', since anti-fragility encompasses both survivability and increased resilience.

Is the reactive management paradigm the best basis for Risk Management and risk education? What are the pros and cons for an anti-fragile approach to Risk Management, and what is the place of Risk Management in system development?

The argument for the current conventional approach to Risk Management can be made partly on historic grounds, and partly on grounds of simplicity and perhaps ease of control, without the need for the constant awareness of senior management. The argument would be that these would only be involved when needed, hence reducing what could be seen otherwise as an unnecessary excessive drain on their time and attention. However, the numerous repeated and well-publicised failures of Risk Analysis and Management referred to above suggest that this argument itself is tenuous at best, fragile and certainly not anti-fragile.

In contrast, it might be argued that the anti-fragile approach to Risk Management is unnecessarily complex, invasive and over-stretching. If we cannot make the current simplistic approach to Risk Management work adequately, why on earth should we consider a more intellectually challenging and complex approach?

Why, indeed? And the education issue is also significant. Since risk is everywhere, in all our operations and processes, we need an approach and rules for Risk Management that are simple for everyone to comprehend and follow. Whilst these arguments are valid, they miss the point.

With the current approach, the emphasis is on following due process, awareness of risks in an existing or potential system, and the audit trail. With the anti-fragile approach to Risk Management, the emphasis will be on the constant desire and aspiration to develop and operate systems and organisations that are self-improving through challenge, and us all taking responsibility for doing this. For current Risk Management to work, we have to be able to conceive the risk. In the anti-fragile approach to Risk Management we don't, since it is based on applying good precautionary system and organisational design principles to systems architecture and management, in order to protect the system and the organisation. Our risk minimisation approach hence incorporates an element of sensible avoidance, as well as constant learning.

The relatively new approach of Positive Risk Management recognises the importance of human factors and individual differences in propensity to taking risks. It has developed from the work of various academics and professionals who have expressed concerns about the rigour of the wider Risk Management debate, or who have made a contribution emphasising the human dimension of risk. It recognises that any object or situation can be rendered hazardous by the involvement of someone with an inappropriate disposition towards risk; whether too risk taking or too risk averse, and that risk is inevitable and ever present. Each individual has a particular orientation towards risk; timid, anxious, fearful, or perhaps adventurous, impulsive or oblivious to danger. Finally, Positive Risk Management recognises risk taking as essential to all enterprise, creativity, heroism, education and scientific advance. More conventional Risk Management places little emphasis on human factors. The approach has been criticised as, for example, researchers at the University of Oxford and King's College London found that the concept may not work in practice. In a four-year organisational study of Risk Management in a leading healthcare organisation, Fischer and Ferlie (2013) found major contradictions between rules-based Risk Management required by managers, and ethics-based self-regulation favoured by staff and clients. This produced tensions that led to a heated and intractable conflict which escalated, resulting in crisis and organisational collapse.

The biggest human factor in risk is resistance to change. The current way we do Risk Analysis and Management is protected by inertia, limited comprehension of the real issues, vested interest and fear of the unknown.

Talking to risk professionals can be difficult. Nicholas Taleb tells the story of being hired in 2006 to explain to the board of executives of the Parisian bank, Société Générale, his ideas of Black Swan risks. His talk was on how what he calls 'pseudo' risk techniques, commonly used to measure and predict events, have never worked, and how we need to focus on fragility. He describes the experience as:

'I was like a Jesuit preacher visiting Mecca in the middle of the annual Haj – their "quants" and risks people hated me with passion … I was like a Martian … who brought this guy here?'

And yet, it is clearly time for change. Risk Analysis and Management continue to fail, sometimes spectacularly. We need a broader view. We need anti-fragility. The good news is that developing the concept through to practical application within your organisation is not hard. It just takes remembering what we are trying to achieve with Risk Management; going back to first principals.

The Traditional Concepts of Strategy and the Paradigm Shift to Anti-Fragility

It is apparent that the fragility, robustness and potential anti-fragility of an organisation depends critically on its strategy. As with the broader issue of governance systems, strategies themselves may be fragile, robust or anti-fragile, and may have features of each. Whilst a robust strategy can withstand varied circumstances within the external and internal environment, an anti-fragile strategy is a form of strategy that improves as the result of being stressed, not once but on an ongoing basis. In contrast, a fragile strategy does not survive the first contacts with reality.

We live in a world where, of necessity, our views of strategy have been changing (Minzberg 1979). Henry Mintzberg of McGill University's name comes up immediately in any discussion of strategy. Whilst Max McKeown (2011) argues that 'strategy is about shaping the future' and is the human attempt to get to 'desirable ends with available means'. Mintzberg defined strategy as 'a pattern in a stream of decisions' in contrast with an older view of strategy as planning. Mintzberg's fame in the strategy field is largely associated with his well-known Ten Schools of Thought, which define plausible models of Strategy Formation, in terms of deliberate strategy and emerging strategy. He distinguished between deliberate and emerging strategy in 1979, as follows:

> For about eight years now, a group of us at McGill University's Faculty of Management has been researching the process of strategy formulation. Defining a strategy as a pattern in a stream of decisions, our central theme has been the contrast between 'deliberate' strategies, that is, patterns intended before being realised, and 'emergent' strategies, patterns realised despite or in the absence of intentions. Emergent strategies are rather common in organisations, or, more to the point, almost all strategies seem to be in some part at least, emergent. To quote the expression so popular on posters these days, 'Life is a journey, not a destination'.

Clearly, in a faster moving world, a solely deliberate strategy may be too rigid for circumstances, so that strict adherence to it would make the organisation fragile, whilst an unplanned ad hoc set of decisions with no planning would, perhaps, be deficient and fragile in its contribution to achieving objectives, due to its lack of coherence. Planning has the advantage to help structure analysis and thinking about complex problems, encourage questioning, encourage a longer-term view, enhance coordination, improve communication, provide agreed objectives, involve people and provide a sense of security; all of which contribute to robustness or anti-fragility.

However, this second case is not the way the emergent strategy concept is typically used, and in general terms emergent strategy, with some initial planning and constant replanning, is likely to be more anti-fragile in a fast-moving global joined-up world. Thus, we can see the emergence of emergent strategy as anti-fragile in response to the need to reflect the fast-moving requirements of the business's markets and environments in which strategic plans do not last long.

Also crucial in relation to the extent of anti-fragility of strategy are the more general nature and parameters of the strategy development and management activities, reflecting the characteristics defined in Mintzberg's Ten Schools of Thought, but also more broadly and openly the strategy assessment criteria within the EFQM Excellence Model. The EFQM defines strategy as how an organisation delivers its Vision and Mission, assuming that this is done in a balanced stakeholder way. In terms of assessing organisational strategy, the EFQM Model, through its sub-criteria, examines four primary dimensions, each of which can help characterise the strategy and its development and management processes as fragile, robust, anti-fragile or, as in general, something of a mixture. These dimensions cover:

- how, and the extent to which, strategy is based on the needs and expectations of stakeholders, and of the external environment;

- how, and the extent to which, strategy is based on internal performance and capabilities;

- how strategy, and supporting policies, are developed, reviewed and updated;

- how strategy, and supporting policies, are communicated, implemented and monitored.

We shall consider the impact of each of these four areas on fragility and anti-fragility of strategy, and on organisational fragility and anti-fragility, in turn, starting with the first. If strategy is based in an appropriately balanced way on all key stakeholder groups needs and expectations, this is a robust feature. If this is constantly or frequently reviewed and updated then this is an anti-fragile one, particularly if the effectiveness of the strategy to date in terms of these needs and expectations is reviewed as part of this updating process. Similarly, well-structured and founded attention to the requirements of the external environment is at minimum robust and, if constantly ongoing and improving, is anti-fragile. A lot, however, will depend on the methods by which this is done – are these methods of identification of needs and strategy development fragile, robust or anti-fragile?

For the second area, related to internal performance and capabilities, the arguments are very similar to the first, whilst for the last two areas the position appears slightly different, although somewhat similar to each other. For the first of these, the primary concern is the fragility, robustness or anti-fragility of the strategy developing, reviewing and updating methods – are they frequent, timely and well founded, and by implication do they actually happen? For the last area, fragility, robustness or anti-fragility will depend on the fragility or not of the communication; monitoring and implementation methods employed; and also, by implication, on the extent to which communication, monitoring and implementation actually happen.

Returning to our definition of anti-fragile strategy at the start of this section remember, however, that an anti-fragile strategy is a form of strategy that improves as the result of being stressed not once but on an ongoing basis. So, the strategy has to be deployed in order to be stressed and in order to be improved. This is typically at multiple levels in the organisation, possibly initially on a top-down basis. Part of this deployment will be the opportunity for emergence of bottom-up strategy at operational levels, as to be robust or anti-fragile operational strategies should reflect both organisational objectives and operational reality.

Anti-fragility is a paradigm shift to the current formation of strategy. Unlike previously, the question is not, 'Is it a good strategy?' nor, 'Is it a good strategic planning and implementation process?' rather it is, 'Is the current strategy, and strategic planning and implementation process, improving from being stressed, not once, but on an ongoing basis?' With this paradigm, stressing the strategy, and strategic planning and implementation process, is not to be avoided, it is to be pursued.

Change Strategies

There are also two other senses in which the EFQM Excellence Model can contribute to the discussion of anti-fragile strategy; corresponding to basing strategy on it, or basing a change strategy on it. In practice, there is not too much difference between the two, since a proper strategy based on the EFQM Excellence Model properly applied is, perforce, a neverending change strategy, since the model essentially requires it.

Basing strategy, or a change strategy, on using an excellence model approach, such as using the EFQM Excellence Model, or a somewhat more limited alternative such as the Balanced Scorecard, is to some extent itself anti-fragile. This is because, as explained in Chapter 1, the EFQM Excellence Model and other excellence models referred to, are fundamentally anti-fragile in nature, as they incorporate a number of key anti-fragile features: use of the model is typically based on self-assessment principles, with approaches updatable in real time; it incorporates learning loops; there is explicit consideration and balance across the stakeholder groups; there is clear measurement; it covers the quality and deployment of the Leadership, Strategy, People, Partnership and Resources, and Processes, Products and Services provided, as well as the Results achieved for all stakeholder groups. The whole model is also reviewed and improved on a two-year cycle, using learning obtained from users.

Clearly, we would like change strategies, as well as strategies more generally, to be anti-fragile. Much of our discussion about strategies applies to them also, although with some caveats. We shall not discuss these in detail here but let us discuss the general points. Perhaps most importantly, change strategies are frequently seen as one-off interventions, like transformation projects. As such, the only meaningful way one could be described as anti-fragile would be if the transformation project or change strategy repeatedly gets stronger through being stressed. In this case, it will be the change programme or project, rather than the organisation, that is anti-fragile. Anti-fragile projects and project management are of interest because a very large proportion of real projects experience partial or full failure against objectives, with cost and time overruns and none or limited delivery of desired outcomes. This is at least as true for change projects as well as construction and R&D ones. For these, often objectives are unclear and project management weak.

Thinking more widely, and recognising that there is no end to change, if a change strategy is seen as ongoing, without end, constantly learning and improving based on the real world challenges it experiences, then it is anti-fragile. The most forward-thinking organisations now, correctly, look at change in this way. Many organisational change strategies based on use of the EFQM Excellence Model, or its alternatives, are of this nature. There is, of course, a large cultural aspect to this which we shall discuss in the next chapter.

In either of these cases, finite-duration or ongoing, use of the EFQM Excellence Model, or a sensible alternative as the basis of a change strategy has, from the discussion in Chapter 1 and at the beginning of this section, a large number of anti-fragile aspects. But, does it pay off? Do organisations using the EFQM Excellence Model, or alternatives such as the Malcolm Baldrige National Quality Award Model, as the basis of a strategy or change strategy themselves become more robust or anti-fragile by using it? There is evidence to suggest that they do.

The key early research on this topic was undertaken by Vinod Singhal and Kevin Hendicks at Georgia Tec in the 1990s (Hendricks and Singhal, 1999). They used publicly available data to compare performance of excellence award winners and other companies in their sectors and found that award-winning companies have superior performance on share price and usual financial measures for up to five years following an award. This made them the perfect investment portfolio, outperforming alternatives! Such superior performance was based on what appeared to be an 'investment in excellence' phase prior to them winning the award, and provided evidence that companies that took the pursuit of excellence and the use of the Baldrige Model seriously outperformed rivals. But, does this mean that they are more robust or anti-fragile? To a limited extent, yes; it provides limited evidence of anti-fragility as award winners are getting stronger on share price and other accounting measures year on year, in comparison to the competitors, although we do not know that they are improving through being stressed. However one could argue that the excellence models induce stress through challenge in their use of the model and possible self-assessment.

My own research team, then at the Centre of Quality Excellence within the University of Leicester, repeated the research, working with Vinod Singhal, for the EFQM Excellence Model in Europe. Our research was funded by the EFQM and the British Quality Foundation (BQF) (see Bendell, Boulter and Dahlgaard, 2013). Data was collected during 2005–2006 for award winners at the European, national and regional levels across Europe, over the period 1990–2004. The methodology used was similar to the earlier US study. As with the earlier North American study, matched pairs of companies were used, so that for each award-winning company a comparable company was identified and selected. These were chosen so that each had the same country of incorporation of its parent company as the award winner to which it was matched, it had accounting data available over the same study period as for the award-winning company, it had at least the same first digit industry code as classified by Datastream, and it was closest in size to the award winner, as measured by total assets at the fiscal year end before the award-winning company first won an award, with the constraint that the ratio of value of assets was always less than a factor of three. Numbers were reduced due to a requirement for the companies to be publicly listed, plus the need to find a suitable match pair. Overall analysis was thus based on population of 120 award-winning companies, and their comparison companies. Of these, 85 were European head-office companies (70.8 per cent), and 35 were non-European head-office companies (29.2 per cent).

Our study looked at key performance measures including:

- share value, measured by the buy and hold returns, which was the primary measure;

- revenue/sales measures;

- cost measures;

- operating income measures;

- other accounting based measures.

Some of the key findings are shown in Figure 2.1.

What do these findings tell us about companies utilysing the EFQM Excellence Model, and its impact on robustness and anti-fragility? The share value data, sales data, total cost over sales data and assets data all suggest growing comparative strength over time. This is also true for additional measures not shown. Further, some of these measures, like growth in assets, are particularly important in our consideration of strength. There are also differences between the levels of award. European award winners grow in strength considerably faster but by definition, because of standards and competition, they are likely to have been challenged or stressed much more at the European award level, than by the national or regional award processes.

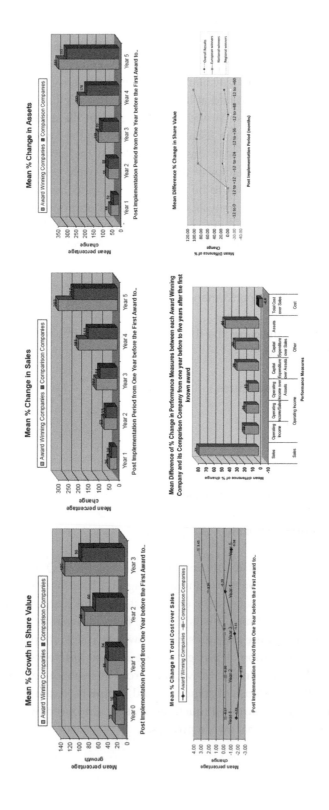

Figure 2.1   Results of Centre of Quality Excellence (University of Leicester) Study 2005–2006

Distinguishing Fragile and Anti-Fragile Strategies and Structures

Organisational structure also has an impact on fragility. Clearly some structures and structuring decision processes are more robust than others, but where does anti-fragility come in? A decision to restructure is frequently taken either in response to a perceived threat, or a perceived opportunity. Functional, Divisional or Matrix structures represent very different forms of organisation, and their fragility or robustness will be determined by their appropriateness for the internal and external circumstances of the time. Anti-fragility of the structure will be determined by the extent to which, and the smoothness with which, the structure changes in response to changes in these external and internal environments. A key consideration here is do such structural changes lead or lag the needs? Too late will typically imply some fragility and catch up. Too early can also introduce at least temporary fragility.

There are well-known fragility issues in particular organisational structures. Growing organisations frequently have periods when large numbers of direct reports to the senior officer of the company develop as the organisation grows, before it is eventually restructured. This may introduce fragility since it can overburden communication channels, decision-making processes, information flow and leadership, management and learning processes. Typically, this fragility may be compensated for, to some extent, through informal human culturally-based factors that can shortcut official channels.

Other structures have different issues. The complexity of responsibilities, reporting and relationships in matrix structures have been criticised by many, including Tom Peters, whilst rigid hierarchical silo structures may have deficiencies in information flow and decision making, and may not have the flexibility to cope with changes in the external and internal environment. Spreading learning is a particular problem for project-based organisations. All of these represent sources of fragility.

An anti-fragile structured organisation will, in contrast, not just be constantly reviewing and adjusting its structure but is also likely to have loose, quickly redefinable, somewhat informal, team relationships to allow it to do so.

There is also the question of size of organisations. Through anti-fragility Taleb has given a coherent theory to 'small is beautiful'. Elephants, he says, are fragile, and mice are not. As we saw in Chapter 1, the view obtained from Soft Systems Thinking is slightly different. There are advantages and disadvantages in terms of organisational fragility and anti-fragility to both large and small organisations. Whilst complexity in large systems, decision making and communication channels can be real problems, the potential for collection and application of useable information to improve performance, robustness and anti-fragility, is enormous. This is recognised in our current preoccupation with Big Data, although as yet it seems we are just not very good at fully exploiting it.

If small is beautiful, then we must also consider the networking of organisations to produce value. This then, in turn, leads us to think of the fragility, robustness and anti-fragility of such networks. We shall return to this matter, in the context of supply chains, in Chapter 6.

What else can we say on the difference between fragile and anti-fragile strategies and structures in practice? Essentially, we are looking for rules to enable exploitation of opportunities, whilst avoiding the fast tracks to extinction. That is hard as, without risk, there is no opportunity. So, what can we do? The author wishes to suggest that a number of rules have emerged from the previous discussion and his practical experience. These are:

1.   To progress towards anti-fragility, our organisation needs to be subject to stresses and progressively gain strength from these. Principally, we want to design it and manage it to progressively gain in strength from being stressed, rather than protect it from stress.

2.   In doing this, we need to work to ensure that the stresses are both proportionate and relevant to the development of strength for survival. Since these aspects are hard to ensure in a world exposed to Black Swans, we also need to apply precautionary principals, such as the deliberate creation of diverse stresses, to provide some protection.

3.   Our management, leadership and stakeholders need to be fully aware of the conceivable risks the organisation is facing, and the existence of as yet unknown Black Swans, that may impact on its survival. To achieve this, the collection and dissemination of full, timely, valid information is required, as is the ability to see the Big Picture.

4.   The management of risk should have a genuine enterprise-wide perspective, be the concern of the leadership team and not be delegated to middle or lower management, and not be ritualised into a compliance-driven 'tick box' process.

5.   There are some simple things that we can do immediately to ensure the integrity and anti-fragility of the organisation's governance. These include training board members and other key stakeholders in their responsibilities.

6.   Organisational strategy needs to be emergent, but based on planning and re-planning.

7.   Based on empirical evidence, as well as theory, change strategies based on the EFQM Excellence Model, or well-founded equivalents, appear to be anti-fragile.

8.   We will often rely on people, rather than systems and processes, to provide robustness and anti-fragility in relation to inherent weaknesses in our organisation, or ones created by unforeseen stress. We need to develop their ability to do this, support them in the process, and incorporate longer-term solutions into systems and processes.

How Does This Work for You?

Every organisation is different, as is every change agent. The above rules, and each of the arguments so far or later in this book, are not prescriptive. That would make them fragile. They may be moderately robust. To make them anti-fragile, we need to use them as working hypotheses defining what is current and hopefully best practice thinking, to be refined, developed and replaced as we understand more. This is true, not just for your individual learning cycle, but for your organisational one and our collective societal one.

So, please think about these ideas. What works for you, and what does not? And why? And, please let the author know (tony@servicesltd.co.uk or tony@theanti-fragilityacademy.co.uk).

Chapter 3
Developing Anti-Fragile People and a Culture of Anti-Fragility

Developing Anti-Fragile People

Previously, we have identified people as key to providing robustness and anti-fragility in relation to inherent weaknesses in our organisation, or ones created by unforeseen stress. People are both a major exploitable source of anti-fragility and a major source of fragility in themselves. Management and leadership's task should be to make it the former rather than the latter.

The reasons for this apparent contradiction are complex, and interpretation of it depends on which approach to, or theory of, management the organisation's business model reflects. The Classical Approach to management focuses on Scientific Management (or Taylorism), Fordism and Bureaucracy, and places emphasis on purpose, formal structure and organisational relationships, division of work, hierarchy of management, authority and clear definition of duties and responsibilities, maintaining specialisation and coordination, technical requirements and common principles of organisation. Associated with Taylor and others, this is essentially a disempowering approach, limiting the individual to defined tasks and role within the organisation. It is concerned primarily with improving the organisational structure as a means of increasing efficiency. Accordingly, organisations being managed according to this Classical Approach, and there are many such around the world, will be possibly highly efficient, but intrinsically fragile, due to the rigidity with which people are used and expect to be used. Even where the business model within the organisation is not a Classical management one, one can still find employees and managers who still intrinsically behave as if it was. Further, the high level of specialisation, and the accompanying *hard-wiring* of plant, particularly within the mass assembly lines created by Fordism, creates further fragility as such plants require high levels of consistent demand, and typically cannot easily adapt to changes in circumstances whether in customer demand, parts supply, supporting resources or broken robots.

In contrast, the Human Relations Approach to management, which could be said to be a reaction against the above, places emphasis on intrinsic employee job motivation and extrinsic rewards, leadership and communication, and organisation structures and practices which facilitate flexibility and involvement. By definition then, this is a less fragile organisational business model, certainly robust and, if there is ongoing improvement, then possibly anti-fragile.

The Systems Approach attempts to merge the Classical and Human Relations Approaches. It is focused on the total work of the organisation, the interrelationships of structure and behaviour, and the range of variables within the organisation. The organisation is viewed within its total environment and emphasises the importance of multiple channels in interaction. Thus, the emphasis on interrelationships, and the broader view of the total organisational environment, reinforces the robustness or anti-fragility seen in the Human Relations Approach.

Finally, the Contingency Approach is an extension of the Systems Approach, based on the principal that the structure of an organisation and its success are dependent upon the nature of tasks which are undertaken, and the nature of environmental influences. Therefore, there is no one best way to structure or manage organisations; rather it must be dependent upon the contingencies of the situation. This has many of the requirements of the anti-fragility concept and, if the organisation is constantly observing its internal and external environments, learning and improving its resilience by doing so, then it is clearly a genuine anti-fragile organisation.

To summarise then; if people work within, or think in terms of, an organisation following a Classical Approach to management, then the people may be a major source of fragility for the organisation, as role and mindset inflexibility, cultural problems, organisational silos, lack of taking of responsibility, managerial inflexibility and potentially slow decision-making processes may result. In contrast, if we have a Human Relations, Systems or Contingency Approach to management embedded in our business model, they should be less of a source of fragility and we will be more robust, and possibly anti-fragile in our human resources.

But how do we motivate and develop each of our people, and our workforce as a whole, to be more anti-fragile and to contribute to our organisational anti-fragility? Motivation is of course an enormous field. There are lots of definitions of what it means but generally motivation is defined in terms of the degree to which an individual wants and chooses to engage in certain specified behaviours, in our case anti-fragile ones.

In terms of definitions of motivation, motivation is typically seen as an individual phenomenon, intentional, multifaceted and predictable. With this view, people's behaviour is determined by what motivates them. Their performance is then a product of both their ability level and their motivation. Extrinsic motivation is related to tangible rewards, such as salary, working conditions, job security and promotion. In contrast, intrinsic motivation is related to psychological rewards, such as receiving appreciation, or a sense of challenge and achievement.   Higher motivational needs include attachment/ affiliation, which is the need for engagement and sharing, feeling of community and sense of belonging; as well as exploration/assertion, which is the ability to play and work, have fun and enjoyment and the need for self-assertion and the ability to choose. Economic rewards, intrinsic satisfaction and also social relationships all contribute to needs and expectations, and hence motivation, within the organisation. Friendships, group working, status and dependency all have a part to play. Frustration may result if there is a barrier or blockage in achieving these goals and this is something we need to manage. So in encouraging the development of anti-fragile behaviours, such as flexibility, we as managers should use all these levers.

It is also true that, amongst the myriad theories of motivation, Maslow's Hierarchy of Needs is probably the best known, although there are other well-established Content theories, focused on what motivates, as well as Process theories, focused on how we motivate. Maslow's model, like some of the other models, recognises that top of the pyramid of what motivates people is self-actualisation, including the desire for personal growth, a challenging job, opportunities for creativity, achievement and advancement, as well as lower-level needs, such as those illustrated by job security, friendly supervision and cohesive work groups. Meeting these high-level needs means actually meeting a need for an anti-fragile job role. So, in essence this means that, inherently, people have a need for pursuing anti-fragility in how they work. Giving people personal responsibility, providing specific challenging but realistic performance goals, providing feedback, using appropriate personal rewards, establishing clear evaluation of individual performance should all also help. Other contributions to anti-fragility that also increase job satisfaction are:

- permitting workers greater freedom and control of the scheduling and pacing of work;

- allowing workers to undertake full task cycles;

- providing workers with tasks which challenge their abilities and make full use of their expertise;

- giving workers greater freedom to work in self-managing teams;

- providing workers with the opportunity to have greater direct contact with clients and customers.

What is a Culture of Anti-Fragility and How Does it Relate to Other Cultural Elements?

Like motivation, the discussion of organisational cultures is a big topic in its own right. Put simply, culture is 'how we do things round here' in the absence of specific instructions or plans. Organisational culture is often defined as the shared assumptions and corresponding behaviour of humans who are part of an organisation, and the meanings that the people attach to their actions. Culture is taken to include aspects such as the organisational values, vision, norms, working language, systems, symbols, beliefs and habits. Organisational culture may also be said to be the pattern of collective behaviours and assumptions that are taught to people joining the organisation as a way of perceiving, thinking and feeling. Organisational culture affects the way people and groups interact with each other, and with customers and other stakeholders.

Large organisations typically do not just have one single homogeneous culture, but also a group of different local, but linked, cultures in different parts of the organisation, possibly with, for example, functional, local and establishment variations. Because of its complexity, this may sometimes be thought of more as a cultural continuum than a distinct set of variants. Diverse and sometimes conflicting cultures may co-exist, due to different characteristics of the management team. The organisational culture may have negative as well as positive aspects. Organisations often have very differing cultures as well as subcultures.

So, what does an organisational culture of anti-fragility look like? For an organisational culture to be anti-fragile it must continually get stronger from being stressed. A strong emphasis must therefore be placed on cohesiveness and determination in the face of adversity, 'the spirit of the blitz', and a neverending quest for growth and resilience. This will be a culture that places emphasis on use of information and collective communication, responsibility, creativity and entrepreneurship, welcoming and learning from challenges, and continual improvement. Further, this emphasis must exist everywhere across the organisation's cultural continuum, with it applying to the inter-group culture, as well as each intra-group one.

But does having an anti-fragile, or any other organisational culture, matter in determining the fragility, robustness or anti-fragility of the organisation? There is evidence that culture and, specifically, certain cultural traits, affect what the organisation achieves long term. This implies that organisational culture affects fragility and robustness, and probably anti-fragility. Based on studying management practices at 160 organisations over ten years, a 2003 Harvard Business School report (Nohria, Joyce and Robertson, 2003) identified that culture does have a significant impact on an organisation's long-term economic performance, and concluded that organisational culture can enhance, or be detrimental to, organisational performance. Specifically, organisations with strong performance-oriented cultures witnessed far better financial growth. A 2002 Corporate Leadership Council study found that cultural traits such as risk taking, internal communications and flexibility are some of the most important drivers of performance. Peters and Waterman (1982) also site innovativeness, productivity through people and the other cultural factors as also having positive economic consequences. Whilst Denison, Haaland and Goelzer (2004) found that while culture contributes to the success of the organisation, not all dimensions were found to contribute the same; the impacts of these dimensions differ by global regions, which suggest that organisational culture is impacted by national culture.

Although his work has been much criticised, Geert Hofstede is a key figure in the discussion of organisational culture. In 1980, Hofstede first published a book reporting his survey since 1967, a study looking for global differences between over 100,000 IBM employees in 50 countries and three world regions in an attempt to find aspects of culture that might influence business behaviour (Hofstede, 1984). He suggested that cultural differences exist between regions and nations, and that awareness of this is important for cultural introspection. Cultural differences reflect differences in thinking and social action, and even in *mental programs*, a term Hofstede uses for predictable behaviour. Hofstede relates culture to ethnic and regional groups, but also to categories such as organisation, profession, family, society and subcultural groups, national political systems and legislation. Hofstede's original theory of cultural dimensions proposed four dimensions along which cultural values might be analysed:

1.   individualism–collectivism;

2.   uncertainty avoidance;

3.   power distance (strength of social hierarchy); and

4.   masculinity–femininity (task orientation versus person orientation).

Personal research in Hong Kong led Hofstede to add 'long-term orientation' as a fifth dimension, to cover aspects of values not originally discussed. In 2010, Hofstede added 'indulgence versus self-restraint' as a sixth dimension, based on co-author Michael Minkov's analysis of data from the World Values Survey.

Can we apply Hofstede's cultural dimensions in considering the implications for organisational anti-fragility? It is clear that the majority of the dimensions can immediately be seen to have an effect on the fragility, robustness or anti-fragility of the organisation. Of particular interest, perhaps, is long-term orientation, since paying attention to, and concern for, the future should have a positive effect on anti-fragility. Similarly, uncertainty avoidance is important, since low uncertainty avoidance cultures accept and feel comfortable in unstructured situations, or changeable environments, and try to have as few rules as possible. These are therefore more equipped for an unpredictable world and are, hence, potentially anti-fragile. The other dimensions also impact. Low power distance, individualism and indulgence combined with high masculinity may possibly be the best anti-fragile combination. The position on the masculinity dimension most suitable to anti-fragility is particularly debatable. Interestingly, since there are identified national and regional differences in cultures on the cultural dimensions, this implies the potential for national and regional differences in organisational anti-fragility; one of a large number of subjects for further research in this new anti-fragility field.

Table 3.1 below speculates on the idealised profile on the cultural dimensions for anti-fragile organisations, and how this compares to identified regional and national positions.

Table 3.1   Hofstede's cultural dimensions and anti-fragility

Cultural Dimension	Anti-Fragile Organisation (speculative)	High	Low	Close to Anti-Fragile?	UK	US
Power distance	Low	Latin and Asian countries, Africa and Arab world	Anglo and Germanic countries	Israel	Middle	Middle, higher than UK
Individualism	Low	North America and Europe	Columbia, Indonesia, Guatemala	Guatemala	High	High
Uncertainty avoidance	Low	Anglo and Nordic and Chinese countries	South and East Europe, and Japan	Denmark	Low	Low
Masculinity	High (?)	Japan, Hungary, Austria, Switzerland	Nordic (very low)	Japan	Relatively high	Relatively high
Long-termism	High	East Asia	Anglo and Muslim countries, Africa and Latin America	China	Low	Low
Indulgence	Low	Latin America, parts of Africa, Anglo and Nordic Europe	East Asia, Eastern Europe and Muslim World	China	High	High

However, Hofstede and later authors acknowledge that organisational culture issues are more complex than just thinking in terms of the dimensions of national cultures. It can be argued that whilst national cultures are embedded in values, organisational cultures are at least partly embedded in practices. In the 1980s, the Institute for Research on Intercultural Cooperation Geert's Institute, conducted a research project on organisational culture, and studied 20 organisational units in Denmark and the Netherlands (Hofstede Centre, 2014). This identified six dimensions of practice (or communities of practice):

1.   process-oriented versus results-oriented;

2.   employee-oriented versus job-oriented;

3.   parochial versus professional;

4.   open system versus closed system;

5.   loose control versus tight control;

6.   pragmatic versus normative.

There is also an acknowledgement that managing international or global organisations involves understanding both the national and organisational cultures. Communities of practice across borders are significant for multinationals and global corporates in order to hold the company together. Frequently, the country of origin's culture is seen to migrate to the multinational or global branches, tempered perhaps to some extent by local regional or national culture.

Considering the above six dimensions of practice in the context of anti-fragility, we can see once again that the organisation's position on them clearly relates to its overall fragility, robustness or anti-fragility. We might perhaps expect an anti-fragile organisation to be results-orientated rather than process-orientated, employee-oriented rather than job-oriented, professional rather than parochial, open system rather than closed system, pragmatic rather than normative, and possibly have loose control rather than tight control.

Management and Leadership for the Anti-Fragility Culture

Let us start this section by discussing what would we expect the conduct of people management activities to be like in an anti-fragile organisation; that is what are the 'nuts and bolts' of managing for anti-fragility? For reasons explained previously, a good starting point for this discussion is the criterion dealing with people management aspects in the EFQM Excellence Model. In terms of people management, the Model embodies the belief that to be excellent an organisation should value their people and create a culture that allows the mutually beneficial achievement of organisational and personal goals. Also, that they should develop the capabilities of their people and promote fairness and equality. They should also care for, communicate, reward and recognise in a way that motivates people, builds commitment and enables them to use their skills and knowledge for the benefit of the organisation. This is a utopian list, but is it anti-fragile? The definition of anti-fragility requires an organisation to improve its resilience by being stressed. Does this wish list correspond to that requirement? Clearly no, or at best, perhaps. It should give some robustness. However, as a paradigm of the EFQM Excellence Model and its alternatives, the criterion should not be seen in isolation.

Elsewhere in the infrastructure of the EFQM Excellence Model, the concept of exposure to stresses through deploying the approach in real life, learning from how well it does, improving it further and repeating this process on an ongoing basis is embedded through the so-called RADAR mechanism. RADAR stands for Results, Approach, Deployment, and Assessment and Refinement. To some extent this is, of course, naturally anti-fragile, although a lot will depend on the mindset with which it is applied; the difference between learning and improving from deployment, and improving resilience through being stressed, is a subtle one. For example, RADAR improvement includes improvement in efficiency and effectiveness, as well as potentially in robustness and anti-fragility; and, whilst within the broad scope, the latter are not explicitly identified by the criteria. There will also naturally be trade-offs between these aspects; as we have already discussed, an efficient solution is frequently not an anti-fragile one. Further, it is unclear to what extent exposure to stress through deployment includes exposure to Black Swans, which are core to the current interest in anti-fragility, as within the normal mindset of the EFQM Excellence Model it may be very reasonable to exclude these as they are unforeseen exceptional circumstances and not core to the routine use of the model.

Consideration of the people-orientated sub-criteria of the EFQM Excellence Model adds some further clarity to the robustness that the model represents and, when integrated with the RADAR logic, its partial anti-fragility. The first sub-criteria broadly covers how people plans support the organisation's strategy and includes how they define the performance levels for people required to meet strategic goals; align these with strategy, structure and processes; involve employees in developing people strategy; appropriately manage recruitment, career development and succession planning; and improve people strategies and plans through employee feedback. Second, there is a focus on the methods whereby peoples' knowledge and capabilities are developed, including skill and competence needs; developing appropriate training and development plans; appropriately aligning and reviewing individual, team and organisational objectives, appraising and helping people improve; and ensuring people have the tools, competencies, information and empowerment to maximise their contribution. The third sub-criteria covers how people are aligned with strategic goals and how they are involved and empowered. This includes developing a supportive culture; encouraging creativity, innovation and entrepreneurship; and involving people in review and optimisation of process efficiency and effectiveness. Fourth, effective communication is covered, including understanding communication needs and expectations; developing communication strategy and channels; communicating direction and focus; ensuring understanding of personal contribution; and enabling and encouraging information and knowledge sharing. Lastly, how people are rewarded, recognised and cared for is covered, including considerations of work–life balance; respect for diversity; health and safety; contribution to society; and mutual support, recognition and care.

Clearly, these clear requirements for consideration, with their emphasis on planning, development, involvement, alignment, communication, review and support, add to the robustness and potential anti-fragility of an organisation truly using this framework, but the previous discussion remains as to whether they are more concerned with efficiency and effectiveness rather than fragility.

So, what of leadership? Firstly, how does the issue of leadership for anti-fragility differ from the management issue above? To quote Field Marshall Sir William Slim:

> *Management is of the mind, more a matter of accurate calculations, of statistics, methods, timetables and routines. Its practice is a science. Leadership is of the spirit, compounded of personality and vision. Its practice is an art. Managers are necessary. Leaders are essential. (Slim, 1957)*

How does this relate to anti-fragility? Clearly, we need leadership to inspire us to develop towards, and run, an anti-fragile organisation; it won't happen by accident, someone will have to lead it.

More modern views of leadership go at lot further in a number of directions; there are numerous models and criteria and we shall look at some of these in the context of anti-fragility below. First, however, let us understand the broad context, through a few more insights:

- '… decisive, he's been radical in making changes and he has the courage to pursue his vision.'

- '… making your team feel valued is one of the keys to successful modern leadership.'

- 'Good leaders need to coach and motivate and then leave people to get on with it.'

- 'Certain decisions will always have to come from the top: the art of leadership is knowing which ones.'

- '… today's leader is as much part of the team as at the front of it.'

- 'Courage, integrity, strategy and vision are all qualities every firm needs to be successful.'

- 'Leadership is needed at every level of the company.'

- 'There's no such thing as a bad team, only a bad leader.'

So, what do these insights tell us about leadership in the context of anti-fragility? Interestingly, and similar to our earlier discussion of motivation, there is an argument to say that there is already some elements of robustness, and potentially of anti-fragility, implicit in what we now judge as good leadership: change, learning, vision, strategy and decision making. As we get into further detail with the models and criteria, this will become more explicit.

In the historical development of modern ideas on leadership, there are a number of keys to this emergence of robust and anti-fragile aspects to the leaders' role (see for example, Northhouse, 2013). Prior to the 1930s, leadership was largely about control and centralisation of power, and the ability to impress the will of the leader on the led, and induce obedience, respect, loyalty and cooperation; essentially a fragile formulation, except that inducing obedience and cooperation gives some robustness. By the 1950s two important themes had emerged relevant to further enhancing robustness. These are the leadership sharing goals with the led and directing the activities of the group towards them, and the ability of the leader to influence overall group effectiveness. By the 1980s leadership was seen as a transformational process, now, perhaps, also revealing some anti-fragile aspects to leadership. Another recent developing theme of further robustness and the possible emergence of anti-fragility in leadership is the formulation of leadership as a process by which a person influences others to accomplish an objective and directs the organisation in a way that makes it more cohesive and coherent. Thus common components included in Leadership today are Process, Influence, Groups and Common Goals; all of which potentially help robustness and anti-fragility.

A clearer recognition of an anti-fragile aspect to leadership comes from considering the Leadership Cycle, based on the common process formulation, since this incorporates an ongoing improvement cycle. Of course, leadership also can be a fragile aspect in an organisation. It can become an end in itself for a leader to extend their power base, or leadership may be judged on the performance and growth of the leader's group or organisation, follower attitudes and perceptions of the leader, the leader's contribution to the quality of group processes or the extent to which a person has a successful career as a leader, rather than the achievement of the objectives of the organisation.

Below, we show a common classification of Leadership theories:

- Great Man theory

- Trait theory

- Behavioural theory

- Role theory

- Transformational theory

- Transactional theory

- Contingency theory

- Situational Model theory

- Path–Goal theory.

According to Great Man theory, leaders are born and not made, leadership had something to do with breeding. This is obviously not an anti-fragile approach, and only robust if enough leaders consistently arise naturally.

Trait theory is based on people being born with inherited traits, with some traits particularly suited to leadership. A trait is a variety of individual attributes, including aspects of personality, temperament, needs, motives and values. Thus people who make good leaders have the right (or sufficient) combination of traits; a *Leadership Gene*. Different authors, however, identify different traits as important for leadership. Again, in general, this theory provides a robust, rather than anti-fragile, approach to leadership. However, if some learning traits are included, or learning is shared between leaders, this will change.

According to Behavioural theory, leaders can be made or trained, rather than being born as leaders, and successful leadership is based in definable, learnable behaviour. So, people can learn leadership from how leaders act, and we can teach people how to be a good leader. Clearly, this can be a robust approach to leadership and, if leaders can extend or improve their learning over time and its application – including learning about resilience arising from unforeseen circumstances – or we can continually improve the distribution and application of such learning in a similar way, then it will be anti-fragile.

Role theory is part of Behavioural theory and, according to it, leaders are influenced by the people around them, playing the leadership role that is put upon them by others. Accordingly, role conflict can come from different people having varying expectations of their leaders, or when the leaders have different ideas about what they should be doing compared to the expectations that are put upon them by followers. Accordingly, this is the basis for a potentially robust approach to leadership.

Transformational theory is about the process of leaders stimulating higher levels of motivation and commitment amongst those that follow them. It is based on the idea that people will follow a person who inspires and motivates them, and who has vision, enthusiasm, energy and passion. It focuses on the relationship between leaders and followers, and encourages shared meanings, values and goals. The leader provides the vision, supports the team and looks out for individuals. Again, it is the basis for a potentially robust approach to leadership.

In contrast, Transactional theory is based on the concepts that people are motivated by rewards and punishments, that social systems work best when they have a clear chain of command, that when people have agreed to do a job part of the deal is that they give up all authority to their manager, and that the prime purpose of a subordinate is to do what their manager tells them to do. The focus with Transactional theory is thus on the management of the organisation, procedures and efficiency, working to rules and contracts, and managing current issues and problems. In common with the related Classical Approach to management discussed at the start of this chapter, by its nature this is an intrinsically disempowering and fragile approach.

Contingency theory sees leaders as being more flexible, with different leadership styles used at different times, depending on the circumstance. It suggests leadership is not a fixed series of characteristics that can be applied to different contexts but rather it tries to match leaders to appropriate situations.

The effectiveness of a leader in a situation will depend on how well the leader's style fits the context. With a large pool of leaders with diverse styles, this would yield a robust approach; potential anti-fragility will depend on whether there is a learning cycle in the process.

Under the Situational Model theory developed by Hersey and Blanchard from the late 1960s, leaders should adapt their style to follower development or 'maturity', based on how ready and willing the followers are to perform required tasks, that is, their competence and motivation (Hersey, Blanchard and Dewey, 1996). There are four leadership styles that should be used (S1 to S4), that correspond to each of the development levels (D1 to D4) of the followers. The four styles are:

- *S1: Telling/Directing*: high directive/low supportive leader. The leader tells the subordinates what, how, when and where to do various tasks.

- *S2: Selling/Coaching*: high directive/high supportive behaviour. The leader still provides a great deal of direction, but also attempts to hear the employees' feelings about a decision, as well as their ideas and suggestions.

- *S3: Participating/Supporting*: high supportive/low directive. The leader's role is to provide recognition and to actively listen, and facilitate problem solving and decision making on the part of the employees.

- *S4: Delegating/Observing*: low supportive/low directive. Employees are allowed greater autonomy because they have both the competence and confidence to do the task on their own.

This is certainly a robust and, potentially, an anti-fragile approach, depending on how it is implemented, whether there is exposure to stress and whether the learning is captured and applied.

With Path–Goal theory, leaders make the paths that followers should take to achieve the goals they have been set, clear and easy, to encourage and support them. Thus leaders should clarify the path so subordinates know which way to go, remove any roadblocks that are stopping them going there and increase the rewards along the route. In practice, the approach will vary depending on the circumstances, including the follower's capability and motivation, as well as the difficulty of the job and other contextual factors. This is robust and potentially anti-fragile if it incorporates stressing, learning and application.

Participative leadership consists of inviting subordinates to share in the decision making. The participative leader consults with subordinates, obtains their ideas and opinions, and integrates their suggestions into the decisions about how the group or organisation will proceed. Potentially this is a robust, or possibly even anti-fragile, approach, depending on the extent of participation facilitated and the extent of ongoing learning.

As with our discussion of people management previously, we can consider the leadership criteria and sub-criteria in the EFQM Excellence Model to begin to explore what anti-fragile leadership in an organisation might be like. The model is based on the concept that excellent organisations have leaders who shape the future and make it happen, acting as role models for its values and ethics and inspiring trust at all times. They are flexible, enabling the organisation to anticipate and react in a timely manner to ensure the ongoing success of the organisation. There are a number of key anti-fragile aspects to this definition; in particular the flexibility of leaders, together with shaping the future and making it happen, and timely anticipation and reaction to ensure ongoing success.

In terms of the sub-criteria, the first is concerned with the method by which leaders develop the mission, vision, values and ethics and act as role models, and includes identifying, setting and communicating a clear direction and strategic focus; uniting their people in sharing and achieving the organisation's core purpose and objectives; championing and role modelling the organisation's values; appropriately fostering development; ensuring ethical behaviour; and developing a shared leadership culture for the organisation and reviewing and improving the effectiveness of personal leadership behaviour.

Second, the model is concerned with how leaders establish and drive improvement of the organisation's management system and performance, including evaluating a balanced set of results to review progress and using all available knowledge; providing an understanding of long and short-term priorities for the key stakeholders, and achieving their confidence; making fact-based decisions; improving performance and providing sustainable benefits to stakeholders; going beyond regularity compliance, and being transparent and accountable to stakeholders and society; undertaking full Risk Management; and developing the underlying capabilities of the organisation.

The third sub-criteria is concerned with engaging with external stakeholders including how leaders respond to their different needs and expectations; how they engage them in generating ideas and innovation; innovating to enhance reputation and attract new partners; how leaders appropriately identify strategic and operational partnerships; and how leaders ensure transparency of reporting to stakeholders. The fourth area is concerned with how the leaders reinforce a culture of excellence with the organisation's people, including how the leaders inspire people and create and promote a culture of involvement, ownership, idea generation, empowerment, entrepreneurship, improvement and accountability at all levels; ensuring people can realise their full potential to contribute to personal and organisational success; appropriately supporting and recognising people in achieving objectives; and promoting and encouraging equal opportunities and diversity.

Finally, the last area is about how the leaders ensure organisational flexibility and effective Change Management, including understanding change drivers; making decisions appropriately; being flexible, realigning organisational direction and ensuring trust; involving and seeking stakeholder commitment; learning and responding quickly; and allocating resources to meet long-term needs.

As with people management, all these detailed EFQM Excellence Model leadership sub-criteria clearly identify and reinforce what we are looking for, to ensure the robustness and potential anti-fragility of an organisation. However, the same issues in relation to anti-fragility remain as we discussed for people; it is unclear how far the criteria go beyond just efficiency and effectiveness improvement to include anti-fragility.

Whilst an organisation attempting to meet the EFQM Excellence Model People sub-criteria, and using the associated RADAR mechanism, will clearly assist the pursuit of organisational anti-fragility, what should be the basis of measuring progress towards this? For this, the answer is largely given by looking at the EFQM Excellence Model People Results criterion.

The EFQM Excellence Model assumes that excellent organisations will need to develop and agree a set of performance indicators and related perception outcome measurements that measure the success of the people strategy and its deployment. It also assumes that the organisation will set clear targets for the most important of these, be able to show at least three years good and improving results, understand the basis for these and anticipate future performance, understand comparative performance with others and accordingly set stretch targets, and be able to segment the results for any specific groups of interest. The performance indicators are those internal measures used by the organisation to monitor and predict people's performance and the efficiency and effectiveness of deployment of people strategy, and to predict the impact on perceptions. Typically, coverage will include appropriate measures of involvement, engagement, target setting, competency, performance management, leadership performance, career development and communications. The perception outcomes may be obtained from a number of sources, including focus groups, surveys, structured appraisals and interviews and they will cover satisfaction, involvement, pride, leadership and management, target setting, competency, career development, performance management, communication and working conditions.

If an organisation wishes to measure its progress towards anti-fragility of its people and people management, the above measurement and monitoring requirements used together with the RADAR mechanism are a good start but, once again, probably have not got quite the right emphasis and do not go quite far enough. The measurement system described is in one sense comprehensive in coverage but varies in focus from that needed to ensure progress to anti-fragility. For example, an interpretation of the system might put maximum emphasis on the efficiency and effectiveness of the deployment of the people strategy, and no emphasis on its fragility. Since we know that efficiency and fragility are often correlated, this deficiency may be particularly fragile. Similarly, there is no explicit consideration of the people's view of fragility of the people strategy and processes in the requirements. In a fast-moving world, where there are issues of layoffs, pension fund problems, skill deficits, transformed roles due to technology shifts and so on, this may again be particularly problematical.

How to Develop an Anti-Fragility Culture

Developing an Anti-Fragility Culture is about change and Change Management required to achieve the culture. We discussed change strategies in Chapter 2, although there, solely in the context of the EFQM Excellence Model. The issues of Change Management are, of course, much bigger. Whatever model of change we take, a key consideration will be the infrastructure that we need to put in place to create the framework for change. Included in this are likely to be considerations of how we gain real management commitment to the changes and change process; how we identify suitable candidates and establish change agents; how we identify

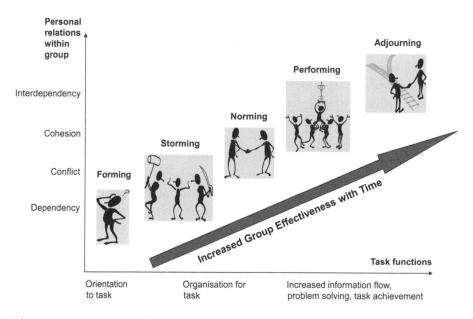

Figure 3.1   Stages of group or team development

and engage the stakeholders involved; how we identify where and what we are going to work on, and in what order; how we identify and establish change teams; and how we identify training needs, and train individuals and teams.

Establishing real and coherent management commitment, or buy-in, is a stage which has, in the past on change programmes, often been done ineffectively and is crucial for success. A starting point is the establishment of a real consensus acceptance of the need for change amongst the senior leadership team. This is typically a facilitated process of information sharing, debate, the emergence of a common view, the building of team ownership, and the creation and deployment of vision. This is similar to the typical team Forming, Storming, Norming, Performing process shown in Figure 3.1 (Tuckman 1965), and may typically suffer from the same weaknesses. Specifically, if the Storming stage, in which the members argue through what they are trying to do and the rules, is not done properly, then the chances of success are poor. Attempts to speed up this crucial step and curtail debate will distinctly limit subsequent team ownership. However, as we shall discuss below, there are also creativity tools which can be used, in a facilitated way, with a team at any level that to an extent avoid some of these issues and do speed up the process.

In the mainstream approach, right from the Forming stage, the process is difficult for a number of reasons. These include conflicting emotions amongst the management team members, for example excitement, anxiety, disinterest or sheer resistance to trying to do this task. Also, loyalties to departments and colleagues and relationships with other team members may interfere with an objective approach, and there may be nervousness about the chances of success. Indeed, within the team there may be sub-groups or factions with unwritten rules, objectives or 'norms' that don't fit with those of the team, for example in terms of behaviour and language. The Forming stage is the orientation phase, at which the set of individuals has not yet gelled in terms of the task, and its characteristics are typically confusion, uncertainty, members assessing the situation and task, testing ground rules, feeling out others, defining goals, getting acquainted and establishing rules.

The following Storming stage is a conflict stage for the team and can be an uncomfortable period. Team members bargain with each other as they try to sort out what each of them individually, and as a group, may want out of the change process. Done properly, individuals reveal their personal and functional area goals and it is possible that hostility is generated as differences in these goals are revealed. Members may resist the influence of other group members on goals and may show hostility. As a consequence, the early relationships established in the Forming stage may be threatened or disrupted. The key personal relations issue in this stage is the management of conflict, whilst the task question is how best to organise to achieve team ownership of the shared vision.

The Norming stage is a consensus stage, where trust is established, and standards set. In this cohesion stage, the members of the group typically develop ways of working to develop closer camaraderie in pursuit of establishing the shared vision. The question of who will do what and how it will be done are addressed. Working rules emerge in terms of norms of behaviour and roles. Possibly for the first time in the management team, a structure is therefore created in which the questions of agreeing expectations and dealing with a failure to meet members' expectations are addressed openly. As personal relations are more cohesive, team members feel that they have overcome conflict, have gelled and typically experience an enhanced sense of group belonging. On the task side, there is typically an increase in data and information flow as members become prepared to be more open about their goals.

By the Performing stage, the leadership team should have developed an effective structure and it is concerned with actually getting on with the job in

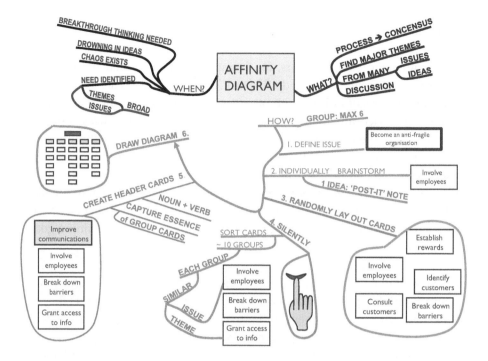

Figure 3.2   Affinity Diagram

hand and establishing the vision. The fully mature group has now been created which can get on with its work. However, not all leadership groups develop to this stage instead becoming bogged down in an earlier and less productive stage. In personal relations terms, interdependency becomes a feature. Leadership team members are now happy working alone, in subgroups or as a single unit. Collaboration and constructive competition occur between them. On the task side, there is a high commitment to the objective, jobs are well defined and problem-solving activities become second nature.

Of course, what works for the leadership team should, properly facilitated, work for the rest of the organisation too, and the above can be used for team development throughout the organisation. For the senior team in pursuit of a cohesive management commitment to a vision, or for lower-level teams doing the same within its own arena, certain creativity tools can be used in a facilitated way that to some extent avoid some of the team-building issues en route and speed up the process. An ideal way to do this is through sequential use of an Affinity Diagram and an Interrelationship Diagram, as illustrated in a simple way in Figures 3.2 and 3.3.

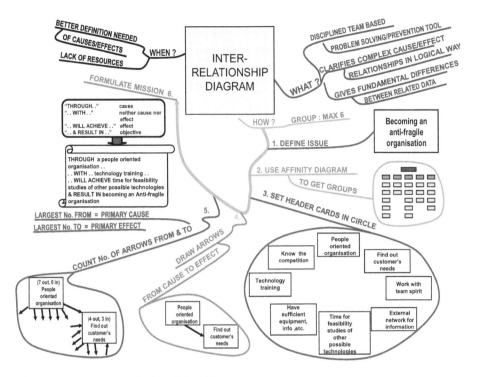

Figure 3.3   Interrelationship Diagram

The first of these two figures illustrates how the Affinity Diagram can be used with a small team of up to six to identify and group the activities where action is required to define the vision. It is an artificial example, both in the naive selection of the issue and in the limited scope in the cards and header card illustrated (typically Post-it notes on the wall), but it does illustrate the process. A key point is that silence should be maintained throughout, enforced by the group facilitator, as members individually brainstorm ideas onto Post-it notes or cards, then randomly lay them out, and then sort the cards into cognate groups. The last of these three stages is particularly difficult to do in silence! Only then can the team talk together to agree the header card for each group, using a noun and a verb and a positive orientation, that is, to make the header card say something we would want to happen, rather than not happen.

Once this is done, reviewed and agreed, the Interrelationship Diagram may be used to construct the vision statement. In this everyone can talk; they lay the header cards in a circle, look for the existence or not of what is only allowed as a single unidirectional relationship between every pair of header cards, draw these, and then count the numbers of out- and in- arrows for each header card.

Using a little common sense, the vision statement can then be constructed by filling in the words from the header cards into the statement:

> 'THROUGH …….. WITH ……., WE WILL ACHIEVE ……..and RESULT IN ……..',

as in the illustration in the figure. In doing this, prime causes are those header cards with the maximum numbers of arrows out, and final effects are those header cards with the maximum number of arrows in. Within reason, it is up to you how many stages you have in between, dependent on the number of people and ideas involved, the number of header cards and the complexity of the vision.

Whilst this creativity tool-based approach avoids some of the issues of team building, and so speeds up the process of developing team ownership, it is more about avoidance than solution. Underlying team issues may well to some extent remain and the team's performance may not reach full potential because of failure to work out early stage issues, lack of clear objectives or understanding of purpose by every team member, and personal and unstated aims or hidden agendas. These will need to be solved or further avoided in the future, so going through the full Forming, Storming, Norming and Performing process in a facilitated way is still a good idea. For good team working we need an appropriate team leadership style as well as clarity of goals, defined roles and decision-making procedures, established ground rules or norms, clear communication, balanced participation, appropriate management of conflict, team member awareness of process as well as the task (the 'How' as well as the 'What'), a systematic approach to problem solving, and a positive environment and climate.

As well as establishing real and coherent management commitment through this process of developing a shared vision and the acceptance of a need for change, management commitment needs to be demonstrated through the leadership team's recognition and communication of the organisational implications, open and visible support for improvement and for the mechanism of change, encouragement of innovation and creativity, enthusiasm for results achieved or to be achieved, championing the change, challenging traditional values and attitudes to overcome resistance to change, and openly demonstrating the relevant leadership qualities. It is argued that such desired organisational change will only occur when the knowledge of the first practical steps to achieve it, combined with dissatisfaction with the status quo and a desired vision of the future, exceeds the combined material and psychological costs of acting.

In defining the infrastructure for change towards an anti-fragile organisation, identifying and establishing organisational change agents at various levels is important. Organisational change agents typically have a mixed role, on the one hand motivational and leadership, and on the other, administrative. This may include identifying and understanding stakeholders and their needs, ensuring the overall goals of the change process are clearly defined and communicated to the relevant teams and stakeholders, communicating boundaries and scope of improvement activities, forming and leading improvement teams, ensuring performance measures are collected and analysed and that assigned actions are completed, championing change and improvement, reporting progress and results to stakeholders, and ensuring the improvement objectives are achieved. It follows that, typically, there is more need for the change agent to be skilled in managing the change process than to be knowledgeable with respect to the substance of the change. Accordingly, to be successful a change agent will need 'soft' management skills related to communication, presentation, selling, negotiating, influencing and providing feedback and support.

So, the big question based on our discussion above is how ready is your organisation for change towards an anti-fragile culture, and what can you do to make it more ready? There are, of course, different extents of change that an organisation may be considering. The change strategy for moving towards being more organisationally anti-fragile may be:

- Developmental: correcting existing aspects of the organisation towards a more anti-fragile culture.

- Transitional: to achieve a known desired state that is different from the existing one, based on unfreezing the current way of doing things, then moving and refreezing.

- Transformational: so radical that it in many senses it may result in a completely different organisation.

Whatever extent of change an organisation is considering, it is inevitable that there will in practice be some resistance to change. This may arise because of fear, due to potential loss of personal standing or job, or increase in workload; the belief that change is being imposed rather than chosen; lack of faith in those making the change; a belief that something important has been overlooked; misunderstanding and lack of trust; contradictory assessments; habit as 'we have always done it this way'; or the economic implications for pay and conditions of service. Some people just have a low tolerance of change.

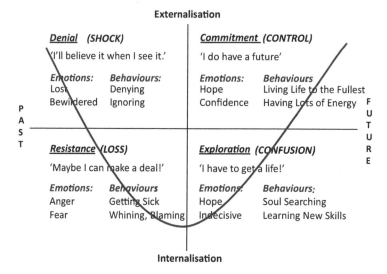

Figure 3.4   Transition Curve

Such change in the work environment can be so traumatic that it is likened to the death of a loved one and the bereavement curve is used to model the stages an individual goes through when it occurs (see Figure 3.4).

Of course, our issue is typically to get our people through this change curve as quickly and effectively as possible (see Figure 3.5).

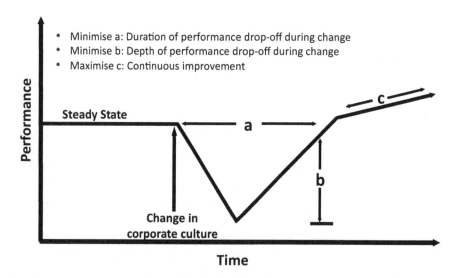

Figure 3.5   Objectives for managing change

In practice, people's reaction to change vary. Some examples are shown in Table 3.2.

Table 3.2   Reactions to change

Disposition to a change. For example, towards organisational anti-fragility	Response to a change. For example, towards organisational anti-fragility.
Commitment	Would like change to happen, will work towards this goal, and create whatever structures, systems and frameworks are necessary to help achieve it.
Enrolment	Would like change to happen, and will devote time and energy to help achieve it within the given frameworks.
Genuine compliance	See virtue in proposed change, do what is asked of them and act within the letter of the framework.
Formal compliance	Understand the benefits of proposed change and are not hostile to it. Do what they are asked but no more.
Grudging compliance	Do not accept benefits of proposed change, do not want to go along with it, voice opposition and hope for failure.
Non-compliance	Do not accept benefits of proposed change, and have nothing to lose by opposing it. Will not do what is asked of them.
Apathy	Just serving time; do not feel involved, neither in support nor in opposition to proposed change.

Typical issues about staff attitudes when facing change are:

• the inability of some staff to recognise that 'room for improvement' is a fact and a way forward, not a criticism;

• the false division between quantity, which they understand, and quality, which they do not;

• frustration with widespread, ineffective team working;

• comfort with the status quo;

• the 'been saying this for years' attitude, which absolves them of responsibility;

- the 'tried that ten years ago and it didn't work then' attitude, which means that they do not need to consider it;

- outmoded practices locked in tradition.

However, managers also have issues when facing change as this often conflicts with custom and practice. These include overemphasis on short-term results, so attacking symptoms of underlying issues rather than directly dealing with them; emphasis on business as usual, and little or no emphasis on Continuous Improvement; failure to integrate Continuous Improvement into business strategy; no clear view on what to improve; failure to integrate Continuous Improvement with normal duties; no clear view of improvement targets; and no clear understanding of the correlation between efficiency and fragility in operations.

Thus, traditional organisational values might be unfortunately summarised in many cases in terms of:

- 'If it isn't broken, don't fix it.'

- 'I don't want to hear the detail just fix it.'

- 'Don't spend too long thinking about it, we need to get stuff out of the door.'

- 'Get it working for now, we can fix it next week.'

- 'It's OK, it's working after a fashion.'

- 'Well, I think this is the problem.'

In contrast, Continuous Improvement and anti-fragile core values will include:

- always look for improvement opportunities;

- management by fact;

- understand root causes before acting;

- avoid blinkered thinking;

- monitor the impact of solutions.

A supportive organisational culture will embed continuous process improvement as part of everyone's job. It will ensure that teams understand that they are empowered to make change happen! Everyone will know why Continuous Improvement is important and everyone will be familiar with improvement tools and use them. Targets, standards and improvements will be clearly communicated.

There are a large number of approaches for managing change. Amongst these, Force Field Analysis, illustrated in Figure 3.6, is of particular interest in the context of developing the anti-fragile organisation. This is based on the concept of driving forces and restraining forces, and the fundamentals that as increasing driving forces can result in an increase in restraining forces, reducing resisting forces is typically preferable. Thus helping a team face up to and deal with a skills deficit or established work patterns is preferable to a manager just pushing harder as this tends to increase resistance. Also, group norms are important forces in their own right. Getting a group to consider these forces in the particular circumstances they face can be both a very good analysis exercise in determining an effective strategy and a good way of developing ownership of an effective solution. It also fits with our remarks previously that through self-actualisation there is a natural need for people to pursue anti-fragility in how they work.

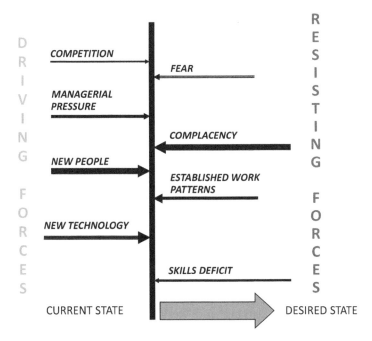

Figure 3.6   Force Field Analysis

Kotter's Recipe for Successfully Managing Change is an eight-step process that can also be applied to pursuit of cultural change towards anti-fragility within an organisation.

The eight steps are:

1.   Establish a sense of urgency: change needs motivation, can we create a *burning platform*?

2.   Create a guiding team: we need to form a powerful group of enthusiasts for the change.

3.   Create vision and strategy: we need to create a vision that will help to guide the change.

4.   Communicate for buy-in: we should use all mediums and vehicles available to constantly communicate the new vision and strategies.

5.   Empower people: to remove the obstacles we need to provide appropriate support and resources.

6.   Short-term wins: we must help create short-term organisational and personal wins.

7.   Consolidating achievements: we should build momentum through consolidating gains.

8.   incorporate the new approaches into the organisational culture: unless these become part of the culture, long-lasting results may not be achieved.

So, some issues to think about in the context of your own organisations;

•   How might you manage organisational culture change towards anti-fragility, and what are the challenges for you? We suggest that you use a SWOT analysis and list your organisational Strengths, Weaknesses, Opportunities and Threats, to help.

•   Identify the Driving and Resisting forces to such change, and construct a Force Field Analysis.

- What responses to change do you expect and who is crucial to managing change towards organisational anti-fragility?

- What strategies will you use to overcome resisting forces and people?

There is an argument to say that developing an organisational anti-fragile culture has a lot to do with developing as a Learning Organisation. A Learning Organisation facilitates the learning of its members and continuously transforms itself. This fits in very much with the reinforcing cycles we discussed in the context of anti-fragility in Chapter 1. It has been argued that learning organisations develop as a result of the pressures facing modern organisations, and this enables them to remain competitive in the business environment. So, this corresponds to becoming more resilient through experiencing shocks. A Learning Organisation has five main features; systems thinking, personal mastery, mental models, shared vision and team learning. The concept of Learning Organisations encourages organisations to shift to a more interconnected way of thinking and become more like communities that employees can feel a commitment to. Again, very consistent with our anti-fragility view.

It is recognised that organisations do not organically develop into learning organisations; there are factors prompting their change. Importantly, as organisations grow they lose their capacity to learn as company structures and individual thinking becomes rigid. When problems arise the proposed solutions often turn out to be only short-term, single loop learning, so that the problems re-emerge in the future. Further, to remain competitive, or for reasons of income, many organisations have restructured, with fewer people, who accordingly need to work more effectively as a team. To create a competitive advantage, companies also need to learn faster than their competitors and to develop a customer responsive culture. This requires cooperation between individuals and groups, free and reliable communication, and a culture of trust. What does this tell us about organisational anti-fragility? Primarily that to achieve it the organisation needs to learn to organise itself to learn at an organisational as well as at an individual and group level. It also suggests that within the organisation we need a diverse community, encompassing diverse thought processes, role preferences and learning styles. This is, of course, not enough alone; anti-fragility includes a lot more.

Developing your Organisational Cultural Template at All Levels of Your Organisation and For All Stakeholder Groups

Why do we want a template, and what is one anyway? In the context we are discussing, a Cultural Template is a typically tabular plan of what we need or intend to change, by when, led by who, with who, with what resource requirements and what desired outcomes. It should be organisation dependent, designed, applicable for all levels of the organisation and for all stakeholder groups, and have an emphasis on Shared Values, Commitment, Flexibility and Learning.

An illustrative pro forma template, for completion, is shown in Table 3.3.

Table 3.3   Illustrative Cultural Template pro forma

Description of Targeted Change	By When	Lead By	Supported By/Links	Resource Requirements	Intended Outcomes

Obviously, the key is in identifying the targeted changes that will help the organisation towards anti-fragility, according to the discussions of the previous section, then completing the rest of the table with the relevant stakeholders, to plan the changes. Such a cultural change template can usefully be applied at various levels in the organisation to plan cultural change; globally, divisionally, departmentally, at the team level or locally. Ideally, such templates should be nested, with ones at lower organisational levels themselves corresponding to further development of targeted changes at the next organisational level up.

In considering the organisation of such organisational cultural changes, we must also consider internal organisational politics, as political alliances and conflicts have a major impact on the reality of achieving planned and intended cultural changes. Stakeholder management is thus crucial. Organisational politics is the use of organisational resources by people or groups within the organisation, such as knowledge, position or networks, to engage in actions that are strategically self-interested. Politics is part of normal organisational life, and typically organisational strategy is fundamentally political. This is because, as a normal part of organisational life, some options are adopted and others are rejected. Thus, typically people and groups desire particular futures, and plan and manipulate accordingly. Some scenarios will be rejected; arguments will be made and data marshalled; moves surreptitiously made and blocked; as a result of which some proposals wither while others flourish. Behind any proposal stand those making it and typically they make these proposals, not from a position of benign neutrality and benevolence, but from a position of self-interest. Managing and aligning stakeholder interests are a key part of this.

An interest can be defined in terms of the relations between actors, discursive rationalities and the structural positions they occupy. The same person, when he or she is a young junior manager, will have differing interests, expressed in terms of different rationalities, from his or her mature CEO self; production managers will differ in their interests and rationalities from marketing managers and so on. Strategic interests emerge when there is something at issue, which divides opinions, on which people take sides. Dominant interpretations of strategic interests will tend to be presented as those that are legitimate for the organisation, even if there is resistance from other representations. Thus political skill is an essential requisite of the change managers' job. It entails using knowledge astutely and procedurally in a manner that best serves the strategic interest one is seeking to advance.

Such strategic interests and politics come from many sources, including:

- structural divisions in the organisation, and the different values, styles and cultures associated with these;

- the complexity and uncertainty attached to the dilemma that strategy seeks to address;

- the importance of the issue for different actors and identities in the organisation;

- external pressure coming from stakeholders or other actors or organisations in the environment;

- the history of past politics within the organisation.

The underlying purpose of such organisational politics involves mobilising support for particular actions by reconciling the differing interests and values. Skill is used to influence decisions, agendas and participation in organisation politics. Political competence means being the kind of change agent who can get things done, despite resistance, because they are skilled at political games. Organisations are designed to be hierarchical social systems in which relations of command and domination, obedience and subordination, are normatively framed in ways that seek to establish these relations as authoritative. In practice, however, authority is not a guarantee against the instability and dynamism that power relations can sometimes unleash. Very often within organisations, relations of power and politics are battles *either to keep things the same or to change*. Those who want things to remain the same usually want this because the current situation suits their interests; those who want things to change believe change is in their interests. In order to appear organisationally legitimate, such politics are typically expressed in terms of organisational, rather than sectional, interests. Legitimacy is added to when contingencies change in the environment that favour one set of interests over another because they are better able to deal with the issues that the new contingencies create.

Micro-politics are strategic attempts to exert a formative influence on social structure and relations in local settings within the organisation. Typically, a strategy, once conceived, struggles to come into being through processes of micro-politics. This process of struggle is one of political change; getting other players to do things that they would not otherwise do. Struggles around and over strategy are creative, as new identities, self-understandings, social relations and products, goods and services are created by them. Strategic struggles occur through communicative action constructed in terms of plans, documents, models, commands and reports.

Any successful strategy will be based on power, as well as knowledge, data, information and advice.

Organisations that cannot manage their power relations may find that their people end up spending more time fighting each other rather than seeking to find common purpose against competitor organisations. In reality, organisational politics is rarely a question of winner takes all; more usually compromises have to be made and coalitions and alliances formed. To be anti-fragile an organisation needs to be able to manage its politics well.

As we did at the end of Chapter 2, it is instructive to identify a number of rules that have emerged from the previous discussion and practical experience. Here though, they are about the pursuit of anti-fragile people, leadership and culture. These are:

1.   As discussed previously, people are both a major exploitable source of anti-fragility, and a major source of fragility in themselves. To develop an anti-fragile organisation, we need to avoid thinking based on the Classical Approach to Management and Transactional theory, both on the part of the organisation and of individual employees and managers. This is primarily an education issue.

2.   In contrast, a number of theories in the area, such as the Contingency Approach and Maslow's Hierarchy of Needs, have a natural affinity with anti-fragility and can help us in achieving it.

3.   An organisation's position in relation to Hofstede's cultural dimensions clearly relates to its overall fragility, robustness or anti-fragility, and could be used to identify areas of fragility and organisational development needs.

4.   In general terms, the EFQM Excellence Model criteria and sub-criteria on leadership, People and People Results support much of the requirements for anti-fragility, but are more focused on efficiency and effectiveness, and so are deficient and need extension.

5.   Real management commitment, and the identification of a shared owned vision, are crucial to the pursuit of anti-fragility and are often not properly established. A facilitated approach to Forming, Storming, Norming and Performing can be very useful to achieve this, as can the use of appropriate creativity tools.

6.   Change can be undertaken at various levels and will always create resistance. Undermining this resistance, typically through providing support and information, is often better than just pushing harder.

7.   To become anti-fragile an organisation also needs to become a
        Learning Organisation.

8.   Internal organisational politics cannot be avoided in considering
        organisational change towards anti-fragility. The change agent
        needs to learn how to be very good at establishing and managing
        alliances with stakeholders in pursuit of change objectives.

Chapter 4

Towards Anti-Fragile Processes and Operations

The Traditional Concepts of Operations Management, and the Central Place of Processes

Operations Management is a very established business school subject that developed as an extension of Manufacturing Management to also include the service sector (Slack, Chambers and Johnston, 2010). What is now called Operations Management was originally about *Production* and *Manufacturing* Management, concerned with *core processes* producing physical products. There was then recognition during the 1970s and 1980s that the management techniques that had developed could be applied to services, and the scope also expanded beyond core processes to include roles such as purchasing and distribution.

The Operations function is the part of the organisation that produces products or services. Processes also produce products and services on a smaller scale and are component parts of Operations. Operations may have various performance objectives dependent on how the organisation competes in its market, but typically these may include:

- quality

- speed

- dependability

- flexibility

- cost.

Today, Operations Management is an area of management concerned with designing, planning and controlling the value adding operations processes and area. It involves responsibility for ensuring that business operations are efficient in terms of using the minimum resources needed, and effective in terms of meeting customer requirements. It is concerned with managing the process that converts inputs (in the forms of information, materials, labour and services) into outputs (in the form of goods and/or services). Operations is not just the sum of its processes, it includes intangible resources, such as:

- the relationships with customers and suppliers;

- familiarity with process technology;

- staff input to new product and service development;

- process integration to support the whole operation.

Operations have strategic impact through reducing costs, increasing revenue, making investment more effective and building long-term capabilities. Operations strategy influences the way in which operations resources are developed to create sustainable competitive advantage. Ryanair, Tesco, Dell and TNT are each examples of inventive Operations strategy. The Operations strategy should identify the broad decisions that will help Operations achieve its objectives, as there is a need to reconcile what is required from the Operations function and how this is achieved through the set of choices made. For example, which products and services shall be produced; which operations technology utilised; what level of demand to plan for; to produce in-house or outsource; how much inventory to hold; and how to measure and report performance.

A core concept of Operations Management is the *four Vs*: Volume, Variety, Variation and Visibility, which determine much of the characteristics of an organisation's operations.

- Volume – for example, high-volume output is associated with a high degree of repeatability and encourages staff specialisation.

- Variety – having a wide range of products and/or services is more complex and costly than a low variety.

- Variation – a predictable constant demand is easier to manage than a variable, or even worse, unpredictable demand.

- Visibility – this is the extent to which the process is directly 'experienced', or can be viewed, by the customer.

There are many ways of describing organisations, including organisation charts. The process perspective analyses businesses as a collection of interrelated processes. Processes provide a useful and informative way of understanding how organisations operate. A central idea of the process perspective is that processes transform inputs into outputs. Inputs include information, materials, facilities and people that are necessary for the process. Products and services differ in tangibility and services may have a shorter stored life, for example a room in a hotel will 'perish' if not sold. Services may also have more customisation and complexity in relation to input requirements for individual jobs. Services and products are to some extent merging, in that often products are sold as part of a service package and services are often now *productised*.

Within the Operations Management field, the concept of processes is crucial at three levels:

1. Operations as an area of the organisation is about the overall management of the set of operations processes.

2. Within Operations, Process Management is about the management of an individual process.

3. Operations need to also be seen within the broader processes corresponding to the Supply Chain and Supply Network, which extend beyond the boundaries of the organisation.

In practice, processes are defined by how the organisation chooses to draw up process boundaries, and there are alternative ways that activities and resources could be defined as distinct processes. *End-to-end* processes satisfy a defined customer need.

Process thinking then, seeing activities as processes that add value for the customers, underpins our view of Operations Management, which is typically concerned with optimising process performance. But what sort of optimisation are we considering? Operations Management and Process Management typically give limited attention to Fragility issues. Once again, in practice much of this optimisation is concerned with efficiency and effectiveness rather than fragility. Accordingly, given the common correlation between optimal efficiency and fragility, the current literature on Operations Management is somewhat artificial compared to some practice, but where applied in practice can lead to overall suboptimal performance. This is a point that is repeatedly raised by Taleb, utilising his examples of Heathrow airport and New York traffic.

Typical Process Fragility Issues

In practice, both Process Management and Operations Management may be fragile, both through design and through operation. How can we make processes, and hence Operations Management, less fragile and more anti-fragile? One method, which we shall utilise below, is to study the Process and Operations Management improvement methods in current use and attempt to improve them. These methods, like QA, Lean Operations, Six Sigma, Lean Six Sigma, Poka Yoke, Process Benchmarking and Theory of Constraints, are typically formulated solely in terms of efficiency and possibly effectiveness.

Typical process fragility issues include more than just the danger of Process Stop. Also included is the danger of:

- the process operating, but with No Output;

- the process operating, but with No Acceptable Output;

- the process operating, but with Performance Below a specified acceptable level, in terms of:
  - delay
  - volume
  - disruption
  - variation.

If performance is below a specified acceptable level due to variation, then this in turn may reflect some unacceptably:

- high-cost jobs;

- high-duration jobs;

- variable number of completed jobs;

- low-quality jobs.

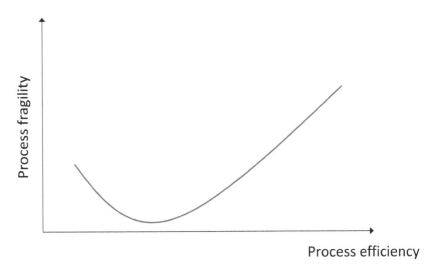

Figure 4.1   Process Fragility–Efficiency Curve

Typically, the less efficient and effective the process is, the more confusion and disruption there is, and with the broader definition of failure, the more fragile it is, and in consequence the greater the opportunity for improvement there is. However, this appears initially at odds with our previous remark, reinforced by Taleb and others, that efficiency and fragility are positively correlated. On reflection, it suggests a U-shaped characteristic for the relationship between process fragility and process efficiency, as shown in Figure 4.1. This is good news, since:

- it suggests that there is an optimum process efficiency to deliver minimum process fragility;

- it allows us to speculate as to whether, in practice, this relationship may be relatively flat, until we reach an intrinsic process efficiency boundary beyond which, as the right hand gradient suggests, the increase in fragility may become severe.

Process Improvement Approaches – Quality Assurance

Quality Assurance (QA) refers to the activity implemented through a Quality Management system to assure the organisation, and its customers, that the organisation has adequate processes to ensure that the requirements for supply of the specified product or service should be fulfilled. It should include systematic measurement, comparison with a standard, monitoring of processes, and an associated feedback loop to correct and prevent errors, as well as ensure continual improvement. This can be contrasted with quality control, which is focused on process outputs. Two principles frequently embedded in QA are: 'fit for purpose', the product should be suitable for the intended purpose; and 'right first time', mistakes should be eliminated. QA includes management of the quality of inputs, including raw materials, assemblies, components, services and information, as well as management, operations and inspection processes.

As we talked about when we discussed risk in Chapter 2, all organisational and system information gathering and feedback loops that potentially use current performance as the basis for control and/or change represent anti-fragility features within their processes, operations and the organisation. So, this will be true for Quality Control and QA systems, such as those to meet the requirements of ISO 9001, as well as for Budgetary Control; Developmental and Evaluative Performance Appraisals; Strategy Review; HSE Assurance; Continuous Improvement, Kaizan, Six Sigma, Lean Improvement, Agile Deployment, Organisational Assessment against the EFQM, Baldrige or Deming Models and, of course, Risk Management activities.

Thus, QA is an anti-fragility feature of our organisations and systems. But, as with Risk Management, this anti-fragility feature is itself often implemented in a fragile way; what we called before second-level fragility. This is because many QA systems, like Risk Management systems, are not necessarily set up or documented to properly capture the value adding processes of the business in a way proportional to risk; carried out with full timely information and critical awareness; based on a holistic view and in the spirit of continual improvement and risk reduction; with the full deployment of senior management attention, leadership and a fully committed QA culture. Unfortunately, being realistic, this is not, in general, the case. Frequently, overview of QA will be in practice delegated to middle management, formalised and standardised, so it is in danger of becoming a compliance-driven ritual with incomplete information, with most importance being given to the integrity of the paper trail for auditing purposes. Having an accredited ISO 9001 certificate is, for many organisations, seen as worth much more than having good QA. The QA system is there to enable the organisation to have a certificate which will satisfy the customers. In consequence, and sometimes due to poor consultancy, the QA system is often fragile, in that, for example, it may be slow and sluggish and inadequately responsive to changing circumstances in operations or the environment. It may, in consequence, not initiate action when it should. In contrast it may largely disregard proportionality to risk and refer all non-compliance, however trivial, up for management review. Essentially, the system may become overburdened, with long delays to update procedures which are, in consequence, worked around or may become ineffective. A QA system is, potentially, the management system for management to plan and control quality and respond to threats. Hence it is an anti-fragile feature of the organisation. If it does not work well though, and falls apart, it is a fragile anti-fragile feature. Many are.

So, as in the case of Risk Management, there is thus again a lack of a holistic approach to Fragility Minimisation and management in current QA practice, and organisational and system design and operation. A good question to think about is: 'What are the differences between a Fragile, a Robust, and an Anti-Fragile ISO 9001 System?'

The answer is that:

- a fragile ISO 9001/QA system can be easily damaged by changes or shocks in the external or internal environment, to make it ineffective or sluggish;

- a robust ISO 9001/QA system is able to withstand changes or shocks in the external or internal environment and keep functioning; and

- an anti-fragile ISO 9001/QA system is more than just robust and, within limits, actually improve its resilience through being stressed.

Thus, an anti-fragile ISO 9001 or QA system merely does what all such ISO 9001 and QA systems are supposed to do, it utilises corrective action, preventive action and continual improvement to improve itself and become more resilient. A system like this is a benefit to an organisation on a journey towards anti-fragility; a fragile ISO 9001/QA system is typically a hindrance.

Process Improvement Approaches –Lean Operations

Let us say at the start that it is well known that the Lean approach is fragile and, as we shall discuss below, inbuilt to the Lean approach there are a number of concepts that inherently imply Process, Operations and Organisational fragility.

These include:

1.   Just in Time (JIT) systems are more fragile than Just in Case, as they are based on Pull rather than Push mechanisms;

2.   single piece flow is more fragile than batch processing;

3.   inventory reduction increases fragility;

4.   focusing on the Value Stream and removing *non-value adding* activities increases fragility;

5.   creating flow or removing or reducing bottlenecks to increase flow, may increase fragility;

6.   focusing on Throughput Efficiency and minimising throughput time, or cost, increases fragility;

7.   considering Overall Equipment Effectiveness (OEE) and maximising utilisation or heavily loading systems to stretch them to exploit their maximum capacity increases fragility;

8.   depending on how it is applied, Lean methodology can reduce organisational agility;

9.   Lean thinking creates an emphasis on process efficiency but as implemented may not cover effectiveness;

10.   the absence of an agreed standard implementation model may mean that Lean is not project-based and/or is applied to the *trivial many* rather than the *vital few*, potentially increasing fragility through complexity. Alternatively, it may be done too quickly to be well founded, for example through naive exclusive use of Blitz Kaizan/Rapid Improvement Events, or too slowly to deliver what is needed, for example through some *system thinking* applications;

11.   Whilst the focus of Lean implementation is typically Operations, frequently its reach does not fully extend into administrative and management areas and the supply chain.

These deficiencies do not mean that the Lean approach cannot make a very real contribution to process, Operations and organisational anti-fragility – it definitely can. As we shall see below, a lot depends on how the Lean approach is implemented. This is not new – we always knew that there were bad implementations of Lean as well as good ones – for example, ones that focused on process changes without considering the people issues; the *toolhead* approach. Like any approach, it was for the naive, inexperienced, misinformed and headstrong, easy to use it wrong. Now, however, anti-fragility gives us a language for capturing the potential fragilities of Lean in a coherent way.

To consider this, we need to first define what Lean methodology is about. Apart from some isolated previous applications, such as production of the Terracotta Warriors in Xeon China and the kitting out of Venetian warships, it is generally accepted that Lean methodology originates from manufacturing, specifically from Toyota in post-war Japan. It was part of the Toyota Production System (TPS), which was dedicated to the *war on waste*. To minimise costs and throughput time through the factory, JIT manufacturing was developed as a pull system, pulling complete vehicles out of the factory on a regular cycle, and hence parts and raw materials in. This lead to reduced inventory and the need to develop supplier partnerships. Further, Jidoka involved intelligent automation (*autonomation*) and identification of defects at source to protect the Lean throughput as well as a move to operator empowerment (Toyota Motor Corporation, 2014). The Toyota Lean approach was then first codified in English by Professors Womack and Jones who documented the Five Lean Principles (see Womack, Jones and Roos, 2007).

These are:

- value;

- the Value Stream;

- flow;

- pull;

- the pursuit of perfection.

Other factors and consequences of Lean are a focus on Supplier–Customer Relationships through JIT; the challenge to traditional operations by replacing batch production by single piece flow; the challenge to the organisational structure to make it less hierarchical; the challenge to the organisational culture to give more empowerment; and the need for management of change.

The concept of Value in Lean thinking is an important one. Value refers to what the customer perceives as he or she wants and gets from your organisation and, in consequence, what they will pay for. As suppliers we need to understand this well. In specific applications it can be more complicated. For example, in public sector processes value should reflect all stakeholders' value perceptions. There is a danger when our internal organisational 'value', that is value to us, overrides our customer's perceived value.

The Value Stream essentially concerns taking the value adding bits of a process and trying to leave out the other bits. It is about understanding the complete process, where a business process is defined as a group of activities performed to deliver or add value.

So, the Value Stream is about identifying and defining the main flow of the value adding activities to achieve the customers' or stakeholders' perceived value of a product or service. It recognises and identifies a process and is typically the first opportunity to identify non-value adding activities in the process, or *muda*, which is Japanese for process waste. A Lean organisation will be mindful of maximising the ratio of added value to non-added value activities. In practise, we can divide up organisational activities into three types:

- Real value added activities, as perceived by the customer or stakeholders:
  - improve efficiency;
  - improve speed of reaction;

- Business value added activities, required to run the business:
  - reduce to a minimum;

- Non-value added activities, do not add customer or stakeholder perceived value nor are required to run the business, that is, muda or waste:
  - eliminate.

For example, in manufacturing, examples of real value added activities are:

- acknowledging a customer order;

- delivering a product;

- processing a customer order;

- providing after sales service.

Examples of business value-added are:

- updating financial accounts;

- updating training records;

- issuing purchase orders;

- negotiating price.

Examples of non-value added activities are:

- rework;

- authorisations and approvals;

- checking and inspection;

- reviews and audits;

- complaint handling;

- processing customer claims/credits.

The concept of process flow is that value must flow through the process continuously. Every step in the process should move at the same speed, with the same capacity and in harmony. We need to eliminate bottlenecks or constraints in the process; these may be due to physical, policy or paradigm restrictions. It is traditional to batch process and excuses for batching can be financial or operational, for example full utilisation of capital equipment, reduced changeovers/set-ups and so on.

Pull is the action of the customer pulling the added value activities through the process to receive goods or service how and when needed; that is at the

98

speed of customer demand. The speed of our processes should wax and wane to reflect this.

The pursuit of perfection is like Continuous Improvement but it is a pull concept rather than a push one. Effective transformation to Lean is achieved when:

- *value* is specified and understood;

- added value to non-added value is maximised and *waste* is eliminated;

- the *Value Stream flow* is smooth and continuous;

- the value added activities are *pulled* in line with customer demand.

But all of this could come to nought if:

- the effort to sustain the transformation falters;

- practices are not in place to develop a Continuous Improvement policy.

So, when the *value-added to non-value added ratio* is optimised, and the activities *flow*, lead times, work in the process (WIP) and inventory can be reduced and the organisation can react to *customer demand* immediately and *changes in demand* can be accommodated readily.

In terms of implementation of Lean, the five stages are:

1.   creating a framework for the programme;

2.   identifying the *Value Stream*, analysing and standardising the process;

3.   streamlining the process to create *flow* of the value-creating steps;

4.   *pulling* the product or service according to customer demand;

5.   continually improving the process in the *pursuit of perfection*.

Value Stream Mapping (VSM) is a simple tool for visualising the *door-to-door* work flows in an organisation. It focuses Lean efforts on improving the whole value chain, rather than optimising the parts, in order to establish flow, eliminate waste and add value. It captures job flows, material movements and information flows in one *Current State* picture and provides a step-by-step approach to creating an ideal *Future State* in which non-value adding activities are minimised. The stages of VSM can be thought of as follows:

1.   Select a product/service – the selection of a product/service, or family of products/services which follow similar process routes.

2.   Current State Map – drafting a Current State Map to reflect work flow, information flow and sequence of processes.

3.   Future State Map – creation of a Future State Map. This requires a lot of knowledge about what is wrong now and what we want to achieve, and how. It is the team's vision of the 'ideal' condition in which wasteful elements have been resolved.

4.   Action Plan – development of an Action Plan. A detailed 'to do list' which prioritises each action to realise the future state.

5.   Implement and monitor progress according to the plan.

6.   Control to keep the gains.

7.   Think about 'what's next'.

To map the Current State process (see Figure 4.2) we start with customer need, for example service level, quantity, order size and frequency, and map each process step using a box – a separate box indicates that processes are disconnected and job flow stops (for example, jobs are moved in batches). We start at the customer end and work backwards, typically using Post-it notes. We then collect process data for each box within the process. Examples of data collected at each stage may be:

- error rate;

- cost;

- times;

- quality problems;

- value added to non-value added ratio (time, cost or number of steps);

- cycle time;

- changeover time;

- batch size;

- number of operators;

- number of product or service variations;

- job size;

- working time (that is, excluding breaks);

- rework/scrap rate.

We also note the location and amount of inventory, and map the supply process in terms of, for example, volume, batch size and frequency.

Considering the Current State Map, we will now identify areas of the process which are most troublesome, in terms of cost, non-value added, time and rework or similar. For these, we drop down below the level of the Value Stream Map and flowchart them, or construct Process Sequence charts to help identify areas for improvement.

Having drawn the Current State Map and examined the causes of the problem, the Future State Map can be drawn with the aims to get one process to provide only what the next process needs when it needs it, to link all processes from the final customer back to initial input, avoid detours in the process and develop continuous flow wherever possible.

Next, the Action Plan breaks the implementation into steps, focusing action first on the pacemaker area that is the most major bottleneck or constraint. The Action Plan needs clear steps, named responsible personnel for all tasks, measurable goals, and checkpoints and milestones. We need to monitor progress, take corrective action and re-plan as necessary. It can be used universally but VSM is easiest to apply for high-volume, low-variety situations with dedicated equipment and people, and simple routings.

(i) Constructing the Current Value Stream Map

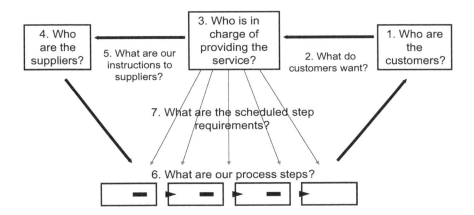

8. What are our process step metrics, standards and performance data?

9. What inventory is there between steps?

(ii) An example of a Current State Map (Automotive Seat Manufacturing)

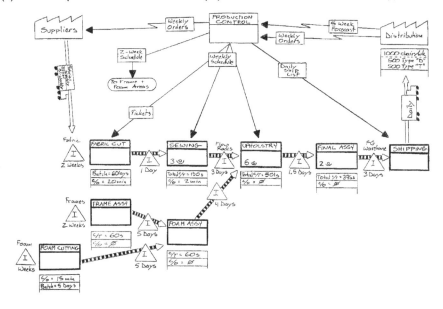

Figure 4.2   Current State Value Stream Maps

Another key concept in Lean thinking, are the Seven Wastes, originally identified by Taiichi Ohno of Toyota and, correspondingly, expressed in manufacturing terms, although they clearly apply to services also. These are:

1.   *Over production* – making, or doing more than is required.

2.   *Waiting* for something to happen!

3.   Unnecessary *transport* of materials or work-in-progress.

4.   *Over processing* due to poor design of services, products, equipment or processes.

5.   *Inventories* that are bigger than they need to be – just in case!

6.   Unnecessary *motion* by people doing their work.

7.   The creation of parts, products or services which have *defects*.

There are, of course, 'new' wastes that we can add to these, like the Waste of Talent, due to:

- Lack of people/skill development.

- Failure to encourage and establish an environment of innovation and creativity.

- Lack of management support.

- Inappropriate systems.

We have now covered the background concepts needed to allow us to realise that the Lean approach, properly applied, is inherently robust or anti-fragile as it uses analysis and study of current real world performance to improve performance. With this in mind we can now discuss the illustrative potential fragility issues with Lean methods that we introduced at the beginning of this section. However, before we do this, there are two further concepts that we need to introduce to be able to return to the list of fragilities created by Lean. These are Throughput Efficiency and OEE. We shall discuss these in turn.

Throughput Efficiency is a useful measure of the waste of waiting. It measures the work content, or value-adding time, of a job as a percentage of time the job is in the system. An illustration of the calculation is shown in Figure 4.3.

$$\text{Throughput Efficiency} = \frac{\text{Work Content}}{\text{Time in System}} \times 100\%$$

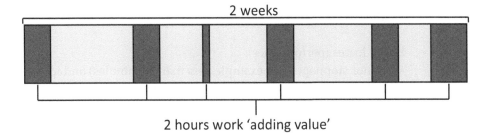

2 hours work 'adding value'

$$\text{Throughput Efficiency} = \frac{2}{2 \times 40} \times 100\% = 2.5\%$$

Figure 4.3   Waste of waiting example

OEE is a key measure associated with Total Productive Maintenance (TPM), which is a holistic approach to having everyone involved in maintaining the processes' integrity. The goal of TPM is ultimately to have Zero Downtime, Zero Speed Losses, and Zero Defects. It works to achieve this through:

- improving equipment/process effectiveness:
  - examines and analyses sources of loss;

- achieving autonomous maintenance:
  - includes both operational and maintenance staff;

- planning maintenance:
  - levels of preventive maintenance and individual responsibilities defined;

- training all staff in relevant maintenance skills:
  - both maintenance and operational staff;

- achieving early equipment management:
  - maintenance prevention through design, manufacture, installation and commissioning.

OEE is thus based on the existence of six potential sources of loss in a process:

- Downtime (availability):
  - breakdowns or unplanned stoppages;
  - changeovers and adjustments;

- Speed losses (performance):
  - minor stoppages (for example, less than 10 minutes) and idling;
  - reduced speed (less than the design speed);

- Defects (quality):
  - scrap or rework;
  - start-up losses during changeover causing reduced yield.

It is calculated as:

$$\% \text{ Availability} \times \% \text{ Performance} \times \% \text{ Quality.}$$

World Class Performance on OEE is typically judged to be anything above 80 per cent.

We can now discuss each of the 11 illustrative fragility issues with Lean that we introduced at the start of this section.

1.   Firstly, the fact that JIT systems are more fragile than *Just in Case* ones is a well-known truism for anyone considering applying Lean methods. JIT reduces inventory and associated holding costs but at the price of potential outages in production, due to changes in demand or disruptions in flow caused by supply chain, quality or logistic problems. This fragility can be reduced by careful progressive planned inventory reduction rather than 'taking the bull by the horns'.

2.   For similar reasons, single piece flow is more fragile than batch processing and it can be tackled in much the same way by progressive planned reduction in batch sizes.

3.   Inventory reduction, with or without JIT or single piece flow, is again much the same and can be tackled in a similar way.

4. Focusing on the Value Stream and removing non-value adding activities increases fragility, as *typically some non-value adding activities may exist as anti-fragile features in the process*. For example, by definition in Lean thinking, a possibly repeated end of process check should be unnecessary if all previous stages have been done properly, so is non-value adding. However, it remains an important safeguard to stop ad hoc or systemic problems getting out to the customers, and subsequently causing major disruption and possible fragility to the organisation. Similarly, duplicated record keeping provides an anti-fragile safeguard against loss or error. Unlike points 1–3 above, where the typical solution is in *how* the Lean approach is implemented, gradual with learning being preferable to 'blunderbuss', the issue here is in general *the extent* to which it should be implemented, or *the modification needed to the optimisation objective*. As we have discussed previously, we need to replace the efficiency objective with an anti-fragility one with an efficiency side constraint.

5. Creating flow, or removing or reducing bottlenecks to increase flow, may increase fragility as removal of bottlenecks may put pressure on downstream fragile parts of the process and the removal of excess capacity at certain stages in the process may reduce the opportunity for maintenance, prevention activities, developmental experimentation and recuperation. As with focus on the Value Stream, the issue here may be *the extent* to which creating flow and bottleneck management should be implemented, or *the modification needed to the corresponding optimisation objective*.

6. The focus on Throughput Efficiency and minimising throughput time or cost can create fragility as it heavily loads the processing facilities, leaves little or no time for verification or review activities, requires constant job movement through the facilities and JIT supply, or possibly on occasion heavy stocks, of inputs. Again, modification may be needed to the corresponding optimisation objective or the extent of focus on these measures may need to be limited.

7. In a similar way, considering OEE and maximising utilisation, or heavily loading systems to stretch them to exploit their maximum capacity, increases fragility as it creates an emphasis on a fully loaded, and fully operational and performing, process at all times.

Again, as well as the impact of loading, this gives no time for verification or review activities, requires constant job movement through the facilities and JIT supply, or on occasion heavy stocks, of inputs. The impact of this maximum loading on the process needs to be considered from a fragility perspective and modification may be needed to the corresponding optimisation objective, or the extent of focus on OEE may need to be limited.

8.   The organisational agility issue is complex. Whilst Lean focuses on the structure of the operational processes to produce the product or service, Agility focuses on the organisation's responsiveness to changes in demand or supply or the wider environment. Not being Agile enough is a source of fragility. Whilst Lean and Agile can go together, particularly if we multi-skill, there are in practice numerous examples of *hard-wired* Lean systems that are not Agile. Such hard-wired, inflexible, inagile systems can include Fordist mass assembly conveyor belt systems which are hard to change when you need to because of the plant involved and major business software systems, which often prove inagile structurally or contractually in service provision, typically resulting in the need for lots of paper between systems. We shall discuss the latter problem further in Chapter 5.

There is also a higher-level sense in which, depending on how it is implemented, Lean methodology can reduce organisational agility. This is the question of using external consultants to 'do Lean to you', or more precisely your organisation, rather than to 'do Lean yourself', by your own people. The latter case requires us to train and develop your people, but properly trained leaves them able to apply the learning elsewhere, more extensively, across the organisation. The former means the organisation remains inagile and relatively fragile, unable to do it on its own and waiting for another consultant intervention.

9.   In a similar sense, it might be argued that Lean thinking creates an emphasis on process efficiency but unfortunately not always, as implemented, on effectiveness. *An efficient but ineffective process, like an effective but inefficient one, will typically create organisational fragility.* Of course, in contrast, a process that is both efficient and effective is at least in some dimensions robust, and hence well on its way to being anti-fragile and contributing to organisational

anti-fragility, provided it improves by being stressed. This is primarily an education issue and, in theory at least, very soluble.

10.   The absence of an agreed standard implementation model for Lean, unlike say Six Sigma, is a big and complex problem. This is an issue that the author is currently grappling with as part of the process of drafting a new Lean, Six Sigma and Lean Six Sigma ISO international standard, to go beyond the guidance standard ISO 13053. There are three main aspects to this issue in the current context. Firstly, despite many using the DMAIC(T) Six Sigma project management approach, or a credible alternative such as PRINCE2, for Lean Improvement activities, in general Lean is not always project based. This may affect implementation effectiveness and hence implementation and organisational fragility; to some extent this is a value judgement based on your views of the needs of effective process Change Management. However, there are strong arguments, supported by theory, that in process Change Management we should:

i.   look to change the process itself ahead of the culture, as this will take longer and follow consequentially on the process change; and

ii. always change processes on a project-by-project basis, within 'fenced-off' areas.

The second point immediately above is largely due to Juran and makes us think of having a programme of projects for process changes.

Secondly, there is the issue of some Lean implementations pursuing the *trivial many* sources of waste, rather than the *vital few*. This is important because such a strategy may increase complexity and fragility, as trying to remove and control many sources of waste, rather than focusing on the few big ones that between them may account for most of the current waste, will stretch resources and human conception. The Pareto Principle suggests that, whilst this is in common use, it is not a good approach.

Thirdly, there is an issue of fragility associated with timescale for the Lean intervention. For instance, it may be done too quickly to be well founded, as through naive exclusive use of Blitz Kaizan/ Rapid Improvement Events. If, as sometimes, these are put in place as a Lean programme, without adequate preparation (such as to identify the pacemaker constraints), or follow up (such as ensuring implementation actions take place), then they do not usually deliver well-founded lasting solutions. As well as fragility from trying to do things too fast, fragility can also come from often so-called *system thinking* consultant-led approaches which take up to two years to deliver, by which time the problem could have killed you, if not your organisation.

11.   Finally, it is commonplace in many applications that the focus of Lean implementation is typically Operations, and frequently its reach does not fully extend into administrative and management areas, and to the supply chain. This unfortunately implies Process, Operations and Organisational fragility because the infrastructure and linkages around Operations may remain sluggish, costly, error prone and full of non-value added.

If properly applied, with continual learning through exposure to application in the real world, the Lean Approach itself should be anti-fragile. Despite this, as we have seen, inbuilt to the Lean Approach there are a number of concepts that inherently imply Process, Operations and Organisational fragility. Many of these are avoidable or reducible through good practice. As previously, the co-existence of fragile and anti-fragile features in a process, system or organisation is not a contradiction; rather it reflects the multidimensional nature of anti-fragility. The Lean Approach can make a very real contribution to Process, Operations and Organisational anti-fragility; but a lot depends on how the Lean Approach is implemented. In practice, whether a Lean implementation is Fragile Lean or Anti-Fragile Lean depends on many factors, including the Organisational Strategy, Structure and Systems, People, Relationships and Culture, Products, Services, Markets, Use of Information and Technology Base. With Lean in particular, the difference between a fragile or anti-fragile implementation may depend strongly on the Operations strategy; hard-wired systems lead us towards fragility, whilst multi-skilling people help lead the organisation towards anti-fragility.

Process Improvement Approaches – Six Sigma

Like the Lean Approach, Six Sigma can be applied in a fragile, robust or anti-fragile way. Also as with Lean, in-built to the Six Sigma concept are a number of aspects that can be associated with fragility, robustness or anti-fragility. The following are common examples:

1.   use of DMAIC(T);

2.   training by rote, not education;

3.   possibly inappropriate statistical toolkit;

4.   Root Cause Analysis sometimes limited;

5.   Software Black Boxes, for example, poor use of Minitab;

6.   role, management and support of Belts;

7.   programme management;

8.   overemphasis on Cost-Down, rather than Profit-Up;

9.   cultural incompatibilities.

Again, as with Lean, before considering these in detail, let us start by defining what Six Sigma is. One way of looking at it, and to see the relationship with Lean, is to ask the question, 'Typically, what do we want to improve about our process efficiency?' To answer this, we should ask in turn 'What can go wrong with our process efficiency?' The answer to this latter question may be concerns about time, cost and accuracy. So we have two issues:

- waste:
  - which is the subject of the Lean approach;

- consistency of products and service (against defined standards):
  - which is what Six Sigma is about. See Figure 4.4.

The Six Sigma Approach originates in the American private sector, originally from Motorola. It was to some extent GE who spread it in both directions along its supply chain and took it into widespread use. GE also marked its widespread

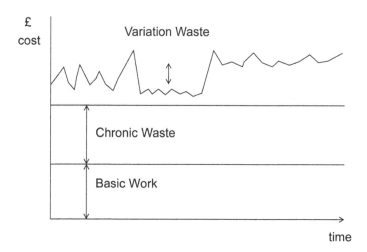

Figure 4.4   Basic work, chronic waste and variation waste

transition into the service sector, through GE Capital, which has subsequently seen its spread across the financial services sector, and more broadly into the service sector. More recently there have been some public sector applications: in healthcare, the courts, Network Rail and so on, but much more limited than public sector applications of Lean.

Six Sigma implementation is project-based, with projects led by trained workforce specialists, called Black Belts and Green Belts. A site expert is a Master Black Belt. The approach is based on use of the so-called DMAIC or DMAIC(T) project management methodology, statistical analysis of data, an extensive process analysis and improvement toolkit and appropriate statistical software, most typically Minitab, to supplement the useful statistical analysis possible in Excel. DMAIC(T) refers to the phases of Six Sigma projects, as follows:

- Define – identify what the problem is.

- Measure – base line current performance.

- Analyse – identify root causes of the problem.

- Improve – define, pilot and implement the solution to the problem to yield improvement.

- Control – burn-in the gains through training, proceduralisation, Mistake Proofing and so on.

- (Transfer) – transfer what was learnt to other similar areas.

Typically, the DMAIC project management methodology is presented as linear, but in practice a large percentage of Six Sigma projects subsequently naturally require redefinition, and possibly remeasurement and reanalysis. This possible need for project redefinition is embedded as part of the extensive ISO Six Sigma Guidance standard, ISO 13053.

The general principles on which Six Sigma is based include it being a strategic programme, driven and supported from the top of the organisation, measured by product or service improvement and savings, with all projects monitored by senior management, all of whom have had appropriate training. The project methodology for the improvement projects uses statistical tools and software (often Minitab), the training approach is Train – Apply – Review, and mentoring support continues to be provided to Black and Green Belts after training.

Six Sigma personnel roles are typically defined to include:

- Master Black Belts, who are technical site experts in the statistical approaches.

- Black Belts, who are typically full-time Improvement Managers or Engineers, who have qualified through about 20 days training and independent assessed project work applying the method.

- Green Belts, who typically spend part of their work time on improvement activities, possibly a minimum of one day per week, and have qualified through six to ten days training and independent assessed project work applying the method.

- Yellow, White and Grey Belts; these tend to vary with the organisation but include team member roles on improvement teams.

- Project Sponsors or Champions.

(i) The Technical Meaning for Six Sigma

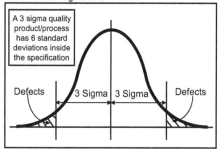

Given the specification, Six Sigma Quality for a product/process metric means that more of the distribution is contained within the Specification than at the 3 Sigma level.

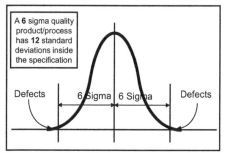

	Yield (% Inside Spec)	DPMO (defectives per million opportunities)
At ± 2 sigma	95.44%	45,600
At ± 3 sigma	99.73%	2,700
At ± 4 sigma	99.9937%	63
At ± 5 sigma	99.999943%	0.57
At ± 6 sigma	99.999998%	0.002

A 3 sigma quality product/process has 6 standard deviations inside the specification

A 6 sigma quality product/process has 12 standard deviations inside the specification

(ii) Effect of a 1.5 Sigma Shift

If the product/process mean now shifts 1.5 sigma ('worst case'), then:

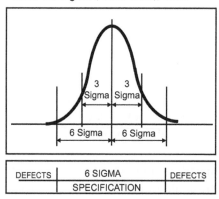

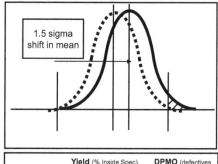

	Yield (% Inside Spec)	DPMO (defectives per million opportunities
At ± 2 sigma	69.15%	308,500
At ± 3 sigma	93.32%	66,810
At ± 4 sigma	99.379%	6,210
At ± 5 sigma	99.97673%	233
At ± 6 sigma	99.99966%	3.4

Figure 4.5   The technical meaning of Six Sigma

There are a number of interrelated current usages of the term *Six Sigma*. These include:

- Its use to describe a statistical or technical target corresponding to six standard deviations to the specification limits either side of the target, or equivalently three non-conformances out of one million opportunities, or *Best in Class*. See Figure 4.5.

- A variation reduction and process improvement programme that uses the project-based DMAIC(T) approach.

- A measurement-based strategy for improvement.

- An improvement 'philosophy'.

The Six Sigma toolkit is extensive, with some commentators counting 141 statistical tools and concepts in the GE approach, and 140 in Caterpillar's. Perhaps the most useful tools include, in particular, the Seven Tools of Quality Control, various Statistical Process Control (SPC) charts, Experimental Design and specifically Taguchi methodology, and Root Cause Analysis. Useful non-statistical tools include Failure Modes Effects and Criticality Analysis (FMECA or FMEA), Quality Function Deployment (QFD), Poka Yoke or Mistake Proofing, and some right brain and creativity tools.

Having introduced the Six Sigma concept, we can now return to the nine potential fragility-related issues with Six Sigma that we introduced at the start of this section:

1.   The use of the DMAIC, and particularly DMAIC(T), project management approach is essentially anti-fragile, since it is a planned, evidence-based, based on application in the real world, approach. The fact that it is often presented as linear, when redefinition of the project, remeasurement and/or reanalysis may in reality be needed, is potentially a fragile feature if implemented in this way, as it will imply that this prescriptive formulation will prevent or delay real discovery of causes or solutions.

2.   In practice, many Six Sigma Black and Green Belt training programmes are based around *training by rote*, rather than education, which by definition is fragile as it is non-adaptive. This delivery method is partly because the toolkit is so extensive; although this itself is based on *how* Six Sigma is taught. With an education approach to understand the basis and interconnections of the tools, providing some insight to the underlying concepts rather than learning specific tool use by heart, Belt candidates can work on a reduced core toolset but have the basis for more broad identification and selection of appropriate tools. This is how the Six Sigma Green and Black Belt courses taught by the author and his colleagues, through Services Limited, are delivered. The other

reason is that, unfortunately, much current Six Sigma training provision is provided by trainers who themselves do not fully understand the statistical basis of the tools they train on. Clearly, whilst practitioner experience is essential for robust Six Sigma training, deep statistical understanding is also crucial for anti-fragile Six Sigma training.

3.   The question of a possibly inappropriate statistical toolkit arises not primarily because of the number of tools in the toolkit, but *what* they are. Largely because of the background of trainers as non-statistical experts, the content of many Six Sigma training programmes are somewhat historical, reflecting statistical methods that the author taught to undergraduates more than 40 years ago. In the last 50 years, the world and statistical methods have moved on. One of the big changes, helped by the development in graphics technology, has been the emergence of graphically-based Exploratory Data Analysis (EDA) techniques, which exploit our visual dexterity to identify and exploit pattern in data for analysis, finding root causes and developing solutions. The EDA approach, being exploratory and based on real world data, is intrinsically robust or anti-fragile. However, rather than incorporate much EDA, many training programmes still rely considerably on teaching formal statistical inference (hypotheses tests) which, being formalised rule-based processes, are intrinsically fragile. A distinct issue is that since there is, as yet, no universally agreed body of knowledge or curriculum for Six Sigma, key tools or concepts have been omitted in some training programmes and hence in some practical applications. This is again fragile but will be addressed by the planned new ISO Lean and Six Sigma standard.

4.   A key part of the Analyse phase in DMAIC(T) is Root Cause Analysis. In some cases, in line with the discussion above, what is taught on Belt courses in this regard is very limited; there is a deficiency of specific Root Cause Analysis techniques beyond the basic *Five Whys* which, anyway, is typically mistaught to select the first answer we think of at each stage. Clearly, this is a source of fragility.

5.   The issue concerning the use of the supporting statistical software packages is, because of the learning by rote mentioned above, that many Belt practitioners do not adequately understand the

outputs the packages produce, do not have the insight to identify ambiguities and contradictions in the outputs and so make erroneous conclusions. This is extremely fragile and, unfortunately, not uncommon. I have chaired conference sessions where Belts go wrong in their analysis at slide two! For all its great advantages, there is a particular danger of this with packages such as Minitab and a good precautionary principle in training Belts is to ensure that they go step by step through the analysis in Excel before trying it in a black box package, so they have a better understanding of the output of such packages.

6.   As we have indicated previously, much of the Six Sigma approach is inherently anti-fragile. However, poor implementation can lead to fragility. The role definitions, management and support of Belts are important for the ongoing contribution, learning, adaptability and responsiveness of the Six Sigma programme. This will determine how fragile, robust or anti-fragile the implemented Six Sigma programme is. A lot of organisations have, in practice, had problems with these. Part of this is the classic emphasis on short-term thinking, as in, 'Let's get started with Six Sigma, we can sort out the detail later.' This typically leads to an evolutionary approach, which is in itself anti-fragile, but creates specific initial and longer-term fragility weaknesses, such as lack of clarity on the long-term career progression of Black Belts; are they to return to, and progress in, line management roles based on their cross-functional learning or are there further development roles within the Six Sigma/Belt hierarchy? In practice, it has on occasion also exposed individuals to a subsequent redundancy risk during hard times since full-time Belts frequently have no direct reports. This is a waste of skill and development, and hence represents fragility. Also, should Black Belts report into a central function as implicitly assumed above or have business unit or process reporting, possibly with dotted-line reporting, to a central coordinator? Do we need a Continuing Professional Development programme for our Belts, which would be potentially an anti-fragile safeguard and, if so, what should it be?

7.   The next point is connected. Black and Green Belts lead Six Sigma improvement projects but who defines, coordinates, monitors and runs the overall programme within which these projects occur? In some organisations there is very little explicit Six Sigma Programme

Management; an obvious cause of fragility. Should it be done on a divisional basis, a process basis, or at a site or corporate level? Who should be in charge, a Master Black Belt or a board-level corporate executive? The answers will depend on organisational circumstances but these should be explicitly considered, determined and reviewed on an ongoing basis to give anti-fragility.

8.   The cost-down or profit-up issue, or the equivalent outcome identification issue in public and voluntary organisations, concerns what outcome measure exactly are we trying to optimise through applying Six Sigma to our process? Clearly, a solution that minimises cost may or may not maximise profit, or the equivalent outcome objective in a public or voluntary sector application. Generally though, cost minimisation is a common objective and will be suboptimal, hence causing fragility. In manufacturing areas, typically the only way to contribute to increased profit is frequently to reduce cost, but in service operations areas it may also be possible to increase revenue. For example, in a telephone contact centre, contact staff may be able to sell additional services as well as handle customer queries, so cost minimisation may lead to shorter call durations whilst profit optimisation may lead to longer ones. Cost minimisation therefore gives the wrong answer, causing fragility.

9.   Six Sigma is very much an American approach, on occasion even called 'a truly American philosophy'. In its origins, it typically focuses on process optimisation and shareholder value, and this may not be compatible with organisational or national culture which might, for example, place greater emphasis on a balanced stakeholder approach, as embedded in the EFQM Excellence Model. These cultural conflicts create fragility.

Process Improvement Approaches – Mistake Proofing

Considering Lean and Six Sigma, a common cause of both waste and consistency problems is human error. Human error is a source of fragility. Hazard Avoidance and Mistake Proofing are inherently robust features of a system as they reduce shocks, reduce their impact or provide a warning. A system that automates this and updates through learning from real world application and hence stress is anti-fragile.

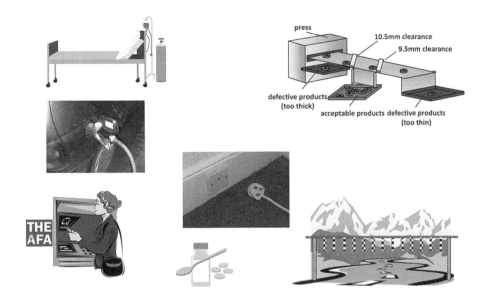

© THE **ANTI-FRAGILITY** ACADEMY

Figure 4.6   Some opportunities for error and Poka Yoke devices

Foolproofing is a long-established idea that was adopted and refined by Shigeo Shingo in the context of Toyota and its suppliers (Shingo, 1986). Originally known as *baka yoke*, the approach to Mistake Proofing that we now call Poka Yoke has been used to great effect in Japan, and its value and potential is now widely recognised in the west. Mistake Proofing is needed because, even with the most conscientious person and best maintained machinery, mistakes will occasionally be made. If something can go wrong, then typically, ultimately, it will! One interesting aspect of Poka Yoke is that typically de-skilling work tends to lead to higher quality, for example giving supermarket checkout staff barcode readers has improved the accuracy of bills. The purpose of Poka Yoke then is to produce goods and services that are defect-free, ensure other processes are error-free, eliminate scrap and rework, reduce costs and improve customer satisfaction.

In engineering and manufacturing areas, Poka Yoke involves creating simple devices to prevent or identify errors. In service or transactional areas it may involve simple devices such as checklists, check digits, colour coding (for example, documents or forms), required fields, drop-down menus, rejecting on data input (for example, in scanning forms) or use of barcodes. See Figure 4.6.

A key concept of Poka Yoke is that everyone makes errors, but since a process error only leads to a product or service defect when it escapes from the process that made it, we can prevent the errors from leading to defects. There are lots of sources of error, including forgetfulness, tiredness and loss of concentration, misunderstanding and misinterpretation, lack of standards, lack of training and experience, identification errors, inadvertent errors, wilful errors such as ignoring a warning light, and deliberate 'mistakes' or sabotage. So, with Poka Yoke we can try to prevent the error, find the error before it leads to a service or product defect, or find the defect as early as possible after that. Defects that do arise in products and services occur for various reasons, as illustrated in Table 4.1.

Table 4.1   Reasons for product and service defects

Manufacturing	Service and Transactional
Missed operation	Omitted processes
Processing errors	Processing errors
Set-up errors	Incorrectly filed documents
Missing parts	Missing information
Worn or broken tooling	Missing document
Raw material variations	Wrong document
Flow-line blockages	Computer files not updated
Measurement errors	Keyboard/data entry errors
Transit damage/loss	Corrupt/failed transmission

To do this, Poka Yoke relies on Source inspection, rather than Judgement or Informative inspection. That is, it involves inspecting the process for potential error sources rather than inspecting the product or service, or looking for deviations from process operating standards. This makes it potentially anti-fragile, particularly if it is done regularly and based on the real world process performance, with learning from process problems taken into account. In contrast, Judgement inspection, being an accept/reject selection for product or service, is detection rather than prevention, so is at best robust. Informative inspection is somewhere in between, reduces defects by spotting the pattern and providing feedback, and may be anti-fragile or more likely robust, depending on whether that feedback is used to improve the process as well as the product, in an ongoing way, based on real process performance.

Thus, Poka Yoke, unlike informative inspection methods like Statistical Process Control, does not require statistical sampling methods, is applicable at every process stage by monitoring potential error sources and, where possible, makes use of instrumentation with immediate feedback, as human personnel are fallible in spotting errors and defects. However, humans are essential to identify and establish the potential error sources.

Red Flag conditions correspond to when an error is particularly likely to occur. Some examples are:

- repetitive work;

- poor process environment;

- exceptional jobs;

- similar but different jobs;

- change of process pace;

- no work standards.

The potential to seriously mistake proof every process within our organisation, in a way that utilises ongoing feedback from these processes in real time, including the impact of unexpected shocks, is an aspirational anti-fragile target operating model. In deploying this, a lot will depend on the efficacy of the source inspection approach, and the identification and response to Red Flag conditions.

The Characteristics of Anti-Fragile Processes, and Doing a Process Fragility Stocktake

Behind the concept of processes in the EFQM Excellence Model is the belief that excellent organisations design, manage and improve processes in order to fully satisfy, and generate increasing value for, customers and other stakeholders. Further, these organisations analyse, prioritise, manage and improve their end-to-end processes as part of their overall management system, including those processes extending beyond the limits of the organisation. These also define the responsibilities of process owners, develop appropriate process performance and outcome measures, and innovate, improve and assess their processes. Combined with the RADAR mechanism, this requirement provides the majority of the requirements conceivable for the processes to be anti-fragile, provided only that the issues about stressing the processes that we have raised before is avoided.

To remind you, a lot will depend on the mindset with which the RADAR concept is applied; as before the difference between learning and improving from deployment, and improving resilience through being stressed, is a subtle one. For example, RADAR improvement includes improvement in efficiency and effectiveness, as well as potentially in robustness and anti-fragility of the processes; and whilst within the broad scope, the latter are not explicitly identified by the criteria. There will also again be trade-offs between these aspects and, as we have discussed, an efficient solution is frequently not an anti-fragile one. Further, it is unclear to what extent exposing our processes to stress through deployment includes exposure to Black Swans, which are core to the current interest in anti-fragility. Given the normal mindset of the EFQM Excellence Model, it may be very reasonable to exclude these as they are unforeseen exceptional circumstances and not core to the routine use of the model.

What then are the characteristics of anti-fragile processes? How do we design such processes and how should we manage them? These are important issues to think through in the context of your own organisation, and a good starting point is to do a stocktake of fragility, robustness and anti-fragility within your current processes.

To undertake a process fragility stocktake, we need to work on a team basis to:

- identify the process taxonomy;

- identify the current fragile, robust and anti-fragile features within each end-to-end process;

- consider human roles, the extent of rule-based processes, risk and opportunities for anti-fragility;

- consider second-level fragility.

As with the previous chapters, let us now consider a number of rules in relation to anti-fragility of processes that have emerged from the previous discussion, and practical experience. These are:

1.   Operations Management and Process Management typically give limited attention to fragility issues, and in practice much of the optimisation of these is concerned with efficiency and effectiveness rather than fragility. Accordingly, given the common correlation

between optimal efficiency and fragility, the current literature on operations management is somewhat artificial, but where applied in practice can lead to overall suboptimal performance.

2.   Typical process fragility issues include more than just the danger of the process stopping, but also the process operating with no output, the process operating but with no acceptable output, and the process operating but with performance below a specified acceptable level in terms of delay, volume, disruption and/or variation.

3.   There may be a U-shaped characteristic for the relationship between process fragility and process efficiency. This would suggest that there is an optimum process efficiency to deliver minimum process fragility and a possible flat area until we reach an intrinsic process efficiency boundary, beyond which the increase in fragility may become severe.

4.   QA is an anti-fragile aspect of our organisations and systems but is often implemented in a fragile way, so that a QA or ISO 9001 system may be fragile or anti-fragile in practice, dependent on how it is implemented.

5.   The Lean Approach is inherently fragile but can make a very real contribution to process, operations and organisational anti-fragility, depending on how it is implemented. The difference between fragile Lean and Anti-Fragile Lean are subtle and complex, and are discussed in detail above, together with how to exploit these.

6.   A similar situation exists for Six Sigma, which is inherently anti-fragile, but can still be implemented in a fragile way.

7.   Poka Yoke Mistake Proofing is inherently robust or anti-fragile. The potential to mistake proof every process in an organisation, utilising ongoing feedback from these processes in real time, including unexpected shocks, is an aspirational anti-fragile target operating model but will depend on the efficacy of the source inspection approach and the identification and response to Red Flag conditions.

8.   As previously, the EFQM Excellence Model criterion and sub-criterion covering processes gives a good summary of many of the requirements for anti-fragility, except that the model is more focused on efficiency and effectiveness, and so must be used carefully.

Chapter 5

The Use of Information and Technology, and the Impact of Innovation

How our Technology and Information Systems Make us Fragile or Anti-Fragile

As with so many of the aspects of the organisation that we have looked at so far, technology can be fragile or robust, and/or hinder or help the pursuit of organisational anti-fragility. This does not just refer to technical fragility of the technology, but also to the full basis for using it on which the current business model is based, which as far as it goes, can be summarised under PESTEL circumstances: Political, Economic, Societal, Technological, Environmental and Legal. Such fragility caused by economic circumstances includes the impact of market conditions, substitution and so on. Whether the technology is fragile, robust or anti-fragile depends on what the technology is, how it is used, and the organisational and external environment.

In a similar way, the organisation's information systems may be fragile or robust, and/or hinder or help the pursuit of organisational anti-fragility. Again, this does not just refer to the technical fragility of the technology but also to the full PESTEL basis for using it on which the current business model is based. Fragility here may include performance information issues concerned – for example, with the integrity of the information provided in the system – a matter that we shall return to in a later section below.

It is a truism based on experience that technologies that start robust, or even anti-fragile, will over time become fragile, as market and technology developments and so on occur. Whilst today we have all now largely developed the conceptual understanding that no technology basis will last forever, perhaps strangely, in organisations, we still often do not appear to take a proactive view on this but exploit our cash cow until, inevitably, but with regret and surprise, serious market decline occurs. This is a consequence of the nature of innovation, whose impact we shall also discuss in a section below. Thus, a technology's anti-fragility is at best temporary and itself fragile. We talked about second-order fragility previously as the fragility of an anti-fragile feature or system in the context of Risk Management and QA; the use of this term is also appropriate here for technology.

In relation to information systems, much of the above argument again also holds. Even information systems that were originally robust or anti-fragile, given enough time, will become fragile, due to changes in the internal and external environment. Again, in organisations we should be constantly on the lookout for this but are often not. Worse, such systems are often, even initially, poorly matched to the full scope of real information system requirements.

It is also apparent that, at this age in human history, our technology and systems, in particular, are causing our organisations and society considerable fragility, arguably at an increasing rate. This fragility is not just in terms of small step changes, with easily manageable consequences, but also large ones, with major disruptive implications. Examples are the invention of air travel, mobile technology, the move from fossil fuels and the development of biotechnology. Part of the reasons for this is, undoubtedly, the extensiveness and complexity of our current technology base, the economic unification of world markets, the competitive creativity inherent in the global business model, the availability of capital, the emergence of emergent business strategy and the change in our mindset towards a more frantic and changing worldview.

Common Deficiencies in Systems and Use of Information and Technology

As part of this increasing pace of change and consequent fragility, at the current time we are subject to a set of generic organisational technology and system issues that represent sources of organisational fragility. These include, in particular, the hard-wired use of technology that restricts the organisation in responding to internal or external sources of change. As well as rigid flow-line systems used in manufacturing, this in turn includes our dependence on large inflexible software business systems that represent major purchase decisions and, once purchased, tend to determine all aspects of organisational conduct.

Tied to this is the related problem that associated with such enterprise software systems is typically a scarcity of supporting knowledge and skills within the organisation. This is because such skills are not core to the organisation's operations and, possibly until now, their business model; they are, additionally, highly expensive and typically in short supply. This increases the dependence on the vendors of such systems, or possibly external expert professional support. This, in turn, causes potential fragility as organisational purchase decisions, efficient and effective usage of such systems, extensions of use and new applications are then all dependent on the efficacy of the technical and commercial relationship with the supplier. Vendor lock-in, possibly created by lack of transparency in system architecture, deliberate system design and/ or commercial arrangements can then leave the organisation with little choice other than to accept high-cost follow-on choices, or to work around these artificial restrictions with human ingenuity and, typically, lots of paper. Again, a source of fragility.

A further but related potential technology fragility issue is the increasing reliance on global systems, with little or no local back up. This is ironic as this development also contains the potential for the solution to the vendor lock-in problem. Whilst offering extensive functionality, efficiency and low cost, such dependency on remote centralised systems, such as Google Drives and remote desktops, may both reduce the organisation's exposure to some local fragility hazards, such as locally induced system failure, whilst at the same time, however remote, increasing the risk to the organisation from more widespread global system failure. With these global Cloud-based systems, it is likely that the organisation's local fragility issues will be reduced, but when such hazards are eventually realised the impact on the organisation may be much greater as it will be part of a much bigger global fragility system failure.

Cloud computing is a business model for enabling convenient, on-demand network access to a shared pool of configurable computing resources (for example, networks, servers, storage, applications and services) that can be rapidly provisioned and released with minimal management effort or service provider interaction. All main IT and software suppliers are now amongst those offering Cloud solutions, including Google, HP, IBM, Sun, Intel, Amazon, Oracle and Dell. There are now three Cloud service delivery models. These are:

- Software as a Service (SaaS):
  - business applications that are hosted by the provider, and delivered as a service;

- Platform as a Service (PaaS):
  - development environments where customers can create and develop applications;

- Infrastructure as a Service (IaaS):
  - delivery of computer hardware (servers, networking technology, storage, data networking space and so on) as a service.

There are also Public Clouds, Private Clouds and Hybrid Clouds. Thus, the recent emergence of Cloud computing as a real business option offers the opportunity for the reduction of fragility due to vendor lock-in and locally induced system failure, but at the cost of a potential rise in global system fragility.

Cloud represents a major technology development, at least as big as the development of the PC.

By its nature, the characteristics of Cloud computing are:

- Elasticity and scalability:
  - practically unlimited computing resources on demand giving agility;

- Utility computing:
  - variable cost using a pay-as-you-go cost structure;

- no long-term commitments:
  - self-service provisioning and automatic de-provisioning. See Figure 5.1.

Overall, there are many benefits:

- scalability and sustainability;

- secure storage and management;

- location independent;

- 24/7 support;

- Agile Deployment;

- virtualised and dynamic;

- pay as you go;

- utility-based, time-sharing models;

- low total cost of ownership;

- high-level computing.

(i) Traditional Fixed Cost IT Model

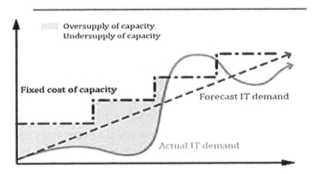

(ii) New Variable Cost IT Model

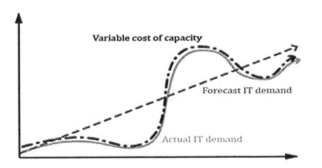

Figure 5.1   **Cost benefit of Cloud computing**

On the other hand, current challenges include:

- Information security and users' privacy:
  - data stored in centralised locations;

- Reliability:
  - seamless user experience given danger of outages;

- high-speed access to the Internet:
  - broadband penetration still lagging in some parts of the world;

- standardisation/regulatory compliance:
  - different standards need to be finalised to allow widespread adoption of Cloud (see, for example, Christauskas and Miseviciene, 2012).

Returning to the issue of fragility associated with vendor lock-in and large purchase decisions, Cloud computing does represent a very real opportunity to reduce periods of frozen organisational systems due to dependency on vendors, the scale of purchase decisions and vendor lock-in. Systems frozen and being worked around, with associated problems of paper fixes between non-compatible systems, escalation of time, confusion and work in progress, is clearly a source of fragility. Automation and integration of systems using Cloud-based products not only eliminates the need for multiple systems with paper fixes between them, but also requires limited technical expertise, allows integration into just *one* managed workflow, and provides 'for free', as a by-product, online process performance information and audit. With products like RunMyProcess or Force, any business manager can purpose-build a software solution that fully automates his or her business processes, just like using Apps on their iPhone or Blackberry.

Thus, Cloud encourages both Leanness and anti-fragility through providing the opportunity to implement real joined-up, end-to-end systems. But Cloud alone does not make an organisation Lean or anti-fragile. In addition, inertias and lock-in mean that Cloud-based solutions are likely to be suboptimal. Thus, there are two options for implementing Cloud solutions in a Lean and anti-fragile way. These are:

- improve towards Lean and/or anti-fragility;

- design for Lean and/or anti-fragility.

When designing a process or system from scratch for Lean and anti-fragility it makes sense to take advantage of the enormous advantages of the Cloud. Cloud computing is one important way of making part of our technology base, and our systems, anti-fragile. However, in doing so one needs to be clear on the system objectives, customer requirements, desired processes, management information requirements and so on as there is a danger of creating an efficient implementation of a non-effective system. This illustrates the fact that the real value added in the development work is typically in the bit you may feel inclined to skim on; the creation of the specification.

Improving towards Lean and anti-fragility is typically easier to do but harder to use Cloud fully effectively with. Vendor lock-in means that it may not be cost effective to remove all the paper between systems. Thus, there is a need for practical realism and skill in designing the end-to-end system.

Identifying the Relevant, Timely and Useable Information We Need for Anti-Fragile Operation

There is a need for organisations to undertake a stocktake of their information, and information systems, from the perspective of anti-fragility. In doing this, the issue is not just the current systems, information provision and their quality but also what are the requirements to support organisational anti-fragility for that particular organisation? The questions to be asked include:

- How do our organisational information and information systems affect our organisational fragility?

- What information is essential to our anti-fragility?

- What aspects of our information systems increase our organisational fragility?

In order to identify the information we need for anti-fragile operations, we need to consider the questions;

- Where do we need it? Why?

- When do we need it? Why?

- What do we need? Why?

- What characteristics must it have? Why?

The answer to the last 'characteristics' question is likely to include: Relevant, Timely, Useable, Adequate and Complete.

   The EFQM Excellence Model, through the RADAR Results and Enabler matrices which define some of the requirements for assessing organisational excellence, also gives us some further insight into what, in general, the required organisational information requirements for anti-fragility may be. These are that:

- regular and appropriate measurements of the efficiency and effectiveness of all approaches and their deployments are carried out;

- results are timely, reliable and accurate, and appropriately segmented;

- output from measurement and learning is used to identify, prioritise, plan and implement improvements;

- the scope of the results measurements is coherent and addresses the needs and expectations of all relevant stakeholders, and is consistent with the strategy and policies of the organisation, and the most important results are prioritised;

- relationships between relevant results are understood, and results are timely, reliable, accurate and appropriately segmented;

- Appropriate external comparisons are made for key results and, based on the evidence presented, there is confidence that positive performance will be sustained into the future.

Again, whilst these are a good starting point for organisational anti-fragility requirements, they emphasise efficiency and effectiveness, rather than fragility, robustness and anti-fragility.

   As well as the RADAR matrices, two sub-criteria in the EFQM Excellence Model deal respectively with what would be expected from an excellent organisation in terms of how technology is managed, and how information and knowledge are managed. For technology, the expectation is in terms of how the organisation develops a strategy and manages the technology portfolio, optimises existing technology and replaces out-of-date technology, uses technology including IT to support and improve the effective running of the organisation, involves stakeholders in development and deployment of technologies, identifies and evaluates alternative and emerging technologies, and uses technology to support innovation and creativity. Since these requirements emphasise an ongoing process of evaluation and development/ improvement they are essentially anti-fragile. However, again the question remains as to how much they explicitly focus on the improvement of anti-fragility, as well as efficiency and effectiveness.

For information and knowledge, the EFQM Excellence Model places emphasis on how this is managed to support effective decision making and build organisational capability. There are specific requirements in terms of how leaders are provided with adequate appropriate information to do this; how data is transformed into information and, where appropriate, into sharable useable knowledge, how access to information and knowledge is provided and monitored for employees and relevant stakeholders subject to appropriate protection of intellectual property and security; how networks are established and managed to identify opportunities for innovation; how the organisation uses innovation to identify new value for customers, ways of working and organisational development; and how process data and information is used to generate innovation. Here there is emphasis on continual development, building capacity and effective decision making; again, good ingredients to take us towards anti-fragility but with the same caveat as before regarding the absence of an explicit focus on the improvement of anti-fragility, as well as efficiency and effectiveness.

From the above discussion of RADAR, a consideration for an organisation if it has the appropriate measurements is, does the organisation then actually use them? Many do not, at least fully effectively. There are a number of tools that have been developed to focus on this issue; one such is the Performance Measurement Maturity Grid.

Table 5.1   The Performance Measurement Maturity Grid

	Low Results Actionability	**High Results Actionability**
High Measurement Aptitude	Analysis Paralysis	Excellence Addict
Low Measurement Aptitude	Ingrained Inertia	The Right Stuff

The Performance Measurement Maturity Grid divides up the assessment of an organisation's use of measurement into rows and columns concerned, respectively, with is it any good at measurement and does it use the outcomes of measurement to take action? (see Table 5.1) The rows concern Measurement Aptitude, which covers the ability to measure. Measurement Aptitude is about the quality, not quantity, of measurement undertaken; so which row an organisation is in is not about how much they measure, but how well they do it *consistently*. Organisations that score high on Measurement Aptitude typically:

- know what they wish to measure;

- have a system in place to measure it; and

- can easily access the right data in a timely way.

The columns measure Results Actionability. This concerns the ability to accept and use the results of measurement, which can be difficult for some organisations in general, and for others when the results do not turn out to be as expected. Whilst debate can be healthy, there comes a time when actions need to be taken and organisations clearly need organisational mechanisms to act upon the results of measurements.

The Performance Measurement Maturity Grid shows four quadrants, with qualitatively different characteristics. In the top right, 'Excellence Addicts' typically correspond to organisations that are always looking for ways to improve, constantly tweaking performance, embrace the results of measurement and have a positive change culture. Organisations in the 'Right Stuff' quadrant, bottom right, typically have the ingredients with which to act; executive involvement, an open attitude and culture with regard to measurement, and the necessary organisation structure and processes. However, they often lack hard data and metrics on which to base sound decisions, do not know what to measure or how to collect the data, and typically they may have had a change in leadership or a change in their environment.

In contrast, organisations top left, in 'Analysis Paralysis', typically measure well but have no organisational buy-in or acceptance to act on the results. They lack clear management directives, have a defensive culture, and often conflicting agendas from many stakeholders, so that there is an opportunity for 'terrorists' to derail the efforts. There also may be an organisational disconnect between the data collection and actions taken. Such organisations may have lost sight of the ultimate goal, and may be 'measuring for the sake of it', that is, as an end in itself. Finally, 'Ingrained Inertia', bottom left, describes organisations that may not be measuring at all or, whilst they measure a lot, it takes them a long time to get actual data. There may be no organisational momentum or executive support to accept and act on the results of measurement and the people doing the measurement may be far removed from decision making and lack influence. This can result in no buy-in at executive, or any, level to the data collection effort, and subsequent resistance from people that have access to the data.

To be a robust or anti-fragile organisation, it needs to be measuring well and using the measurement well. If it is not, it should put this right. If an organisation is in the 'Ingrained Inertia' quadrant, what should it do first: improve measurement or improve actionability? Clearly the latter, since the route through 'Analysis Paralysis' is a hard and dangerous one; one would not want one's organisation to get stuck there!

Benchmarking

In discussing the information requirements suggested by the EFQM Excellence Model, we mentioned the need for comparisons with external performance. This is the subject of Benchmarking. Benchmarking has been prevalent in the west for over 30 years. It is an essential part of any serious quality or performance improvement strategy, and is an aspect of the EFQM Excellence Model and its relatives. However, the 'Benchmarking Boom' of management interest of the 1990s has long receded and now Benchmarking is frequently seen as just another tool in the armoury of Quality Management. Back then, the author's FT book on *Benchmarking for Competitive Advantage* (1997) was a best seller, ultimately published in six languages, and two editions. To some extent it is a big mistake to see Benchmarking as just another tool. Benchmarking is an ongoing management process, a philosophy or world view based on open thinking, a culture or the way we should do things round here – not just a tool. It needs to be developed wisely within any organisation serious about pursuing excellence or anti-fragility. The reason that organisations need Benchmarking is that, typically, they do not really know how good they are. Nor do they know, for sure, who is better, or who the best is, and how they can become as good as or better than the best. There are also issues of the need for Continuous Improvement, the marginal approach frequently taken to management by just focusing on improving on previous figures rather than comparing performance to the best, and, frequently also, the need for major process re-engineering.

The contributions Benchmarking can make to anti-fragility, as well as excellence, Six Sigma, ISO 9001 and Lean thinking, are of greater importance now than ever before but only if it is applied correctly. With the growth of the Internet and publicly available information, we have seen a *growth in bad practices* in Benchmarking that hurt rather than help the serious pursuit of anti-fragility and excellence. We shall discuss these a bit more below. The key concept of Benchmarking is learning from the success of other organisations. The method once again originated in Japan and in many senses can be seen as an approach at various points going back through Japanese history. However, a key point in the story is the late 1950s when Japanese industrialists visited thousands of US and European companies with a view to studying production methods. They identified best practices, transferred methods between industries, acquired patent rights and for the first time started to develop modern industries.

However, the Benchmarking method was not transferred into the west until after 1979, when the Xerox Corporation was experiencing a rapidly diminishing market share. Patent protection had just run out on the black and white photocopier. In consequence Xerox, who had had a monopoly in the 1960s, was under severe competitive pressure from the Japanese who, it seemed, could sell more reliable machines for less than Xerox could make them. By studying the activities and methods of its successful joint venture in Japan, Fuiji–Xerox, Xerox was able to identify improved practices, understand through the Japanese the systematic process of learning from other organisations, and save itself. Thus, Benchmarking became a corporate programme across Xerox and entered western management practice.

Benchmarking is about moving from 'business as usual' thinking, focusing on improving on last year's performance, to comparing to the market leaders instead. David Kearns, who was CEO of the Xerox Corporation at that time, defined Benchmarking as: 'The continuous process of measuring products, services and practices against the toughest competitors or those companies recognised as industry leaders.'

Another useful quote, that very much explains what Benchmarking is about, and has been used repeatedly to motivate its application, originates some 2,500 years ago, from the Chinese warlord, Sun Tzu: 'If you know the enemy and know yourself, you need not fear the result of a hundred battles. If you know yourself but not the enemy, for every victory gained you will also suffer a defeat. If you know neither the enemy nor yourself, you will succumb in every battle.'

Based on these definitions, Benchmarking then is clearly an anti-fragile aspect of organisational practice as it involves ongoing learning and implementation of improvement, from studying the performance of organisations that are doing better than your own organisation – always assuming, however, that it is done right. It is often not.

Benchmarking can be applied at a variety of levels within the organisation, ideally in a hierarchical way. Strategic benchmarks can be developed for corporate priorities as well as benchmarks for annual plan objectives. At the process level, we can focus on the performance of the vital few process areas and develop operational benchmarks to study, to improve these. In this regard, Xerox identified four types of Benchmarking;

- Internal Benchmarking;

- Competitor Benchmarking;

- Functional Benchmarking;

- Generic or Process Benchmarking.

Internal Benchmarking is the identification of other sites, divisions, departments and so on within your organisational group from whom there is real potential to learn, because their performance in the specific characteristic of interest that you are studying greatly outperforms that of your part of the organisation. Clearly you are more likely to get cooperation than trying to do this with a competitor, although this can still be a difficult issue. The downside is that since there is usually some tendency for best practices to be shared, you are unlikely to discover major paradigm shifts in thinking and performance this way.

Not surprisingly, Competitor Benchmarking is much more difficult. Often competitors will not cooperate to share best practices, and, if they do, they may infringe competition law. However, typically much can be gleaned from public domain sources and, if the organisation is definitely performing much better than your own in the specific characteristic that you are studying, then anything obtained is likely to be of interest. The comparative level of performance, if extreme, can also provide the 'emotional event' for the organisation, or your 'burning platform', that forces you to look up and take note; bringing forward the stress on your system in order to improve and gain resilience. Hence such Benchmarking is clearly anti-fragile.

Functional Benchmarking is the comparison of performance of a functional area of your organisation, such as HR, Design or Catering, with a similar but superiorly performing unit elsewhere. This, of course, may be a non-competitor in a completely different business area and so is much more likely to cooperate in sharing best practices both ways than a direct competitor.

Finally, we have Generic or Process Benchmarking, where we compare performance of a process within your organisation with that of a superiorly performing, but similarly purposed, process elsewhere. Again, this may well be with a non-competitor so, again, is more likely to get cooperation.

In all of these approaches, a key consideration is to ensure that we identify the most appropriate organisation, or organisational area, to compare to and, certainly, one that has much better performance than us. Otherwise, there will be nothing to learn and it will not help our pursuit of anti-fragility.

We said earlier that, with the growth of the Internet and publicly available information, we have seen a growth in bad practices in Benchmarking that hurt, rather than help, the serious pursuit of anti-fragility. More generally, there are, as with all somewhat subtle management approaches, lots of pitfalls to Benchmarking. Some of the more common ones are:

- overambitious plans;

- using the wrong team;

- poor choice of partner/benchmark organisations;

- poor preparation;

- legal impediments;

- timescales;

- resource issues.

These are all fairly obvious deficiencies, well known to the author and confirmed by various surveys around the world. Being unrealistic on what is to be achieved is a common starting error and, in the extreme, has led to organisations trying to benchmark every one of their processes at once, consequently with considerable problems of resources and timescales. Related is being unprepared, having not done adequate deskwork to find out about them when making contact with a potential Benchmarking partner. Sometimes it is the wrong partner, chosen for convenience and ease of access rather than performance and the ability for us to learn from them. We may also use the wrong Benchmarking team, perhaps corporate 'seagulls' rather than people working in, or owning, the process, hence contributing to real problems to getting good ideas from the benchmark organisation accepted locally. All these, of course, represent potential fragilities of our Benchmarking process.

But there are other, more subtle, problems too. The Benchmarking word is frequently misunderstood and misapplied. Problems include:

- Organisations or teams that think Benchmarking is about showing that they are the best so there's nothing to learn. If this is true, then they have selected the wrong Benchmarking topic – no organisation is best at everything!

- Confusing compilation of 'League Tables' with Benchmarking – the key learning that will help create anti-fragility is knowing 'how' the top performers achieved their superior performance.

- Confusing benchmarks with predetermined standards – finding out how well others are performing and who's the best is again key to your organisation progressing towards anti-fragility.

- 'Industrial Tourism' – to be efficient and effective Benchmarking needs to be a focused, planned, managed and controlled process, not a tour of interesting places and waiting for divine inspiration.

- 'Scatter Gun Surveys' – like League Tables, sending out questionnaires or emails en masse is not Benchmarking. Instead desk research is needed to identify the best to compare to and more considered approaches made.

- 'Cosy Clubs' – joining a Benchmarking club can be good personal development, not to mention fun, but it is not in itself Benchmarking, which requires a much more highly focused, planned and controlled project approach.

- Proprietary Surveys – these are typically like the Scatter Gun Surveys but also suffer from lack of transparency, due to commercial considerations.

- Google searches and the use of non-validated data – whilst Google is a wonderful tool, can you always trust the integrity of what you find though using it?

It is partly because of the existence of Google that Benchmarking is particularly relevant now. It has been said that:

> If you Google it, you get a million answers ... but, if you ask a Librarian, you get the right answer!

Actually, I found that Googling 'Benchmarking', I got about 16,400,000 results in 0.19 seconds. The point, however, is that you cannot, in general, trust the sources. Anyone can put up an item or contribute to a wiki. In looking at information sources, we should look for accuracy, authority, currency, objectivity and audience – but we do not have the ability to do this well with web sources. Unfortunately, websites do not always check facts and are not necessarily trustworthy. Thus, we need a proper, systematic, rigorous, verifiable Benchmarking process and not to rely on naive Googling. Despite what some people call it, naive Googling is not Benchmarking – and it's certainly fragile.

There is one final point to make about Benchmarking and anti-fragility. As with many of the ideas around excellence, much Benchmarking activity and theory focuses on process efficiency and, to a slightly lesser extent, effectiveness. Whilst, in theory, Benchmarking also includes the anti-fragility of the processes and systems, in practice this may be neglected. Measuring and comparing efficiencies is relatively easy, measuring and comparing the ability to increase resilience by being stressed is, of course, more complex. We have potential issues of defining anti-fragility metrics. But it is easy to compare fragility, rather than anti-fragility, by considering metrics such as lost time, number of process stoppages, breakdowns and so on.

How Innovation Changes Things

Innovation, of course, is about change. It is part of the reason why, as we have discussed above, any technology's anti-fragility is at best temporary and itself fragile. Innovation may be defined as the creation of novelty that provides economic value through the creation of new products and services. Within this definition, product innovation means creating new products or services, whilst process innovation is about doing things differently. For product innovation, we can also distinguish between radical innovation, which fundamentally changes the products offered, and incremental innovation, which makes small and Continuous Improvements to an existing product.

In his 1942 book, Joseph Schumpeter coined the term *creative destruction*, for the 'process of industrial mutation that incessantly revolutionises the economic structure *from within*, incessantly destroying the old one, incessantly creating a new one'. With this view, the key role in creative destruction is reserved for technological innovations that can make existing products, designs and processes redundant. Hence any incremental improvements to these are also made redundant through creative destruction. There are many examples of this in recent history – the horse and buggy, the typewriter, telex, the fax machine, the police whistle and so on.

Interestingly, it appears that large companies do not frequently invest in such *disruptive technologies* because, as they tend to be simpler and cheaper, they thus promise less profit. They may also develop in fringe markets that are not currently important to the big players. So, the existence of disruptive technologies represent sources of fragility for these large companies which, to counter these, need to have a developing portfolio of other products and an ongoing stream of new ones. According to Tidd and Bessant (2007), such sources of disruption to established markets include:

- The emergence of new markets: for example, the SMS industry grew out of nowhere into a billion-dollar industry with a high profit margin. Originally, SMS was added to mobile phones as a minor function but teenagers started using it to avoid the peak tariffs of mobile phone providers (that is, substitution).

- The development of new technologies: for example, the advent of the computer, which posed a serious challenge to typewriter manufacturers and other office equipment providers.

- New legal, societal and political rules: for example, the tobacco industry that has had to adapt to regulation of prices, distribution and promotion, as well as law suits.

- The creation of new business models: for example, companies such as Amazon and eBay that have reinvented whole industries.

- The identification of new needs and behaviours: for example, the emergence of the diet industry or the now rapidly growing healthy lifestyle industry, providing fitness centres, personal trainers, fitness equipment, health food, and detox and activity holidays.

- Unthinkable events: for example, September 11, and the emerging security industry. Following the 9/11 terrorist attack, a whole new business sector has now emerged.

In contrast to these, most developing technologies are *sustaining technologies*, which improve the performance of existing products rather than lead to their replacement. Such sustaining technologies do not produce real innovation.

In such disruptive innovative times, organisations need strategies for dealing with disruption to minimise its potential impact on organisational fragility. Suggested aspects to approaches include:

- strategies should be emergent, with the organisation adapting and learning quickly;

- a high tolerance for ambiguity should be allowed, as the rules only emerge over time;

- organisational culture should support and encourage curiosity-driven behaviour;

- risk taking and tolerance of (fast) failures should be high;

- weak ties and peripheral vision are also important.

There are rationalist and incremental approaches to innovation strategy. The rationalist approach is based on a linear model, whereby you scan the external and internal environment, decide on a course of action summarised in a plan and then implement that plan. However, a purely rationalist approach has severe limitations as the complexity of the environments is extremely high, so that it is difficult to develop a clear view. In addition, whilst innovation is about the future, the rationalist approach takes the status quo as its starting point and hence may be fragile. In contrast, an incremental strategy relies on a step-by-step, trial-and-error approach whereby small steps are accompanied by frequent and quick feedback loops that constantly evaluate development, and mistakes are seen as learning opportunities. Hence, this is an anti-fragile approach.

Pfeffer (2007), amongst others, argues that, like organisational strategy, innovation in a large organisation is also an inherently political activity as it almost invariably threatens the fragility of the status quo. Also, Deborah Dougherty (2008) identified three properties of large and complex innovative organisations – *fluidity*, *integrity* and *energy* – as part of her *design science*. *Fluidity* refers to dynamic ongoing adaptation across product teams, businesses, technologies and capabilities. Fluid organisations are more loosely, rather than tightly, coupled and innovative organisations should not be bureaucratic ones. *Integrity* implies that integration is prized as a principle structuring thought and action, and also as an outcome of that thought and action. *Energy* means that innovative organisations continually energise, enable and motivate people. These organisational features are at least robust and are potentially anti-fragile.

The concept of the Ambidextrous Organisation was developed by Tuschman and O'Reilly (1996). These create specialist subunits within the larger parent organisation, each with unique processes, structures and cultures that are specifically intended to support early stage innovation and are comprised of one or more innovation teams. These are set up to support the unique approaches, activities and behaviours needed when launching a new business or product. Thus, the Ambidextrous Organisation characterises an entity that is capable of simultaneous incremental *and* revolutionary innovation, and is thus particularly anti-fragile.

We shall briefly talk about two further recent developments in the theory of innovation. Firstly, the concept of the co-creation of value is associated with Prahalad and Ramaswamy (2000), who have identified that, due to technology, consumers are more connected than before, as interests groups, communities and social networking sites such as Facebook and other social groupings, connect users with each other globally. Thus, consumers are more informed as higher connectivity means that information travels faster and that more information is accessible to more people. Consumers also feel more empowered and are typically more active. Thus, core competencies are no longer owned exclusively within the firm and this can be a source of both fragility and anti-fragility, dependent on whether the benefits of an increased creative environment are eclipsed or not by the potential commercial threats.

The second recent development is related to the fact that earlier, the concept of Open Innovation was pioneered by Erich von Hippel, Henry Chesbrough and others, from the 1980s onwards. Open Innovation is based on allowing companies and multiple stakeholders to interact and co-create; hence networks, eco-systems and innovation communities become important strategic resources because they allow co-creation. Chesbrough and Appleyard (2007) differentiated between four distinct *open strategies* that organisations may employ to benefit from Open Innovation. These are:

- With a *deployment* open strategy, Open Innovation increases what is available to the user and they pay for the enhanced service. For example, IBM makes money from training and consulting on open source software applications.

- With a *hybridisation* open strategy, firms invest in and remain in control of the intellectual property of add-ons to products developed in the open.

- With a *complements* open strategy, a supplier sells a product or service that is related to the use of the open source content. For example, a mobile phone supplier may benefit from the availability of free open software for the mobile.

- Finally, with a *self-service* open strategy, the community develops a service for its own needs, and no one monetises its value.

Again, Open Innovation and open strategies give a potential for reducing fragility and increasing anti-fragility as the openness allows a more creative environment. However, commercially, such an environment may also represent challenges for a company, adding to fragility.

Implementing Anti-Fragile Information and Technology-Based Systems

Information and technology are two distinct but related areas that can make or destroy an organisation. They create competitive advantage but they also are often the failure points in the success of an organisation's unique strategy. The need to implement them well is large. Part of the difficulty is *the relative rigidity, inflexibility and lumpiness of technology and information management decisions*; typically change in these is only possible with heavy investment, long change cycles and major purchase decisions. So, if we get it wrong, it will be costly and time consuming to put right – time we may not have. This is reflected in the Deloitte's Layer Model, where Technology and Information appears almost at the bottom of the layers; only Physical Assets are further down within the organisational model, and hence typically have more inertias to change.

Thus, our issue is not just the pursuit of what the right information and technology structure is to minimise fragility and maximise anti-fragility within our organisation, it is also *how we assure that the decisions made are the right ones*; the fragility, robustness and anti-fragility of our technology and information capital and related decision-making processes. Whilst *applying the concepts of fragility, robustness and anti-fragility to decision making* puts us in mind of our discussions regarding governance and risk, it clearly raises new issues about the decision-making process itself. This is an area not particularly well understood within organisations and consequently may cause fragility. We shall discuss the issue here.

In general, decision making is the process by which managers respond to opportunities and threats by analysing options and making decisions about goals and courses of action. Decisions are of two types. These are decisions in response to opportunities, for which managers seek ways to improve organisational performance and decisions in response to threats, which occurs when managers are faced by events adverse to the organisation. There is another sense too in which there are two types of decisions. Programmed Decisions represent a routine, almost automatic process, where managers have made similar decision many times before and there are rules or guidelines to follow, for example deciding to reorder office supplies. In contrast, Non-programmed Decisions are more unusual situations that have not been often addressed in the past, where there are no rules to follow since the decision is new. These decisions are made based on information and a manager's intuition and judgment, for example, should the organisation invest in a particular new technology? Clearly, Non-programmed Decisions, normally being more major in terms of the consequences of making the wrong decision, are greater threats of fragility to the organisation than programmed ones.

Also, real decision making has to be made under conditions of risk and uncertainty. Decision making under certainty is when the decision maker knows with reasonable certainty what the alternative choices are and what outcomes are associated with each alternative. Decision making under risk is when the availability of each alternative and its potential payoffs and costs are all associated with risks. Finally, decision making under uncertainty is when the decision maker does not know all the alternatives, the risks associated with each or the consequences of each alternative. This gives us the biggest likelihood of fragility.

The decision-making process in general terms, consists of the following steps:

1.   recognise the need for a decision;

2.   frame the problem;

3.   generate and assess alternative options;

4.   choose among alternatives;

5.   implement chosen alternative;

6.   learn from feedback.

The Classical Model assumes that all necessary information is available to the manager to allow them to list alternatives and consequences, that the manager can process this information adequately and that the manager knows the best future course for the organisation. In contrast, the Creative Model sees the process in terms of preparation, incubation, insight, verification and implementation. The options considered in decision making need to be feasible and satisfactory, with affordable consequences and based on legal, ethical, economic and political positions. In terms of the behavioural aspects of decision making, the Administrative Model of Decision Making recognises that when faced with a decision situation, managers actually use incomplete and imperfect information, are constrained by bounded rationality and tend to satisfice, so that they end up with a decision that may, or may not, serve the interests of the organisation. Incomplete information exists due to many issues, including ambiguous information, time constraints, information costs, bounded rationality, satisfying, escalation of commitment and coalition.

In decision making, the manager's individual beliefs about right and wrong behavior, or ethics, combine with the organisation's ethics to create managerial ethics. These concern the relationships of the firm to employees, employees to the firm and the firm to other economic agents. Various cognitive biases exist in managers, including Prior Hypothesis Bias, Representativeness, Illusion of Control, and Escalating Commitment.

Many decisions are made in a group setting. Groups tend to reduce cognitive biases and they can call on combined skills and abilities. However, there are some disadvantages with groups. One is Groupthink, whereby we get biased decision making resulting from group members striving for agreement. This often occurs when group members rally around a central manager's idea and become blindly committed without considering alternatives. The group tends to convince each member that the idea must go forward. The advantages of group decision making, compared to individual decision making, include:

- additional information and knowledge are available;

- more alternatives tend to be generated;

- more ownership and acceptance of the final decision is likely;

- enhanced communication of the decision may result;

- generally, better decisions emerge.

On the other hand, disadvantages are:

- the process takes longer than individual decision making so it is costlier;

- we may end up with compromise decisions, resulting, for example, from indecisiveness;

- the group may be dominated by one person;

- there may be Groupthink.

Correspondingly, there are various methods to improve group decision making, including:

- Devil's advocacy: one member of the group acts as the devil's advocate and critiques the way the group identified alternatives, pointing out problems with the alternatives selected.

- Dialectical inquiry: two different groups are assigned to the problem and each group evaluates the other group's alternatives.

Top managers then hear each group present their alternatives and each group can critique the other.

- Promote diversity: we increase the diversity in the group so that a wider set of alternatives may be considered.

In practice, one can increase the effectiveness of group decision making by being aware of the pros and cons of having a group or team, rather than an individual, make the decision; by setting deadlines for when decisions should be made; by avoiding problems with dominance, by managing group membership; by having each group member critically evaluate all alternatives on an individual basis; by not making the manager's position known too early; by appointing a group member to be a devil's advocate; and by holding a follow-up meeting to verify the decision.

It follows from the above that human decision making, particularly where not codified or explicitly rule-based, is particularly fragile. Incomplete or imperfect information, cognitive biases and ethics, as well as the environment of decision making, all impact on the decision made. Individual diversity in process, approach or standards can affect the outcomes and potentially endanger the organisation. In general terms, this risk of fragility can typically be reduced by careful planned use of group decision-making processes, providing more robustness – but disadvantages and risks remain.

The pursuit of an anti-fragile decision-making process would require a level of explicit monitoring of, and learning from, the decision-making process that is currently not realistic within most of our organisations. This is, however, an aspirational aim. And it is consistent with the old saying that; 'Good judgement comes from experience but experience comes from bad judgement.' Clearly, individuals and organisations do learn in this way, and gain resilience, and it would be possible to build reviews of decision making more explicitly into appraisal and personal development processes at all levels, in pursuit of anti-fragile decision making.

As in the previous chapters, we now identify rules and patterns in relation to the anti-fragility of the use of information and technology which have emerged from the previous discussion and practical experience. These are:

1.   Technology and information systems can be fragile or robust, and/or hinder or help the pursuit of organisational anti-fragility. However, technologies and information systems that start robust,

or even anti-fragile, will over time become fragile, as market and technology developments and so on occur. It follows that a technology's anti-fragility is at best temporary and itself fragile.

2.   Currently, technology and systems are causing considerable organisational fragility with major disruptive implications. This includes the hard-wired use of technology, such as rigid flow-line systems used in manufacturing, and the large inflexible software business systems that represent major purchase decisions and, once purchased, tend to determine all aspects of organisational conduct.

3.   Cloud computing represents a significant opportunity to reduce this dependency on major purchase decisions associated with large software systems, as well as, perhaps to a lesser extent, a concern that it will increase reliance on global systems, with little or no local back up; hence potentially trading a decrease in local fragility for an increase in global fragility, and the opposite for anti-fragility.

4.   The relevant EFQM Excellence Model sub-criteria and the RADAR scoring matrices again give considerable insight to the requirements for organisational anti-fragility, in relation to technology and information. However, as previously, their emphasis is primarily on supporting efficiency and effectiveness rather than fragility, robustness and anti-fragility.

5.   The contribution properly conducted Benchmarking can make to organisational anti-fragility in general, as well as specifically in relation to technology and information systems, is large. However, with the development of the Internet, there are considerable dangers in trusting analyses based on public domain data sources.

6.   Measuring and comparing anti-fragility is inherently more difficult in comparison to measuring efficiency or effectiveness as it requires measuring and comparing the system's or organisation's ability to increase its own resilience over time through its experience of being stressed. Accordingly, we have the potential issue of how to define anti-fragility metrics at the local level and globally for the organisation. However, it is easier to compare fragility, rather than anti-fragility, by considering metrics such as lost time, number of process stoppages, breakdowns and so on.

7.   Innovation, especially in the context of disruptive technologies, is a cause of fragility, and organisations need to protect themselves against it and develop anti-fragile approaches. Innovation strategy should be incremental and firms should focus on fluidity, integrity and energy.

8.   There is a relative rigidity, inflexibility and lumpiness in relation to technology and information management decisions. Typically, substantive change in technology and information management is only possible through heavy investment, long change cycles and major purchase decisions. Thus, if we make a wrong decision, it is typically costly and time consuming to subsequently put right, even if we can. Accordingly, we need to consider the fragility, robustness and ant-fragility of our decision-making processes themselves. Human decision making, particularly where not codified or explicitly rule-based, is particularly fragile, but the risk of fragility can typically be reduced by careful planned use of group decision making. The pursuit of an anti-fragile decision-making process would require a level of explicit monitoring of, and learning from, the decision-making process that is currently not realistic within most of our organisations.

Chapter 6

Anti-Fragility and the Supply Chain, Environment and Corporate Social Responsibility

Supply Networks and Supply Chains are Fragile

In this chapter we shall primarily consider the meaning of anti-fragility in the context of developing and maintaining supply chains. To do this we need to define them as well as the underlying concept of a supply network. The supply network is concerned with the network of operations required to deliver the product or service, and includes the chain of suppliers providing inputs and the chain of customers that receive the outputs of the operation, but also includes competitors, collaborators and other firms with which our organisation does not directly interact. From an organisational viewpoint, most of the network may not be under direct control of the organisation, which means that we need to include influencing and negotiating considerations. In the network, depending on what the product or service is, the flow of transformed resources may include materials, parts, information and customers.

Fragility of the supply network can threaten supply of the product or service to the customer due, for example, to harvest failures, national and international political issues, limitations of processing capacity or logistics issues. Much government policy and activity is focused on making these networks robust, or possibly anti-fragile, often from a viewpoint of strengthening the suppliers. There are various developments in the network structure relevant to this. For example:

- disintermediation 'cuts out the middle men', hence putting more resources and control into the hands of suppliers;

- coopetition (cooperative competition) within a cluster of similar businesses may assist them to attract more customers.

There is also the question of vertical integration and what the scope of the organisation, within the supply network, should be. This is about consideration of:

- direction – expand by buying suppliers or customers, or contract by selling part of business;

- extent – how far the business should take vertical integration.

So-called balance between stages occurs where one operation produces only for the next stage in that network and fully satisfies its requirements, hence implying exclusivity of relationship. However, this may be fragile as there is not spare capacity nor alternative sources of supply. Also, operations may exhibit economy of scale effects, whereby operating costs reduce proportionally as the scale of capacity increases, or diseconomies of scale as complexity costs increase, and a larger unit is more likely to be underutilised. Over time, as demand changes, capacity of operations needs to be changed and balanced to reflect this.

Supply chain management is the management of relationship and flows of information, products and services between the string of operations and processes, inside and outside the organisation, necessary for the organisation to deliver the final product or service to the end customer and satisfy them. The management of an organisation's supply chain will dictate its delivery performance and hence its fragility, robustness or anti-fragility. As with the discussion of processes, appropriate performance measures should include coverage of quality, speed, dependability, flexibility and cost. Clearly, the performance of the chain as a whole, rather than just the organisation's internal operations, is important from the customer perspective in order to ensure that the products and services are appropriate and meets price and delivery requirements, and that the organisation is focused on satisfying these. Doing this for a whole supply chain is clearly more difficult than just doing this internally for operations. This will also be the basis of the customer's view of its fragility, robustness or anti-fragility. These end objectives of the chain help determine the organisation's supply chain management approach. For example, functional and long supplied products and services will typically require Lean supply chains, whilst innovative, fashionable and seasonal products and services typically benefit from more Agile supply chains.

There are two extreme versions of supply chain management relationships within the chain. Transactional approaches select the best supplier for each transaction based on immediate market conditions, which has the advantages that:

- it maintains ongoing competition between suppliers;

- suppliers may supply to many customers, in order to gain economies of scale;

- the organisation retains flexibility to change the number and types of suppliers;

- innovations can typically be acquired more quickly and cheaply than developing them in house.

However, this approach also has the disadvantages that suppliers build up little loyalty to the customers and the ongoing process of choosing a supplier takes continuing time and effort. In contrast, partnership relationships are themselves a compromise between vertical integration and transactional relationships. These have the benefit of relatively enduring inter-firm cooperative agreements which share success and, in the longer term, assists joint coordination of activities. Also, they facilitate joint learning and problem solving, there are many fewer relationships to manage and we can build up information transparency and trust. All supply chain relationships lie somewhere in the spectrum from *transactional* to *partnership*, and it is likely that anti-fragility will require this as, to retain customers, a certain level of guaranteed supply will be necessary, but not at any cost.

In selecting suppliers, there are a range of factors to consider, including their potential performance in terms of quality, responsiveness, dependability, delivery and volume flexibility, cost and quantity available. Also, there are longer-term factors such as their ability to innovate, how easy it is to do business with them, their willingness to share risk, their long-term commitment to supply and potential knowledge transfer. Clearly, supplier selection should reflect overall supply chain objectives and will involve aspects of their technical capability, operations capability, financial capability and managerial capability.

At the current time, there is also considerable economic pressure on western organisations to outsource and offshore parts of what were their in-house operations and support processes. The benefits and disadvantages of outsourcing can be assessed using performance objectives such as quality, speed, dependability, flexibility and cost, although cost is often the dominant factor. Most frequently, offshoring is seen as a form of outsourcing that moves operations to a lower-cost region of the world to reduce overall costs, although this can be on a wholly owned basis rather than an outsourced one. Location of the organisation itself is important because it can have a significant impact on profits, and location evaluation criteria include capital requirements, market factors, cost factors, future flexibility and, of course, risk factors. When a site move is planned the organisation also needs to deal with the transition and continuity of supply.

Also, currently, the debate about single sourcing, and multi-sourcing is of interest. The advantages of single sourcing include potentially better quality, durable relationships with higher confidentiality, more supplier commitment and effort, better communication, easier cooperation on new products or services, and economies of scale. However, the disadvantages of single sourcing are that it creates increased vulnerability to disruption to supply if the supplier fails, volume fluctuations may be more difficult to agree, and there can be a continual upward pressure on prices, if no alternative supplier is available. In contrast, multi-sourcing has the potential advantages of cost reduction through competitive tendering, the ability to switch sources and the potentially wide range of expertise on tap. On the other hand, the disadvantages are that it can be difficult to gain commitment from suppliers, more difficult to assist suppliers to improve quality, more time and effort may be needed to communicate, there are reduced economies of scale and suppliers will be less likely to invest in new processes to support customer needs. Poor supplier selection gives us fragility; good supplier selection robustness. A learning, improving, supplier selection system gives us anti-fragility, especially if we make mistakes to learn from.

Especially with recent globalisation, unsatisfactory supplier relationships are often the result of a mismatch in expectations between what the supplier thinks the organisation wants and what it really wants, or how the supplier thinks it is performing compared to how the organisation thinks it is. Communication can be improved to reduce the expectations gap and the organisation may use its own skills to help the supplier meet its own expectations. Service Level Agreements (SLAs) are formal definitions of standards or dimensions of service, for example defining the services normally provided, periods of availability, maximum response times, special services available on request, performance reporting and what happens if the service standards are not achieved. Such SLAs are working documents and should be reviewed and updated in the light of experience.

Just as supplier development assists robustness and anti-fragility of the supply chain, in a similar way closing the expectations gap for customers can enhance the operation of the supply chain. This can be based on the use of customer complaints or formal feedback data to identify areas for attention. Going forward, improved processes can then manage how customer requirements are captured.

Also worthy of our consideration is that e-commerce and the Internet has enabled a fundamental change in purchasing processes. This has not only affected consumer purchasing and retail but upstream supply processes also. Now, for example, the availability of supplier information makes it easier to choose alternative suppliers, and purchasers can group together to obtain economies of scale. Whether part of e-commerce or more traditional supply chains, logistics services concern the movement of materials and goods, from suppliers, through intermediary stages and ultimately to the customer. These are often outsourced to third-party logistics companies (3PL). There is a range of integration of haulage, storage and packing services with, in the extreme, 'total supply chain management' providers (4PL) taking responsibility for the end-to-end process, often for several customers simultaneously. The Internet enables tracking of deliveries in real time and automatic identification technologies, such as bar codes or Radio Frequency Identification, enable scanning to capture data quickly, accurately improving the ability to track and trace goods in and out of warehouses, shops and so on.

Excellence, Anti-Fragility, Partners and Suppliers

The aspirations of the EFQM Excellence Model include the requirement that excellent organisations plan and manage external partnerships and suppliers as well as their internal resources, and that partners and suppliers are managed for sustainable benefits. So, what is the difference between a partner and a supplier? Partners may, or may not, be suppliers. And suppliers may, or may not, be partners. Unfortunately, the words are often used almost interchangeably in everyday business usage, but this is wrong. Essentially, partnership implies, and requires, a long-term relationship, built on a shared vision of the future. This may be with suppliers, customers or any stakeholder. We probably use the term most frequently with regards to suppliers but we should not use it for transactional relationships in the supply chain, or ones with little shared vision.

The partnership and supplier requirement in the EFQM Excellence Model is about planning and managing the external partnerships and suppliers in support of strategy and operational process effectiveness. This includes effectively managing the environmental and societal impact. In order to do this, part of the requirement is how does the organisation segment and differentiate partner and supplier groups, and effectively manage the distinct groups? Also, the requirement covers how the organisation: builds sustainable relationships with its partners and suppliers based on openness and trust; establishes extensive networks from which they identify potential partnerships; sees partnerships in terms of jointly enhancing value and systematically enables the delivery of enhanced value to stakeholders through synergies and seamless processes; works together with its partners to achieve mutual benefit and supports partners and suppliers with expertise, resource and knowledge to achieve shared goals. As previously, this is an impressive list of practical requirements that does much to take the organisation towards an anti-fragile world. Specifically, it implies an aspect of ongoing management, building sustainable relationships and working towards mutual benefit, enhanced value and shared goals. Together with the RADAR requirements, it also covers an ongoing loop of improvement, based on learning from the real world deployment of the approaches. However, it again emphasises effectiveness and does not explicitly cover fragility and anti-fragility issues beyond a possibly implied presumption that an effective approach is not a fragile one. This means that there is no explicit consideration of how and to what extent the organisation develops anti-fragile mechanisms in relation to its partnerships and suppliers, improves the improvement cycles nor even explicitly considers the fragility risk.

Managing the Supply Chain, and the Information Requirements for Anti-Fragility

A key part of the consideration of fragility of supply chains concerns their information requirements. Supply chains need information to work effectively and efficiently, and good quality information flow is also an underlying requirement for anti-fragility. Customer requirements are passed through the supply chain in the opposite direction to the products or services they provide. If suppliers do not receive market information or forecasts, or receive misinformation, then there will be errors and delays in supply that will impact on customer satisfaction and organisational performance. This effect gets worse the further back in the supply chain you go, and is analogous to the so-called *Bull Whip* effect. With this, demand fluctuations become progressively amplified as their effects work back up the supply chain, so that a slight variation in end customer demand eventually leads to major process stop/start oscillations in far upstream processes. The Bull Whip effect, and the errors and delays in supply we referred to above, can all be reduced by information sharing, aligning planning and control decisions, improving flow efficiency and better forecasting. This will reduce fragility of the supply chain, if systemised will increase its robustness and, if the information system is designed to capture and apply on an ongoing basis, the learning from operating it in a suboptimal way,should help develop its anti-fragility.

Absence of market information, however, is not the only source of fragility in supply chains. Capacity management concerns the management of mismatches between demand and the ability to supply, in order to satisfy current and future demand. Capacity is the achievable output volume in relation to demand and measures of capacity reflect the ability of an operation or process to supply demand. It depends on the product or service specification, the output that an operation can achieve in a defined unit of time and the actual product or service mix. Unfortunately, the theoretical capacity is not achieved in practice due, for example, to process stoppages or scheduling difficulties. This is called leakage, which is a source of fragility.

To deal with leakage we need to understand how demand might vary. There are two categories of variation:

- unpredictable, which requires a quick organisational response or demand will be missed;

- predictable, which the organisation should be able to plan for.

Thus, to improve on the current supply chain leakage, the organisation needs a balance between better forecasting and improved operations responsiveness.

The most common approach to planning supply chain capacity is the concept of base capacity. This is the level from which capacity is adjusted up or down. The higher the base level, the less capacity variation is needed to satisfy demand. But setting the level too high is wasteful, although setting the level too low means that on occasions demand cannot be met. There are three key factors in setting base capacity. These are the relative importance of the operation's different performance objectives, the perishability of the operation's outputs and the degree of variability in demand or supply. There are three main types of capacity management plans:

- Level capacity plan:
  - under this, the processing capacity is fixed at a uniform level, regardless of fluctuations in demand forecast;

- Chase demand plan:
  - here we match the processing capacity to the varying levels of forecast demand;

- Manage demand plan:
  - with this, instead of varying supply, we attempt to change demand to reduce its fluctuations.

Potentially, fragility may arise from not fully utilising the capacity of the supply chain available and the corresponding lack of efficiency. Yield management is a particular approach, used in the hospitality sector, which aims to use the capacity to its full potential. It is used where;

- capacity is relatively fixed;

- the market can be fairly clearly segmented;

- the service cannot be stored in any way;

- the services are sold in advance;

- the marginal cost of making a sale is relatively low.

For example, airlines overbook flights, expecting some no-shows, and only discount those that are not busy. Also, Cumulative Demand and Supply Curves may be used for outputs that can be stored and enable consequences of alternative capacity plans to be illustrated; to meet demand as it occurs, the cumulative production total must always exceed cumulative demand.

Inventory management is another part of the supply chain management issue affecting the fragility of supply chains. As we touched on in Chapter 4, the dilemma of inventory management is how to balance the costs of holding stock with the implications for customer service of not holding adequate stock. In the context of the supply chain, the usual optimisation decision is typically seen in terms of decisions about order quantities which will minimise the total cost of stock holding and stock-outs. Looking at this from a fragility perspective, however, may give different answers as the impact of these downsides on fragility will not necessarily reflect those on cost. It is difficult to properly cost the impact of a hazard on organisational fragility, as *this will be at best an expectation, not reflecting the worst case due to environmental circumstances.* For example, a stock-out may, or may not, have a much bigger impact on organisational fragility than the cost of holding extra units does; *cost is not a good proxy for fragility measurement.*

Resource planning and control concern managing the allocation of resources and activities to ensure that the supply chain processes are efficient and reflect customer demand. The core mechanics of this, on the interfaces with customers and suppliers, are loading the jobs into the process, scheduling them, prioritising and sequencing them, and monitoring and controlling them and the supply chain. Decision mechanisms are also needed for the planning and control information system, as well as staff.

The customer interface concerns demand management, which covers the interfaces with individual customers as well as the market more broadly. Activities for this include negotiation with customers, order entry, demand forecasting, customer communication, updating records, post-delivery customer service and the logistics of physical delivery. In many senses this customer interface defines the customer experience and customers' perceptions. It represents the public face of the organisation and line of visibility for customers in terms of how much they can see into it. Managing customer expectations is particularly important early in the relationship and managing their perceptions becomes more important as it progresses. Thus, the customer interface should reflect the organisation's objectives through prioritisation of customer types and differential encouragement for them, and trading-off service and efficiency. The customer interface also acts as a trigger, with receipt of an order triggering the processes. Three common strategies are resource the process to orders, produce to order and produce ahead of order.

At the other end of the supply chain process, the supplier interface exists to inform the suppliers to make available products and services when needed which, as we have discussed above, will affect the end customer experience. Again, there is a need to manage supplier's expectations and perceptions.

Between the two interfaces, the supply chain planning and control system reconciles supply and demand through the timing and level of the loading, sequencing, scheduling, and monitoring and control activities:

- loading concerns allocating tasks to resources;

- scheduling specifies when operations do things;

- sequencing specifies the order; and

- monitoring and control checks and adjusts to meet the plan.

The supply chain planning and control system integrates human and technology-based automated decision making. Computer-based supply chain planning and control systems are now common but decision making is still done partly by people. As we have seen previously, people are better at 'soft' qualitative tasks and provide flexibility, adaptability and learning. They also facilitate communication and negotiation, and can contribute intuition. These human skills, in practice, add considerably to the anti-fragility of resource planning and control, and the supply chain.

This is particularly important as resource planning and control systems involve the management of a vast amount of information. Ideally, in pursuit of anti-fragility, the organisation should avoid duplication and integrate the information and decisions from all relevant functions. This is the basis of Enterprise Resource Planning (ERP) which aims to be a complete enterprise-wide business solution, consisting of software support modules such as marketing, sales, design and development, production, inventory control, procurement and distribution, facilities management, quality, HR, finance and accounting, and information services. ERP is typically seen as having the potential to significantly improve company performance through enhanced visibility, forcing improvements to processes, improving process control, encouraging Continuous Improvement, creating more sophisticated communication, integrating the whole supply chain and installing discipline. However, in practice, off-the-shelf ERP software systems can have many of the fragility issues that we have discussed more generally about large inflexible business systems and vendor lock-in.

The development of much of western economies within the service sector raises an additional issue concerning the information requirements for anti-fragility of the supply chain. Typically, as above, in supply chain management we think of information flow in the opposite direction to job flow, as necessary to ensure the efficiency, effectiveness and minimum fragility of the supply chain. In some circumstances, however, information itself is more intrinsically a part of the product or service supplied, and hence of the individual jobs flowing through the supply chain. Operations and supply chains providing services, in contrast to those supplying manufactured products, often have greater information requirements, sometimes associated with individual human characteristics and records of the recipient of service. This is particularly true, in the extreme, when contrasting high-volume, low-variety manufacturing with public services. The provision of this information is often poor and has a major impact on the efficiency, effectiveness and fragility of the supply chain.

This *information (sub) supply chain* is much more problematical than the rest of the supply chain within which it is embedded for a number of reasons. Typically, the provision of this information will be personal data provided by customers themselves and other stakeholders, such as different government agencies. Often the data will have to be acquired, checked for currency, otherwise verified and assembled, prior to supply. Unlike the supply of parts or materials, this will typically involve at best an implicit contract, or SLA, for supply. There will typically be no explicit stated quality requirements. Frequently, the requirements of supply, terms of supply and need to supply are not adequately known, articulated, communicated nor understood. Apparent vested interest on behalf of the information supplier, real or in reality counterproductive to their own interests, may prevent, delay or corrupt the information supplied, or all three.

The impact of all this is that service provision performance overall is poor, and considerable effort within the organisation has to be dedicated to identifying, researching and closing these deficiencies and rescheduling and completing jobs. The resulting impact on workplace complexity, management overhead, communication, record keeping and staff morale is major. Such a process is typically neither efficient, effective nor anti-fragile. Many Lean programmes have been targeted on improving situations of this type, but not always effectively. Often a requirement to provide 'clean' information prior to the job being admitted to the operations process is unilaterally placed on the information provider, sometimes with penalties for non-compliance. The downstream process then is much more controllable and in isolation shows much better performance on efficiency indicators. However, real effectiveness of the whole process will not be improved, unless the information supply process is actually improved and integrated properly into the end-to-end process. The first part of this is an education issue but also changes the organisation's relationship with the information provider. With the increase in online services and user-responsible processing this is also becoming more important. An anti-fragile approach to this situation would focus on the development of the relationship with information providers, reducing their disempowerment, integrating them into the end-to-end process and developing mutual learning and improvement; every information provider who does it wrong would be an opportunity to improve the system.

Anti-Fragility, the Environment and Corporate Social Responsibility

In focusing in this chapter on anti-fragility of the supply chain, we shall also consider, more widely, the impact on the environment and the place of Corporate Social Responsibility (CSR). The environmental impact of the supply chain and the broader issues of CSR, such as child labour and Fair Trade, are related to anti-fragility considerations in a number of ways and at a number of levels. Firstly, they impact on organisational fragility, robustness and anti-fragility through the impacts of public, customer and stakeholder perceptions; an organisation's public positioning on such issues is important to its success and longevity. Secondly, the fragility, robustness or anti-fragility of the environment itself, and/or of society, and/or the economy, are affected by the organisation's operations and supply chain, and other dimensions. Thirdly, we ask whether the organisational environmental management system itself, and its CSR equivalent, get stronger by being stressed. Here, we shall focus primarily on the first and third of these. We shall return to the second broad area in the final chapter.

A requirement of the EFQM Excellence Model concerns an organisation effectively managing the environmental and societal impacts of their supply chains. To do this they need to implement an effective strategy to manage their own buildings, equipment, materials, natural resources and utilities well, but they should also consider the impact of external partners and suppliers. The model specifies that usage of all tangible assets – such as buildings, equipment and materials – should be optimised, and that their lifecycles and physical security should be effectively managed. The organisation should also be able to demonstrate that they effectively manage the impact of their operations, and one would presume those of their suppliers, on public health, public safety and the environment. They should measure and manage any adverse impacts of their operations on the community and their people, and again this should be extended to cover those of the rest of their supply chain. Finally, the organisation should adopt and implement appropriate policies and approaches, exceeding legal requirements, to minimise their local and global environmental impact.

It is clear that this set of requirements, combined with the RADAR mechanism for ongoing targeted improvement through deployment and learning, should go a long way to ensuring robust and anti-fragile environmental management of operations, and to a lesser extent the supply chain. It should also assist the anti-fragility of the organisation by being conceived publically as good practice. As previously, there is an emphasis on optimising the use of assets, effective management, measurement and minimising adverse impact. However, the emphasis on the supply chain rather than operations is limited, there is little here on the wider societal issues, and the usual questions remain in relation to there being no explicit emphasis on increasing the resilience of the environmental management system and the public perception of the organisation, rather than their efficiency and effectiveness.

To discuss the broader societal issues, let us first define CSR. Around the world there is increasing interest in CSR for organisations of all types and sizes. Such interest exists within the business sector itself, for instance the activities related to the European Union (EU) Business Alliance on CSR, the Organisation for Economic Co-operation and Development (OECD) Guidelines for Multi-National Enterprises and the UK Institute of Chartered Accountants. UK Government interest is illustrated by the Millennium Development Goals and the subsequent International Strategic Framework for Corporate Social Responsibility. Momentum has been building since the World Summit on Sustainability in Johannesburg in 2002 and there are a number of countries like the UK who have a government minister with specific responsibility for CSR.

It has been argued that CSR is primarily about the behaviour of private sector organisations and their contribution to sustainable development goals. However, as evidenced by the EFQM Excellence Model criteria, the approach and values of good organisational citizenship are also relevant to other organisations, including those in the public or voluntary sector. Many governments internationally are now requiring Sustainable Development Action Plans from each ministry as part of their commitment to actively promoting corporate responsibility and accountability commitments made at the World Summit on Sustainable Development.

The UK Government has regarded itself as a leading advocate of CSR. Part of the reason for this is undoubtedly the economic argument for CSR. For instance, the March 2006 European Commission Communication on CSR stated that CSR can make a significant contribution to the competitiveness of the European economy and the Lisbon strategy for growth and jobs. In consequence, the European Commission Communication aimed to make Europe a 'pole of Excellence' on CSR.

There are many formal definitions of CSR and these all reflect the idea that it is about how companies and other organisations lead and manage their people, resources and business processes to produce an overall positive impact on society. Clearly, organisational strategy is a key element of this. Other more limited definitions include:

> *Corporate Social Responsibility is the continuing commitment by business to behave ethically and contribute to economic development while improving the quality of life of the workforce and their families as well as of the local community and society at large. Holme and Watts (2000)*

Partly reflective of the variety of definitions of CSR, there are different frameworks for CSR in use internationally. Arguably, amongst the most robust is the European Foundation for Quality Management (EFQM) Framework for Corporate Social Responsibility. The Framework is built around the well-established EFQM Excellence Model and extends aspects of its interpretation in the context of CSR.

Here, instead of focusing on this, we shall consider the core Society Results criterion of the EFQM Excellence Model to provide further guidance over and above what we saw for the environment. The requirement here is that the organisation develops an agreed set of internal performance indicators and outcome perception measurements to ascertain the success of deployment of their societal and ecological strategy; sets clear targets for the most important results based on stakeholder needs, and delivers on these; demonstrates understanding of causality for the results obtained and anticipates future performance; compares results to those of similar organisations and sets targets accordingly; and segments results to understand needs of specific stakeholders. The organisation should use appropriate sources, possibly including surveys and public meetings, to obtain this society perception data which should indicate society's perception of the effectiveness of the implementation of the organisation's societal and environmental strategy. The performance indicators are internal measures used to monitor and improve these perceptions. This clearly extends to the results for environmental management to CSR and, with the RADAR mechanism, goes a long way towards anti-fragility. As usual, from the anti-fragility viewpoint, the potential deficiency is the lack of explicit emphasis on increasing the resilience of the societal and ecological strategy rather than its efficiency and effectiveness. Coverage of the whole supply chain is also not explicit, other than 'responsible sourcing and procurement performance' indicators, and once again it is not explicit whether learning from deployment will include major stresses or if these could be excluded as 'exceptional'.

Reducing Fragility by Design and Management of Supply Chains

In order to now take stock of some of the issues covered in this chapter, let us briefly consider a few questions:

- Why are supply chains fragile?

- How can we make them less fragile?

- How is fragility related to information in the supply chain?

- How can we reduce fragility by design of supply chains?

- How can we reduce fragility by management of supply chains?

- What are the benefits?

Based on our discussions to date, the answers to these questions are not particularly difficult but they may be insightful. Supply chains are inherently, or at least comparatively, fragile because they rely for their working on linkages and relationships which go beyond the boundaries of the organisation and which, in consequence, rely for their efficacy on the goodwill, rationality and self-interest of multiple organisational players outside the organisation itself. This can easily go wrong, particularly where the supply chain crosses multiple national boundaries. Both the internal and external hazards facing a supply chain are in general, by definition, more numerous and more complex than those for operations within an organisation.

Organisations use various mechanisms to attempt to minimise and control this fragility. This is partly about ensuring good quality information and information flow. It is also about the design of the supply chain and how it is managed. For example, the use of single or multiple suppliers, partnership or transactional relationships, the extent and direction of vertical integration, outsourcing and/or offshoring, capacity management and inventory management. Best practice should take account of:

- planning;

- simplicity;

- real-time information flow;

- feedback;

- limitations of rule-based process design;

- human role.

The benefits are immediately apparent; reducing fragility is an end in itself. However, it is also the basis for developing robustness and pursuing anti-fragility.

Now, in line with our approach in the previous chapters, we can identify rules and patterns in relation to anti-fragility and the supply chain which have emerged from the previous discussion and practical experience. These are as follows:

1. Supply networks and supply chains are fragile because they rely on linkages and relationships which go beyond the boundaries of the organisation, and on the goodwill, rationality and self-interest of many other organisations. This can go wrong, particularly where the supply chain crosses multiple national boundaries. Both the internal and external hazards facing a supply chain are, in general, both considerably more numerous and more complex than those for operations within an organisation.

2. There is an extensive theoretical and practical literature on the design and management of supply chains. Organisations use various mechanisms to attempt to maximise the efficiency and effectiveness of supply chains, and to minimise and control their fragility. This is partly about ensuring good quality information and information flow. It is also about the design of the supply chain and how it is managed.

3. Good quality information flow is an underlying requirement for anti-fragility in the supply chain; if suppliers do not receive market information, or receive misinformation, then there will be errors and delays in supply that will impact on customer satisfaction and organisational performance. These can all be reduced by information sharing, aligning planning and control decisions, improving flow efficiency and better forecasting.

4.   The relevant parts of the EFQM Excellence Model criteria, together with the RADAR mechanism, are once again extremely helpful in giving a good summary of many of the requirements for anti-fragility. Here, the relevant parts include the Partnership sub-criterion; the sub-criterion covering the management of tangible assets such as buildings, equipment and materials; and the Society Results criterion. As previously, whilst these requirements cover the improvement cycles to efficiency and effectiveness, achieved through deployment and learning, the improvement in resilience that is anti-fragility is not explicitly addressed.

5.   The discussion of inventory management in this chapter illustrates an issue about using the cost of failure/fragility as a measure. It is difficult to properly cost the impact of a hazard in creating organisational fragility as this will be at best an expectation, not reflecting the worst case due to environmental circumstances. For example, whilst we can use total cost of stockholding and stock-outs combined to minimise total cost and identify optimum stockholding, we cannot sensibly calculate the cost of organisational fragility such a stock-out might lead to since it will depend on the environmental circumstances. In some circumstances, it may kill the organisation, in others it will not. Instead we use an average cost, averaged over various environmental possibilities. In reality, a stock-out may, or may not, have a much bigger impact on organisational fragility than does the cost of holding extra units; cost is therefore not a good proxy for fragility measurement.

6.   As previously, human skills are again crucial to developing anti-fragility within the management of supply chains.

7.   The information (sub) supply chain is more problematical than the rest of the supply chain within which it is embedded as, typically, data is provided by customers themselves and other stakeholders with, at best, only an implicit contract. Frequently, the requirements of supply, terms of supply and need to supply are not adequately known, articulated, communicated nor understood, and the vested interest of the information supplier may prevent, delay or corrupt the information supplied.

8.   The environmental and societal/CSR impacts of the supply chain are related to anti-fragility at a number of levels:

- they impact on *organisational* fragility, robustness and anti-fragility through the impacts of public, customer and stakeholder perceptions; an organisation's public positioning on such issues is important to its success and longevity;
- the fragility, robustness or anti-fragility of the *environment* itself, and/or of *society*, and/or the *economy*, are affected by the organisation's operations and supply chain;
- the *organisational environmental management system* itself, and its *CSR equivalent*, may be fragile, robust or anti-fragile, and get stronger by being stressed.

Chapter 7

Fragility in Relation to Markets, Products and Services

What Makes Our Product and Service Portfolios Fragile or Anti-Fragile, and Why?

At the most basic level, Porter's Five Forces Model gives us a way at looking at the fragility, robustness or anti-fragility of a product or service offering. The origins of the model dates to 1979 when the *Harvard Business Review* published an article by a young economist and associate professor, Michael E. Porter, entitled 'How Competitive Forces Shape Strategy'. It was his first article for the *Harvard Business Review* and it revolutionised business thinking. Since then, Porter's Five Forces have been a key concept in both academic research and business practice. The model identifies five forces in the organisation's micro-environment that affect its ability to be successful (see Figure 7.1). These are:

1. Supplier Power – for example, how easy is it for suppliers to drive up prices?

2. Buyer Power – for example, how easy is it for buyers to drive down prices?

3. Competitive Rivalry – what is the level and strength of competition in the market?

4. Threat of Substitution – how likely is it that your customers, or others, will find a different way of satisfying the need that you currently provide a product or service for?

5. Threat of New Entrants – how easy is it for new competitors to enter your market?

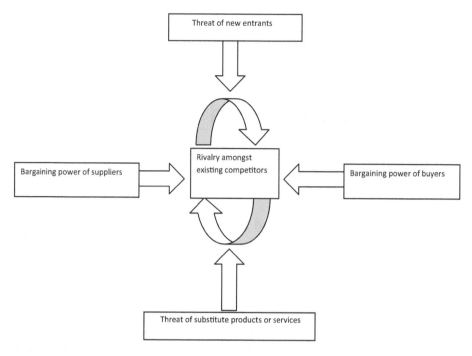

Figure 7.1   Five forces that shape industry competition
Source: http://hbr.org/2008/01/the-five-competitive-forces-that-shape-strategy/.

It follows that our product and service offerings may be fragile for all of, or any of, the five above reasons. Supplier power may make it uneconomic for us to continue to supply this product due to price, or they may, for their own objectives, want to restrict who we sell it to. Similarly, buyers may drive our margins down so far that we go out of business, or place impractical or unacceptable restrictions on the specifications of what we supply. Too much competition can make us very fragile if we cannot identify clear competitive advantage. The threat of substitution is, in a sense, another sort of competition, but here our fragility comes from alternative and possibly innovative products and services that take away the need for what we provide – the refrigerator replaced the icebox and the motorcar replaced the horse and cart. Finally, the threat of new entrants makes us fragile as it threatens our existing market.

For our product and service offerings to be robust we should have each of Porter's Five Forces under control. This means that we would need to understand well our existing and potential suppliers, customers and competitors, as well as the potential substitute product/service offerings due to technological or business innovation. On the basis of this understanding we would also need to have an advantageous position in relation to each of the five forces that is inherently strong against suppliers or customers trying to renegotiate and which is proof against competitor rivalry, new entrants and substitution. This is a demanding requirement and – because products and services other than the most basic foodstuffs, materials and services, all appear to have a finite lifecycle – if our products/services are robust now, they are unlikely to stay so indefinitely. This links to our previous discussion of a robust or anti-fragile technology becoming fragile over time.

Anti-fragility of our products and services on this basis would be hard to obtain and, with only extreme exceptions, unlikely to be retainable for very long, as it requires a continuing ability to continually learn from, and counter, incoming threats of competition, substitution or supplier power, and increase resilience through doing so. Accordingly, it appears more appropriate to consider potential robustness and anti-fragility, not of individual product and service offerings, but of the organisation's portfolio of these. For large complex organisations this, of course, may be within a product or service range, market, trademark or brand. The exceptions, however, where anti-fragility appears to have been achieved largely at the individual product offering level, for example Coca Cola, are particularly interesting.

For achieving or pursuing anti-fragility in the context of a portfolio of products and/or services, additional anti-fragility is created by the design and management of the portfolio. Just as we discussed near the beginning of the book how the biological diversity of the members of a species helps its survival, a similar argument can be made in the current context for the spreading of market and environmental risks. The design and constant readjustment of the content of the portfolio to reflect opportunities and threats provides an additional level of protection (robustness) and potential to exploit opportunities (one level of anti-fragility).

The Boston Matrix (illustrated in Figure 7.2) is a well-known tool that provides a basis for an organisation to select the markets it should be in and to examine the likely financial performance of the members of its product and service portfolio. The Matrix was developed by management consultants at the Boston Consulting Group in the early 1970s. It, places products and services into four categories based on their market share and market growth:

1.   *Cash cows* are products or services that have high market share in a slow-growing industry, and these typically generate cash in excess of the amount of cash needed to maintain the business. Hence, they are a source of robustness.

2.   *Dogs* are products or services with low market share in a mature, slow-growing industry. These typically break even, generating just enough cash to maintain the business's market share. Though this should provide jobs and possible indirect business benefits, from an accounting point of view such a unit is a liability, not generating cash for the company and depressing the return on assets ratio. Since this is used by many investors to judge how well a company is being managed, dogs are a source of fragility and it is argued that they should be sold off.

3.   *Question marks* or *problem children* are products or services with a low market share in a market with high market growth. Many businesses start from here as they have the potential to gain market share and become stars, and eventually cash cows when market growth slows. However, if question marks do not succeed in becoming market leaders then, possibly after years of cash consumption, they will degenerate into dogs when market growth declines. Question marks, therefore, could be sources of either future fragility or robustness and must be analysed carefully in order to determine whether they are worth the investment required to grow market share.

4.   *Stars* are products or services with a high market share in a fast-growing industry. They may be successful question marks that have become market leaders in high-growth sectors. Typically, the desire is that, longer-term, stars become the next cash cows but to do this they require high funding to fight competitors and maintain growth as the market growth declines. Otherwise, when growth slows, they will become dogs. So, stars are at least temporarily a source of robustness, but may become a source of fragility over time.

In any market, the organisation's positioning of its products and services is also important to the fragility question. Michael Porter's name is also associated with three generic strategies used by organisations to achieve and maintain competitive advantage. One definition of competitive advantage is that when a number of firms compete within the same market, one firm possesses a competitive advantage over its rivals when it earns, or has the potential to earn, a consistently higher rate of profit. Thus, competitive advantage gives a company an edge over its rivals and an ability to generate greater value for the firm and its shareholders. Competitive advantage may arise from internal

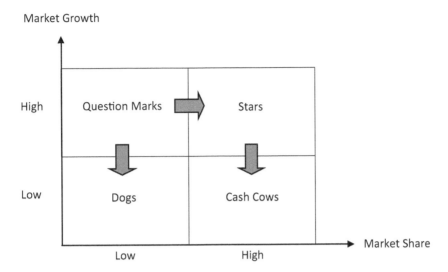

Figure 7.2   Boston Matrix

or external sources of change. Internally, some organisations have greater innovative and creative capacity whilst, externally, changing customer needs, changing prices and technological changes lead to differential impacts between firms, and some firms exploit change faster and more effectively.

The main problem with competitive advantage for a firm is its sustainability which is clearly linked to fragility, and firms work hard to protect it. Essentially, this is by establishing barriers to imitation, such as obscuring their superior performance, relying on multiple sources of competitive advantage to establish causal ambiguity, signaling aggressive intentions to would-be imitators, exploiting all available investment opportunities and basing competitive advantage on resources and capabilities that are immobile and difficult to replicate. Competitive advantage differs between trading and production markets; in trading markets, information, superior diagnosis and lower trading costs can give competitive advantage, whilst in production markets, it may be a barrier to imitation or innovation. In general, competitive advantage divides into cost advantage (similar products at lower prices) and differentiation advantage (a price premium from different features, skill and capabilities). This largely corresponds to Porter's three generic strategies for competitive advantage which are cost leadership, differentiation, and market segmentation or focus. The third strategy, market segmentation or focus, is not really a separate strategy as such but describes the more limited scope over which the company may compete based on cost leadership or differentiation (see Table 7.1).

Table 7.1   Porter's generic strategies

	Low-Cost Competitive Advantage	Differentiation/Uniqueness Competitive Advantage
Broad market scope	Cost leadership	Differentiation
Narrow market scope	Cost focus	Differentiation focus

Empirical research suggests that firms with a high market share are often quite profitable, as are many firms with low market share. However, the least profitable firms are those with moderate market share; this is sometimes referred to as the *hole in the middle* problem. Porter's explanation of this is that firms with high market share are successful because they pursue a cost leadership strategy, firms with low market share are successful because they use market segmentation to focus on a small but profitable market niche, but firms in the middle are less profitable, and presumably fragile, because they do not have a viable generic strategy. Later research has suggested that companies pursuing a combined differentiation and low-cost strategy may be more successful, and less fragile, than companies pursuing only one strategy.

As well as positioning, strategic marketing, Customer Relationship Management (CRM) and brand management will also impact on product/ service portfolio fragility, and organisational fragility. A marketing strategy is an internally integrated, but externally focused, set of choices about how the firm addresses its customers in the context of the competitive environment, and strategic marketing is about identifying and evaluating the choices the organisation faces in establishing their market position. It has been said that marketing is too important to be left to the marketing department, and this resonates with the view that strategic marketing is about:

- understanding customers' real wants;

- managing long-term customer relationships, rather than single transactions;

- focusing on the customer as the source of profit, rather than the product;

- attracting new customers, and maintaining and cultivating the existing customer base.

This is clearly, in general, a robust approach to the market and, if based on continual learning and improved CRM based on experience, a potentially anti-fragile one.

CRM is a business process that reaches across many organisational functions, concerned with achieving improved customer satisfaction through the development of effective and lasting relationships with customers. It aims to attract and win new customers, nurture and retain existing customers, attract former customers back, improve the customer experience, grow revenues, reduce the costs of marketing operations and customer service, and increase the efficiency of customer-facing processes. Again, this is a robust and potentially anti-fragile approach but, in practice, proprietary software systems may be subject to many of the issues associated with large inflexible business systems and vendor lock-in that we have discussed previously.

According to Aaker, Brand equity is: 'A set of assets (and liabilities) linked to a brand's name and symbol that adds to (or subtracts from) the value provided by a product or service to a firm and/or that firm's customer.' Brand equity is created through building four relationships between the brand and the consumer. These are:

- Brand awareness: do people know the brand?

- Loyalty: does the brand have followers?

- Perceived quality: do people perceive the brand as of quality?

- Brand associations: which socio-cultural profile do people relate the brand to?

A brand can provide an identity as it: tells people what it is, by virtue of the characteristics by which it is recognised and known; acts as a social marker; is simultaneously about sameness and difference; tells us what something is and, equally, what something is not. Very few brands achieve the status of an 'essential' identity – one that is constant and unchanging – but this would presumably be an anti-fragile one. Companies acquire brands in order to gain instant access to markets, and branding commands an influence across all organisational units. A corporate brand is made up of four distinct elements:

- a strategic vision, which expresses top management's aspiration for the organisation;

- the organisational culture, which expresses how employees enact values, beliefs and basic assumptions;

- the stakeholder images developed by outside stakeholders, including customers, media, and others;

- the brand identity, which emerges at the juncture of the above three perspectives, as a reflection of how the organisation perceives itself.

Strategists often believe the brand is something that can be created and manipulated by top management. Interpretation of the brand will be framed by the cultural, social and political context in which they are seen. Brands are dynamic platforms or arenas on which negotiations about identity take place. Strategic marketing and branding assist strategists to:

- identify what customers really want;

- identify profitable market segments;

- identify reliable distribution channels;

- identify a unique positioning for the company, and its products and services;

- align products and corporate brands;

- develop valuable brand equity.

The above discussion has important implications for the company's marketing mix, which is the definition of products/service characteristics and distribution, promotion and pricing strategies. It follows that both a brand, and the marketing mix, can be fragile, robust or anti-fragile. Anti-fragility will require continual learning, development and improved resilience on the basis of experience in the market.

Distribution is one of the four elements of the marketing mix. This is the process by which a product or service is made available for use or consumption by a consumer or another organisation as a user, directly or indirectly, through intermediaries. The organisation's marketing and sales channels will also be important to its fragility, robustness or anti-fragility, and it has been argued that there are more than 40 marketing and delivery channels that marketers need to manage. Many organisations use a mix of different channels; for example, they might complement a direct salesforce, calling on the larger accounts, with agents, covering the smaller customers. In addition, it has been argued that online retailing or e-commerce is leading to *disintermediation*; the removal of intermediaries. Intermediaries are interdependent organisations involved in making the product or service available for consumption and include merchants who buy and resell products, and agents and brokers who act on behalf of the producer but do not take title to the products or services. Retailing via mobile technology, smartphone or m-commerce is also a growing area.

To have robust distribution, the organisation needs to design the most suitable distribution channels for its products and services, then select and manage appropriate channel members or intermediaries. The organisation may also train staff of intermediaries and motivate the intermediary to sell the firm's products. The firm should monitor the channel's performance over time and modify the channel to enhance performance; this will introduce some anti-fragility. The firm can also use positive actions to motivate the intermediaries, such as offering higher margins, special deals, premiums and allowances for advertising or display. However, channel conflict, a source of fragility, may arise where, for example, one intermediary's actions prevents another intermediary from achieving their objectives.

Excellence, and Anti-Fragility of Products and Services

Satisfying and generating increasing value for customers is clearly an underlying concept in the EFQM Excellence Model, and Adding Value for Customers is, in fact, one of the eight Fundamental Concepts of Excellence, on which the model is based. To achieve this the model looks at four main aspects. The first aspect is about the development of product and services to create optimum value for customers and considers how the organisation uses creativity, innovation and understanding of the potential impact of new technology, and customer feedback, to enhance the product and service portfolio; the stakeholders' involvement in product and service development; and the potential impacts on economic, societal and ecological sustainability.

The second aspect deals with how products and services are effectively promoted and marketed, covering aspects such as definition and implementation of the value proposition and business model, and ensuring their sustainability by balancing the stakeholder requirements; defining unique selling points, target customer groups, market positioning and distribution channels; developing marketing strategies, and effectively market well; and ensuring they have the capability to fulfil their promises.

The third aspect is concerned with how products and services are produced, delivered and managed. This considers areas such as how the products and services are produced and delivered in line with the stated value proposition, to meet or exceed customer expectations; ensuring staff are adequately equipped in all senses to maximise the customers' experience; managing their product and services' lifecycles, including reuse and recycling, and the impact on public health and safety and the environment; Benchmarking product and service delivery performance; and involving their stakeholders in maximising the efficiency and effectiveness of their value chain.

Lastly, the model looks at how customer relationships are managed and enhanced, including identifying their customer groups, and anticipating and responding to their differing needs and expectations; identifying and meeting day-to-day and long-term customer contact requirements; building and maintaining an open trust-based and transparent dialogue with all customers; at all times monitoring and reviewing the experiences and perceptions of customers, and responding effectively and in a timely manner; and advising customers on the responsible use of products and services.

These four areas, as always with the EFQM Excellence Model, have an impressive coverage of key aspects needed for anti-fragility of products and services, and customer relationships. Specifically, they include fulfilling promises, adequate resourcing, balancing stakeholder requirements, sustainability, lifecycle management, monitoring and Benchmarking, and the use of customer feedback to improve, in addition to the linked but separate RADAR requirements. Again, however, fragility perspectives of the offerings are not explicitly addressed, apart from the physical lifecycle management considerations, and instead efficiency and effectiveness are stressed.

The EFQM Excellence Model also has a criterion concerned with Customer Results. This is similar in nature to that we have already considered for People Results. The requirements are concerned with how the organisation develops and agrees a set of performance indicators and related perception outcome measurements that measure the successful deployment of strategy, based on the needs and expectations of the customers. It also assumes that the organisation will set clear targets for the most important of these, be able to show at least three years good and improving results, understand the basis for these and anticipate future performance, understand comparative performance with others and accordingly set stretch targets, and be able to segment the results for any specific customer groups of interest. The performance indicators are again those internal measures used by the organisation to monitor and improve performance, and the efficiency and effectiveness of deployment of the customer strategy, as well as to predict customers' perceptions. Typically, coverage will include appropriate measures of delivery, customer service and relationships, complaints, compliments and recognition. The perception outcomes may be obtained from a number of sources, including customer surveys, focus groups, vendor ratings, compliments and complaints. We may also add blogs. They may include aspects related to reputation, product and service value, delivery, customer support and relationship, and customer loyalty and engagement.

As with people management, if an organisation wishes to measure its progress towards anti-fragility of its product and service offerings, the above measurement and monitoring requirements used together with the RADAR mechanism are a good start but, once again, do not have quite the right emphasis, and do not go quite far enough. The measurement system described is in a sense comprehensive in coverage but varies in its focus from that needed to ensure progress to anti-fragility. For example, an interpretation of the system might put maximum emphasis on the efficiency and effectiveness of the deployment of the customer strategy, with no emphasis on its fragility. Since, as we have discussed, efficiency and fragility are often correlated, this deficiency may be particularly fragile. In addition, there is no explicit consideration of the customer's view of fragility of the customer strategy and processes in the requirements. In a globalised, e-enabled world, this could be a major, and dangerous, omission.

Again, as in our discussion for people management, there is a reference above to customer segmentation in our discussion of the EFQM Excellence Model criteria in relation to products and services. Customer segmentation is the process of dividing a market into distinct groups with distinct needs, characteristics and behaviours, to whom the organisation might provide separate offerings or marketing mixes. This is true whether the organisations' customer groups cover one or both of:

- consumer customers, who typically purchase goods and services for use by themselves, and by those with whom they live;

- business customers, who purchase goods and services for use by the organisation for which they work.

Typically, firms may segment markets or customers according to a combination of the following types of segments:

- geographic segmentation;

- demographic segmentation;

- psychographic segmentation;

- behavioural segmentation.

Targeting is the process of evaluating each market segment's attractiveness and selecting one, or more, segments to enter. For each segment, the growth potential can be estimated by looking at current and predicted future market size, growth rates, market share and the extent to which a product or service may evolve; for example, as new technology become available. Analysis of competitive intensity includes evaluating the number and strength of competitors, ease of entry to reach the specific target segment and an evaluation of potential substitute products, as well as studying competitor's strategies. Segments selected for targeting will depend on the organisation's knowledge of the segment, the existence of exploitable marketing channels to exploit it and the extent to which the needs of the target market align with the organisation's overall strategic direction and capabilities.

The EFQM Excellence Model requirements on Customer Results essentially include the ability to segment the results obtained for any specific customer group of interest. This will assist targeting and mitigate against fragility issues associated with lack of awareness of segments or their trends; it is thus a step towards robustness. To progress to anti-fragility, this ability needs to get better over time, through being challenged. This is a demanding requirement.

Customers and Customer Service

In real terms, defining who the customer is, is not always clear. This is particularly true in the public sector where who is ordering, who is paying and the recipients of the service are often very different, but it is true also for organisational purchasing where the purchaser and the users may be in very different parts of the organisation. A robust approach needs to consider the interests of both. Another difficulty is that, in the public sector, rather than just stakeholders there can be multiple customers within the same transaction, each with different needs and expectations. For instance, when a policeman arrests someone, who is the customer? The suspect or 'backdoor customer' taken to the cells at the back of the police station, the victim, witnesses, society, the courts, the government or so on? All of these have separate needs and expectations out of this transaction. *Whilst having much in common with that for the private sector, the question of fragility for public sector organisations has distinct and subtle differences*, of which this is one. Also, of course, such public sector organisations are more risk averse, and typically subjected to lower likelihood and magnitude of risks. However, the recent financial crisis reminds us that they still cannot ignore these risks.

Whether our organisation is providing product, service, or product and service – and whether it is in the private, public or voluntary sector – there is a strong argument to say that customer service is the core of the transaction. We have realised for a long time that manufacturing includes an element of service and that there is an emerging tendency to bundle service with product, and for the distinction between product and service to disappear. Over the last decade, Service Dominant Logic has emerged, to see service as the fundamental basis of exchange, rather than goods, as traditionally used. Whilst service is the fundamental basis of exchange, it is provided through complex combinations of goods, money and institutions, so that the service basis of exchange is not always obvious. In a sense, goods are a distribution mechanism for service provision; both durable and non-durable goods derive their value through use, that is, through the service they provide. In this view, the firm can only offer value propositions and the customer is always a co-creator of value. Enterprises can offer their applied resources for value creation and together with customers create value, following acceptance of value propositions by the customer. Because service is defined in terms of customer-determined benefit, and co-created, it is inherently customer-oriented and relational, and value creation is collaborative. Value for the beneficiary is unique, idiosyncratic, experiential, contextual and meaning laden.

This places a heavy requirement on organisations to develop robust and anti-fragile customer service. However, to many of us this is currently an area of considerable disappointment; many large consumer-facing organisations display rigid fragile customer interfaces, with disempowered staff, restrictive technology/systems, lack of holistic ownership of the total customer experience, lack of adequate customisation and communication, inadequate access to

Direct recipient of service

	People	Things
Tangible actions	**Services directed at people's bodies:** e.g. Health care Passenger transport Beauty salons Exercise clinics Restaurants Haircutting	**Services directed at goods or other physical possessions:** e.g. Freight transport Equipment repair & maintenance Janitorial services Laundry and dry cleaning Landscaping & Gardening Veterinary care
Intangible actions	**Services directed at people's minds:** e.g. Education Broadcasting Information services Theatres & Museums	**Services directed at intangible assets:** e.g. Banking Legal services Accounting Insurance

(Left axis label: Nature of the service act)

Figure 7.3   Service classification
Source: Based on Lovelock, 1983.

useable data; and a reliance on information from, processing by, and a tendency to blame, the customer. Authority and the ability to make ad hoc exceptional decisions, or substantially change the system, in these organisations are often high up, and often not easily accessible to the front line or customers. This appears to have been a trend with technology, is not robust, and certainly not anti-fragile. In a Soft Systems Thinking sense, the feedback from the customer experience on the front line is not just being delayed, it is not getting through. Anti-fragility requires fast feedback. Sporadically, or regularly, measuring general perception is not enough; the organisation needs specific feedback on the systems, the interfaces, the products and individual customer's experiences. Until now, the consumers have been too disempowered in the face of the organisation for this to threaten its fragility but, as we have discussed elsewhere, that may be changing through emerging customer networking and organisation.

Degree of interaction and customisation

	Low	High
Low	*Service factory:* Low Cost Airlines Trucking Economy Hotels	*Service shop:* Hospitals Auto Repair Other Repair Services
High	*Mass service:* High Street Retailing Traditional Schools Canteen	*Professional service:* Doctors Lawyers Accountants Architects

(row axis label: Degree of labour intensity)

Figure 7.4   Service Process Matrix
Source: Based on Schmenner, 1986.

There are various ways to classify services from the perspective of fragility, robustness and anti-fragility. One system we may consider utilising, due to Lovelock (see Lovelock, 1983), splits the service act into tangible and intangible actions, and into whether the service is directed at a person's mind and body, or at an asset. This is illustrated in Figure 7.3.

Services with tangible actions, where the direct recipients are people, are likely to have more direct observed feedback than ones with intangible actions, or those directed at 'things'. Hence in an a priori sense they may be more fragile, but because of the level of direct observation they may have already been engineered to be more robust or anti-fragile than in the other three quadrants. It is in these, that *dormant undiscovered fragility, or undiscovered failure,* may lie waiting.

The Service Process Matrix, due to Schmenner and illustrated in Figure 7.4, instead creates a two-by-two classification on Labour Intensity, and Interaction and Customisation, which differentiates the Service Factory, Service Shop and Professional Service from Mass Service.

Here, Professional Service may appear most robust and potentially anti-fragile of the types of service job since the high labour intensity and interaction/customisation may well also have associated with it a skilled, empowered and, within professional boundaries, flexible, workforce so that service can be adjusted to meet need. However, the overall Professional Service provision may also be the most fragile as it uses a lot of labour and needs a lot of customisation, so may be under cost and time pressure. Similar issues exist in the other three sectors, also. See Figure 7.5.

Another key concept to consider in the context of organisational fragility, robustness and anti-fragility is service development and the specification for service design. In developing a service, or specifying a service design, there are three elements that an organisation should consider. These are:

1.   the service concept;

2.   the package of service elements;

3.   the delivery system.

The service concept is the set of service features and characteristics which will enable the organisation to meet customer needs and have the potential to enable a differentiated position against competitors. The package of service elements is the bundle of goods and services provided as the basis of providing service and consists of four features:

1.   The Supporting facility – the physical resources in and through which service is provided. Consideration may include: location, interior design, supporting equipment, architectural appropriateness and facility layout.

2.   The Facilitating goods – the materials purchased or consumed by the buyer during service. Here consideration may include: consistent quality, quantity and selection.

3.   The Explicit services – the benefits readily observable by the customer from service. Consideration may include: adequacy of training of service personnel, comprehensiveness of service, consistency and availability.

4.   The Implicit services – the psychological benefits the customer may observe because of the service. Consideration may include: attitude of service, atmosphere, waiting, status, sense of well-being, privacy and security, and convenience.

The service delivery system is the method in which the product or service is delivered to the customer. The brand image and the attitude of the staff must also be considered to ensure that these issues are aligned with the concept.

In considering service development then, our organisational analysis has three dimensions: the fragility, robustness and anti-fragility of the service concept; the package of service elements; and of the service delivery system. Historically, many services have been developed without explicit systematic consideration of these aspects and, in consequence, show fragility in various dimensions. To some extent this is a hierarchical phenomenon, with fragility in the concept potentially causing greater overall fragility to the service than, in turn, that at the service package level or at the delivery system level.

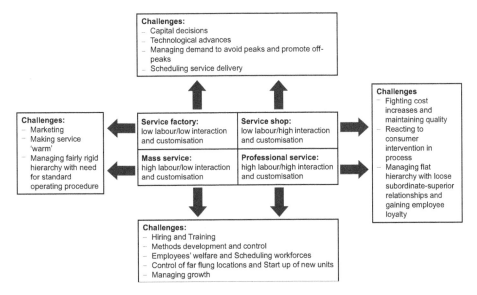

Figure 7.5   Possible fragility challenges
Source: Based on Schmenner, 1986.

Conversely, the need for robustness and anti-fragility at this level is greatest. Within the service package it is easy to forget implicit services and this has also often caused service fragility, as under the introduction of the Best Value policy for local government services in the UK.

Whilst it has critics, the so-called Gap Model, or Servqual, is one of the most important concepts of service quality. Developed by Zeithaml, Parasuraman and Berry in the 1980s (Parasuraman et al., 1985), the model highlights the main requirements for delivering high service quality and identifies five common gaps that cause unsuccessful delivery. To do this, it defines service quality in terms of the discrepancy between the customers' expectations and their perceptions of what they receive. Key factors that influence these customer expectations are word-of-mouth communications, individual personal needs, past experience and external communications. If service as delivered does not meet customers' expectations, this creates a gap that results in poor service quality and, in consequence, fragility of the service provision and its parent organisation. Originally the model was based on ten aspects, or determinants, of a service gap. These are:

1.   Competence, or the possession of the required skills and knowledge to provide the service.

2.   Courtesy, or consideration and appearance of contact personnel, manifesting as politeness, respect and friendliness.

3.   Credibility includes trustworthiness, belief and honesty. It involves having the customer's best interests at prime position.

4.   Security, or feeling free from danger, risk or doubt including physical safety, confidentiality and financial security.

5.   Access, or approachability and ease of contact, such as convenient operation hours and locations.

6.   Communication means informing customers in a language they understand and listening to customers.

7.   Understanding the customer is about understanding customers' individual needs, providing individualised attention and so on.

8.   Tangibles are the physical evidence of the service, including the physical facilities, tools and equipment used to provide the service, and the appearance of personnel and communication materials and presence of other customers.

9.   Reliability, or the ability to provide the promised service in a dependable and accurate manner, first time and on time.

10.   Responsiveness, or employee's readiness and willingness to help customers in providing prompt timely services.

Subsequently, in the early 1990s, the authors refined the model to the reduced set of service characteristics:

- reliability,

- assurance,

- tangibles,

- empathy, and

- responsiveness.

These spell out acronym RATER and provide a simplified model for quantitatively exploring and assessing customers' service experiences that has been widely used by service organisations.

The Gap Model, which is illustrated in Figure 7.4, gives us an interesting insight into the issue of fragility, robustness and anti-fragility of the service provision. The set of ten determinants show the complexity of the dimensions in which service fragility may occur. Underlying causes behind these probably mean that in many circumstances they are correlated. For example, some are likely to be at least partly service design fragility problems such as access and tangibility. Others are clearly service delivery and management fragility problems; for example, courtesy, credibility and responsiveness. For a particular organisation, examination and identification of which of the gaps are the most major, together with in which dimensions, will, by implication, identify the most major sources of fragility and indicate where robustness and anti-fragility needs to be introduced.

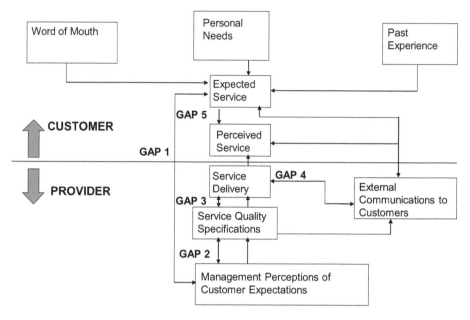

Figure 7.6   Conceptual model of service quality

Service Blueprinting provides a holistic view of the whole process of service and interfaces of customer relationships and hence can assist new product or service innovation, design or redesign. The technique was first introduced by Lynn Shostack, a bank executive, in the *Harvard Business Review* in 1984 (Shostack, 1984). Essentially it is a flowcharting method which separates the *Front* and *Back Office*. This allows the organisation to think through detailed elements of service, and their interaction, in order to deliver customer satisfaction. Included in a Service Blueprint are:

- Customer actions: the sequence of activities that customers undertake as part of the service delivery process.

- Front office, onstage or visible contact employee actions: these face-to-face actions between employees and customers are separated from the customer actions by a *line of interaction*.

- Backstage, back office or invisible employee actions: a *line of visibility* separates the onstage from the backstage actions. Anything that is above the line of visibility can be seen by the customers, while everything under the line of visibility is invisible for the customers. A good example of a backstage action is a telephone call, which is a front stage interaction between an employee and a customer but they don't see each other so that the employees' action, like updating a record, is largely backstage.

- Support processes: an internal line of interaction separates the contact employees from the support processes, which are all the activities carried out by individuals and units within the company who are not contact employees, but which need to happen in order for the service to be delivered.

- Physical evidence: these are all the tangibles that customers are exposed to that can influence their service quality perceptions. Typically, for each customer action and every moment of truth, the physical evidence that customers come into contact with is described at the top of the Service Blueprint.

To apply Service Blueprinting then, we need to identify all activities that make up the complete service package, clearly separate the front and back offices and support processes, identify potential failure points and determine the timeframe for activities based upon customer expectations. What is the link to fragility? The front and back office will both exhibit fragile, robust and potentially anti-fragile features. In addition, so will the support processes. The customers' actions may also introduce fragility. Overall, however, the integrity of the whole service – its fragility, robustness or anti-fragility – depends also upon the holistic interrelationships of these elements. A major part of that is about information and communication (see for example, Minzuno et al., 1991).

The last technique we shall look at here in the context of the fragility of customer service is somewhat more general in scope and originates from the Japanese manufacturing sector in the 1960s. Essentially, Quality Function Deployment (QFD) brings together the voice of the customer and voice of the business, and assists an organisation to determine what they need to accomplish to satisfy, or even delight, their customers. Whilst it can be utilised in a simple format to focus service provision, its original formulation was in terms of linking product design and manufacture; clearly, QFD is relevant to the fragility issues that arise in both areas.

In the product design and manufacture context, QFD is a method to map customer wants into design quality, to deploy the functions forming quality and to deploy methods for achieving the design quality into subsystems and component parts, and ultimately to specific elements of the manufacturing process. Beginning with the initial structured table, commonly termed the *house of quality*, the QFD methodology focuses on determining the most important product or service attributes or qualities. These are composed of customer needs and expectations (see Figure 7.7 (i)). A simple service example, for a retail laundry, is shown in Figure 7.7 (ii).

Once the attributes and qualities have been prioritised, QFD deploys them to the appropriate organisational functions for action, as shown in Figure 7.7 (iii). Thus, QFD deploys customer-identified qualities to the responsible functions of the organisation. A number of QFD practitioners have claimed that using QFD has enabled them to reduce their product and service development cycle times by as much as 75 percent, with equally impressive improvements in measured customer satisfaction.

What can we say about QFD and organisational fragility, both in the context of service provision and in terms of linking product design and manufacture? By bringing together the available information, such as prioritised customer wants and the relationship between these and the technical requirements, and forcing us to collect additional information – perhaps such as the competitive and technical evaluations with benchmarked performance – QFD forces a more fact-based linked approach to design and manufacture, or service provision. It creates a clear thread through concept to delivery of product or service that means we retain clarity of why we are doing it this way. Hence, the QFD approach assists robustness in both arenas and, if there is ongoing review and updating of the product or service based on using it, it is potentially anti-fragile.

Taking Stock of Your Current Situation

With the discussion of anti-fragility in the context of markets, products and services we have largely completed our journey through the aspects and dimensions of the organisation, looking at them anew through the lens of anti-fragility. But in many senses, this chapter is what it is all about – the organisation exists to provide products and services.

In the final chapter, we shall consider briefly a large number of remaining issues. These will include Local and Global Fragility and their interrelationship, including the organisation's impact on the global anti-fragility of the economy, society and the environment. We will discuss the implications of this for the organisation, individuals, government and global institutions. We will also briefly consider developing reliable and timely awareness of opportunities

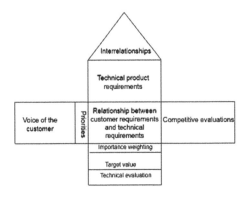

(i) The House of Quality

(ii) QFD Example for Retail Laundry

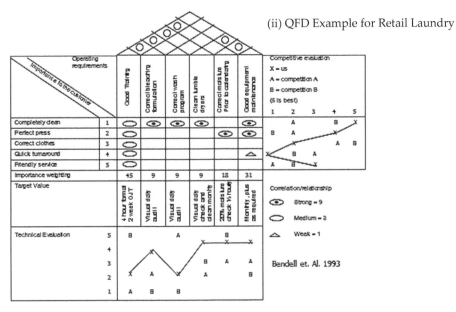

(iii) Waterfall Relationship of QFD Matrices

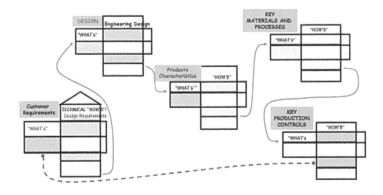

Figure 7.7   Quality Function Deployment

and threats, and using external information and systems to reduce fragility. A key remaining area is the creation of metrics of anti-fragility. We shall discuss defining an overall organisational fragility, robustness and anti-fragility profile, and the establishment of an organisational summary fragility metric. As well as this, we shall consider common pitfalls of fragile organisations, including not knowing that they are fragile. We shall review what we have learned and what is different now about our model of the organisation. Finally, we shall focus on identifying what we still don't know and the research needed to close the gap, and who you should tell.

Before we do all this, however, please reflect. At the end of Chapter 1, I asked you to undertake a simple stocktake. Now is the time to repeat it or, if you haven't done it before, to do it for the first time. To remind you, I suggested there, based on what you knew then, to take stock as to how the concept of anti-fragility applies to organisations in which you are a stakeholder. Is your organisation currently fragile? In what dimensions? I pointed out that there are no absolute answers to these questions but the aim is to help to get you thinking about where your organisation is now and where you would like it to go. I suggested accordingly that you tried the short quiz below to help you get thinking. You would then total your score and think about how you could increase it. I suggest you now repeat the test and compare your answer to before. Is it different? In what way? And why?

A Basic Fragility Test for Your Organisation (score out of 100):

- How good are our current approaches to managing the organisation? (0–10)

- Do we include deliberate diversity of approach and deployment? (0–10)

- How aware are we as an organisation of our environment? (0–10)

- Do we learn as an organisation? (0–10)

- Do we implement what we learn? (0–10)

- Do we learn fast? Fast enough? (0–10)

- Do we have the infrastructure to learn, and apply our learning? (0–10)

- Do we evolve? (0–10)

- Do we have the infrastructure to evolve? (0–10)

- How optimised are our processes? (0–10; 0 = maximum optimisation)

Finally, let us do our usual review of rules and patterns in relation to the anti-fragility of markets, products and services which have emerged from the previous discussion in this chapter and practical experience. Relevant here are:

1.   Partly because most products and services have a finite lifecycle, and even if they are robust now they are unlikely to stay so indefinitely, anti-fragility of product and service offerings is more appropriately considered on the basis of a product or service portfolio, rather than in terms of individual products and services.

2.   In the language of the Boston Matrix, *Cash cows* are a source of robustness, *Dogs* are a source of fragility, *Question marks* could be sources of either future fragility or robustness, and *Stars* are at least temporarily a source of robustness, but may become a source of fragility over time.

3.   As always, the EFQM Excellence Model has an impressive coverage of key aspects needed for anti-fragility of products and services, and customer relationships. Specifically, they include fulfilling promises, adequate resourcing, balancing stakeholder requirements, sustainability, lifecycle management, monitoring and Benchmarking, and the use of customer feedback to improve, in addition to the linked but separate RADAR requirements. Again, however, fragility perspectives of the offerings are not explicitly addressed, apart from the physical lifecycle management considerations, and instead efficiency and effectiveness are stressed. In addition, there is no explicit consideration of the customer's view of fragility of the customer strategy and processes.

4.   Whilst having much in common with that for the private sector, the question of fragility for public sector organisations has distinct and subtle differences. Public sector organisations are more risk averse, and typically subjected to lower likelihood and magnitude of risks. Also, in the public sector, who is ordering, who is paying and the recipients of service are often very

separated and there can be multiple customers within the same transaction, each with different needs and expectations.

5.   Many large consumer-facing organisations display rigid fragile customer interfaces, with disempowered staff, restrictive technology/systems, lack of holistic ownership of the total customer experience, lack of adequate customisation and communication, inadequate access to useable data, and a reliance on information from, processing by, and a tendency to blame, the customer. Authority and the ability to make ad hoc exceptional decisions, or substantially change the system, in these organisations are often high up, and often not easily accessible to the front line or customers. This is certainly not anti-fragile.

6.   Different types or classifications of service have different anti-fragility issues. For example, services with tangible actions where the direct recipients are people are likely to have more direct observed feedback than ones with intangible actions or those directed at 'things', and hence may be more fragile. However, because of the level of direct observation, they may have already been engineered to be more robust or anti-fragile. In contrast, services based on intangible actions and/or where people are not the direct recipients of service, may contain *dormant undiscovered fragility,* or undiscovered failure. Also, Professional Service may appear more robust and potentially anti-fragile than Service Shops, Service Factories or Mass Service, since the high labour intensity and interaction/customisation may well also have associated with it a skilled, empowered and, within professional boundaries, flexible workforce. However, the overall Professional Service provision may also be the most fragile as it uses a lot of labour and needs a lot of customisation, so may be under cost and time pressure.

7.   In considering service development, the organisational fragility, robustness and anti-fragility each have three dimensions corresponding to the service concept, the package of service elements and the service delivery system. To some extent this is hierarchical, with fragility in the concept potentially causing greatest overall fragility to the service. Conversely, the need for robustness and anti-fragility at this level is greatest. Within the service package, it is easy to overlook implicit services and this also often causes service fragility.

8.   The Gap Model gives us with an interesting insight into the issue of fragility, robustness and anti-fragility of the service provision. The set of ten determinants shows the complexity of the dimensions in which service fragility may occur. Underlying causes behind these probably mean that in many circumstances they are correlated. For example some are likely to be at least partly service design fragility problems such as access and tangibility. Others are clearly service delivery and management fragility problems, for example courtesy, credibility and responsiveness. For a particular organisation, examination and identification of which of the gaps are the most major, together with in which dimensions, will, by implication, identify the most major sources of fragility, and indicate where robustness and anti-fragility needs to be introduced.

Chapter 8
Your Place in a Fragile World

Local and Global Fragility and their Interrelationship

Previously in this book we have touched on, in passing, a number of aspects about global and local fragility, and their interrelationship. We shall now discuss them more explicitly here. As discussed in Chapter 1, in considering soft systems thinking, all systems form part of larger systems within a complex hierarchical whole. Fragility, robustness and anti-fragility can exist in any subsystem at any level in this hierarchy and be embedded in any characteristic and/or part of that subsystem, and in its interfaces. Hence, we all live in a very fragile world ... which in turn is part of a fragile universe ... and then, who knows what above it. But it is, presumably, fragile.

To be practical, let us limit ourselves here to the world. Do we approach our world as if it is fragile? The author argues strongly that we do not. Largely, we assume that things will very much go on as before. This is not typically because we have prudently taken precautions to help 'ensure' it does, but because we have an inbuilt belief, a need to believe perhaps, in its stability. We teach this to our children in terms of their deterministic (right and wrong, cause and effect, fundamental laws of nature, historical and assumed to continue) schooling.

We embed it into the current financial system based on the historical, simplistic, system of double entry booking keeping, developed for Venetian merchants in the fifteenth century, tweaked to try to retain some relevance today, and are surprised when it is not effective, efficient nor robust. But even then, when it fails, we don't move very quickly to do something about it – lack of understanding, inertia, fear and vested interest all get in the way. So we lay down controlling regulations, tighten laws, develop codes of practice in the hope of developing some robustness, when the underlying fragility is, in fact, embedded many layers down, untouched, in the underlying postulates and assumptions of the system; it is these that need to change.

The lack of fragility of the world is the basis of our engineering, strangely still fundamentally assumed deterministic, with the occasional stochastic add-on. When it fails, we blame nature for environmental excesses that we could not be expected to take into account. Why? Why should the world remain as it is?

Our science is better, up to a point. Scientific method, based on conjecture and refutation, and the empirical testing of hypotheses, is fundamentally anti-fragile. And yet, in the public conscious, science is a set of known, assumed unchanging rules and laws about how the universe works – forgotten is the fact that these are only human constructions, and then only the best we have so far.

It is not pretty is it? We live in a world that, to quote Taleb, we do not understand. But worse than that, even when we do understand, we do not always act as if we do.

But let us return to local and global fragility, and their interrelationship. In talking about the trend towards the use of Cloud computing for business systems as a way around vendor lock-in to large software business systems, we pointed out that a penalty for this is a *shift in the dimensions of the fragility risks away from an emphasis on local organisational system failure, to global failure* for all user organisations due, for example, to central server failure. It appears that similar trends have, and are, occurring elsewhere in our human systems associated with technology developments; the unification of communication systems' potential impact on globalising financial crises may be another example. Generally, we expect that by increasing the scale of the system, we *reduce the likelihood of failure*, because of the availability of more centralised supporting resources. However, we also *potentially greatly increase the negative impact of failure*. As Taleb says: elephants are fragile, mice are not.

The question is, however, is it worth doing? Is it worth trading a reduced risk of local failure for an increased risk of global failure? For the Cloud example, the answer to this question should be, at least, at two levels: that of the individual organisation whose system provision is being centralised and that of the economy of all organisations whose systems are centralised together. At the individual organisation level, the answer may be that it is, if the likelihood and impact of system failure occurring and affecting it are both reduced. However, this is not typically the basis for making outsourcing decisions, which are more frequently made on a cost basis, and which can give a different answer. For the economy of all organisations whose systems are being centralised, the decision may be more complex as a catastrophic global failure if it occurs can have a disproportionate impact compared to small local failures. This is the problem of all markets, or all power stations, going down at once.

As we said above, fragility, robustness and anti-fragility can each exist in any subsystem or system, at any level in the hierarchy of local and global systems. Ideally, *the feedback supporting anti-fragility at the global level should come in a timely manner from all levels including local* so that maximum learning can be obtained to support maximum anti-fragility. Conversely, *timely feedback from throughout the global system should ideally be used to support learning and anti-fragility at the local level also.*

We shall now use these ideas of global and local fragility to discuss the organisations' impact on the global anti-fragility of the economy, society and the environment, and the converse. Global here may mean national or worldwide. These three dimensions of the sustainability concept are, of course, in general correlated. Extreme economic fragility may cause, or be a consequence of, societal fragility, and environmental fragility may, in turn, follow from, or cause, these. A fragile or failing company in any of these three dimensions, could, for example, through contagion to other organisations, help bring down the global system – such as failing banks. Conversely, they will be affected by the fragility of the global system. How can we minimise these effects so as to protect the global systems from organisational fragility, and organisations from globally fragility, and to consequently make both more robust and potentially anti-fragile?

Returning to the Soft Systems Thinking Model, and Dana Meadows's 12 leverage points for intervening in a system that we considered in Chapter 1, suggests that for a company in a fragile global circumstance, intervention at the organisational level could be made in the form of:

- improving information flow;

- changing the system;

- developing additional Balancing Loops, to protect the organisation from the global 'gathering storm'. These could be created locally, for example finding new markets or reducing exposure, or globally, for example guaranteeing the organisation's credit.

Conversely, to protect the global system from fragile organisations, particularly catalytic ones like failing banks, we may wish to intervene in the system by:

- slowing down certain feedback loops, that, for example, cause panic or spiralling price changes, as well as possibly speeding up others, for example, with valuable data for global control;

- developing additional Balancing Loops to protect the global system from negative feedback/vicious circles created from failing organisations;

- changing the system.

An interesting observation in this regard is that whilst we have been discussing the link between global and local fragility in the context of the three correlated sustainability aspects – economy, society and the environment – normally such consideration is largely restricted to the economic domain. Anti-fragility and Soft Systems Thinking combined give us an insightful view into mechanisms.

Implications for the Organisation, Government, Global Institutions and Individuals

So, what does all this mean for individuals, organisations, government and global institutions? It affects each of the players in a number of ways. However, broadly, all these players will have two common needs in helping them to reduce and manage fragility, and build robustness and anti-fragility. These are developing reliable and timely awareness of opportunities and threats, and using external information and systems to reduce fragility.

Let us consider each player in turn, starting with private sector organisations. These, as we said above, can respond to fragile global circumstances by improving their information flow, trying to change the circumstances and system in which they operate and developing additional Balancing Loops, for example finding new markets or reducing exposure. But, what else should they do in general? It follows from our earlier discussions throughout the book that, to reduce fragility and manage their overall anti-fragility, they also need to coherently and actively manage all aspects of their Governance, Strategy, People, Culture, Processes, Operations, Information, Technology, Innovation, Supply Chain, Environment, CSR, Markets, Products and Services, and Design. That is quite a challenging task. At present, organisations do not have a coherent approach to such a task, although, potentially, an extended ERM approach could be applied. This could place responsibility on the Board for coordination and overall management, as is typical with ERM. The development of reliable and timely awareness of opportunities and threats would then be one specific measurable improvement objective on this system, as a targeted performance could be defined on an annual basis and monitored retrospectively in terms of performance. The linked improvement in the use of external information and systems to reduce fragility could also be a parallel board objective.

For government functions and global institutions, the fragility and anti-fragility issue is at two levels. These are:

1.   For the government function or global institution's defined organisational purpose (micro), with defined purposes, which it is trying to achieve. Fragility here is in terms of it failing as an organisation in being able to achieve this.

2.   For the appropriate macro 'global' system as a whole, based on the aggregation of all of the micro/local organisations or companies that the government function or global institution exists to help, monitor and/or regulate. Fragility here is in terms of failure of the economy, society and/or environment.

Fragility in the first case is about failure of the government function or global institution to operate, whilst fragility in the second case is about failure of the economy, society and/or environment it exists to assist; these are clearly related but distinct. For these bodies, the extended ERM discussed above will be more extensive and complex as a result of these two interrelated aspects.

What of the individual? Your place in a fragile world. This is fascinating, complex, demanding and possibly ethically conflicting. To discuss this we have to summarise you as an individual. But what are you? How can we define you? Most dictionaries seem to approximately define an individual as a single human being – but what roles and functions, what aspects of life does that cover? In considering the organisations' impact on global anti-fragility, we considered the three interrelated dimensions from the sustainability concept – the economy, society and the environment – but pointed out that often practical consideration of the impact of organisations is restricted only to the economic domain. At best, environmental issues are considered separately. So, what about anti-fragility management for a person? Does economy, society and the environment work for them in terms of their intrinsic self-management and personal objectives rather than just their work ones? In some senses, it might be nice to think so – we would really have a sustainability culture. In reality, these are insufficient, as we know clearly enough, for example from Maslow's Hierarchy of Needs.

So, what else should be included and how does this correlate by the roles taken by an individual? Whilst we could consider any standard management classification here, such as a PESTEL, for simplicity of argument we will just supplement the three sustainability dimensions, with political and ethical ones.

Table 8.1 illustrates this, and assumes that the core of an individual's roles can be defined in terms of job, family, involvement in personal groups (for example, voluntary and religious), community and broader society. It also assumes that self-management and personal objectives can be summarised under categories of economic, societal, environmental, political and ethical. The Xs indicate possible associations, and the (X)s weaker ones, but this will vary with the individual – for example, for some individuals family roles and personal group roles may be very associated with personal environmental objectives.

Table 8.1   Individual's roles and objectives

Self-management and personal objectives: / Activity:	Job	Family	Personal groups, for example, voluntary and religious	Community	Broader Society
Economic	X	X	(X)		
Societal		X	X	X	X
Environmental	(X)			X	X
Political			(X)	(X)	(X)
Ethical	X	X	X	X	X

In terms of anti-fragility management for the person, then, we can see the potential for an individual to have anti-fragile aspirations in any or all aspects of their lives; to make their job position, family role, group role, community role and society role, stronger and stronger. The dimensions of this anti-fragility will vary with role, as well as individual, but may include, for example, any of economic, societal, environmental, political and ethical. For the individual to reduce and manage fragility, and build robustness and anti-fragility, they will again need to develop reliable and timely awareness of opportunities and threats, and use external information and systems to reduce fragility. For individuals to reduce fragility and manage their overall anti-fragility, they also need to coherently and actively manage all aspects of their strategy, behaviour, activities, leadership, innovation, supply chains and environment.

In many cases, a major part of this personal anti-fragility will be targeted on keeping and enhancing job role in turbulent times. What should the individual do to be anti-fragile in this respect? Enhance skills, keep up to date, be politically and culturally well embedded in the organisation, select a robust or anti-fragile organisation to work for, and a robust or anti-fragile role.

However, with human individuals, there is a particular challenge. This is where roles come into conflict with the self-management and personal objectives, values and beliefs. It is the question of anti-fragility of job at what price? There appears to be an increasing trend, particularly for senior mature employees, to come into conflict with organisational values later in their careers in both the private and public sectors. This can occur for many reasons – changes of organisational direction or key outcomes required, key performance indicators (KPIs), priorities or senior management teams; changes of ownership and takeovers; changes in technology or process; disempowering of customers, or in other ways reducing their position; disempowering of staff. Such conflict of personal and organisational values, with associated issues of loss of status and respect, can be very traumatic and cause the member of staff to exit. This implies that, in such circumstances, anti-fragility of job role is not the ultimate concern, it is subjugated to something higher.

The Metrics of Anti-Fragility

We commented earlier that it is harder to measure anti-fragility than efficiency. Even for a process it is conceptually somewhat difficult to measure. This is intrinsic, since anti-fragility is a second-order characteristic of the process; efficiency is about the process speed whilst anti-fragility is about the rate of decline of the tendency to fail. Thus, a clue to the definition of anti-fragility measurement is to see *anti-fragility as measured by the rate of decline of fragility due to exposure to stress*. As this definition is a rate of decline, we will also need to specify a current fragility level in order to parameterise anti-fragility. Table 8.2 shows some illustrative measures for fragility, robustness and anti-fragility associated with different aspects of the organisation.

Table 8.2   Illustrative measures

	Efficiency	Fragility	Robustness	Anti-fragility
Process	Throughput rate, OEE.	No. of breakdowns, lost time.	Uptime.	Rate of decline in number of breakdowns, and lost time.
People	Utilisation, output per head.	Absenteeism, turnover.	Attendance, retention.	Rate of decline in absenteeism, and turnover.
Technology	Utilisation, output.	Failure rate, non-availability.	Availability.	Rate of decline in failure rate, and non-availability.
Information	Timely, reliable, accurate.	Delay, inaccuracy.	Timely, reliable, accurate.	Rate of decline in delay and inaccuracy.
Supply Chain	Throughput rate, OEE.	Number of breakdowns in supply, unsatisfied demand.	Continuation of supply.	Rate of decline in number of breakdowns in supply and unsatisfied demand.
Markets	Sales, transaction times.	Lost transactions.	Continuation of sales.	Rate of decline in lost transactions.

Whilst to define the above measures the denominator of the rate of decline for anti-fragility can be taken as stress level, it is more useful here, for the moment, to take it as time. This is because using time enables us to establish easy to measure metrics which can be used to monitor the anti-fragility of the organisation. If we do this it is apparent that the relationship between anti-fragility, as we have defined it above, and fragility is a *negative equivalent* of that between velocity and distance. That is, velocity is the rate of increase of distance travelled with time and anti-fragility is the rate of decline of fragility with time. This is a useful insight but to develop it necessitates that we define some additional terms.

Until this point, we have taken a largely intuitive, and standard, usage of the word 'robust' in terms of inherent health and strength, and the ability to withstand stress. The definition we gave in Chapter 1 was: Robust refers to systems and organisations that are able to withstand ... changes or shocks in the external or internal environment. This has been sufficient for our purposes but now that needs to change, and we shall define three distinct but related kinds of robustness. These are:

- *Pointwise robustness* is the opposite of *pointwise fragility*, and represents the instantaneous strength and the ability to withstand stress, at this particular point of time. Hence, it is a (nonlinear) function of time.

- *Ongoing robustness* is a constant level of inherent strength that is retained within the item, system or organisation, and that does not decline nor increase over time.

- *Declining robustness* corresponds to a level of inherent strength that declines over time, as a result of inherent deterioration through use or environmental damage, or intrinsic deterioration.

Although it is not essential to our argument, it is convenient to define pointwise robustness as a mathematical function R(t), which is scaled or defined to take a numerical value between 0 and 1, with 1 representing perfect robustness, the ability to withstand any shock, and 0 representing no robustness, and failure with every shock. We may also define pointwise fragility as a mathematical function F(t), where F(t) = 1-R(t),which is increasing with t, so that its derivative f(t) = dF(t)/dt is assumed to be non-negative. Those readers familiar with reliability theory, or simple statistical theory, will be familiar with analogous formulations. Figure 8.1 illustrates the terms, and their interrelationships.

Since our argument above is based upon the analogy between velocity and speed, the question arises as to what is the analogy here with acceleration? Since anti-fragility is the *negative velocity* with which fragility declines, we may define the *anti-fragile acceleration rate* as the rate at which this negative velocity changes, which can be positive or negative. For example, for the illustrative anti-fragile upper curve in Figure 8.1 (ii), this anti-fragile acceleration rate has been taken as positive, but it does not have to be, and the curve could downturn if it was negative. If the anti-fragile acceleration rate is zero, it will be a straight line (see Figure 8.1 (iii)).

The above discussion provides an interesting basis for monitoring the ongoing robustness and anti-fragility of organisations. As we discussed above, to define the above measures, the denominator of the rate of decline for anti-fragility was taken as time rather than stress level. What would happen if we did instead take it as stress level, and would the resulting measures be practically useful? The difficulty here is that stress, unlike time, is somewhat badly defined in this context since, as Taleb has pointed out, the effects of stress depends not just on the total magnitude applied but on the pattern and timing. There are thus at least two important parameters, frequency and magnitude, but magnitude is itself multidimensional. So, we can either attempt to construct a composite index of stress to replace time on the horizontal axis, a somewhat difficult task, or we can consider multidimensional extensions of the above diagrams, with multiple independent variables. This is more difficult still.

(i)   Pointwise Fragility, F(t), and Pointwise Robustness, R(t).

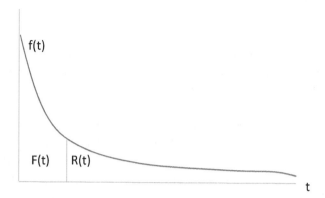

(ii)   Anti-fragility and Robustness.

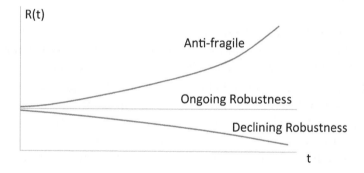

(iii)   Anti-fragile acceleration rate

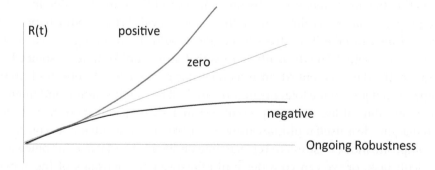

Figure 8.1   Generalisations of robustness, fragility and anti-fragility

There could, however, be circumstances when at least a partial analysis on this basis would be useful. For instance, consider a company whose fragility is in question following unexpected market conditions. Its shareholders are concerned that its robustness is monitored in real time against well understood stresses. In this case, it would be possible to select appropriate stress parameters for either of the two above approaches.

Let us now talk about the overall organisational fragility, robustness and anti-fragility profile of an organisation. Based on our discussions above, we can construct a suite of different anti-fragility and robustness metrics for the different aspects of the organisation. How should these be brought together into a template, scorecard and/or index? One method might be to construct an organisational scorecard based on the EFQM Excellence Model, utilising the nine model criteria in a stylised template to show criterion-based anti-fragility scores as the basis for an overall organisational fragility, robustness and anti-fragility summary index. Alternatively, it might be worth retaining the EFQM Excellence Model structure, or something similar but extended, and show scores on two or three key summary metrics for each criterion. Such extension of the structure could be introduced to highlight certain key fragility/robustness/anti-fragility differentiators, such as information and technology, which are relatively low level in the model. However, the EFQM Excellence Model, and its equivalents, were not designed to summarise organisational fragility issues and, as we know, are somewhat deficient for these purposes. The development of an organisation-specific fragility, robustness and anti-fragility roadmap and progress measure, based on the organisation's particular circumstances and starting position, would be very worthwhile.

Common Pitfalls of Fragile Organisations

This could be a very long section – in a sense the whole book has been about the pitfalls of fragile organisations. Where do, and why do, fragile organisations fail? It is not the purpose of this book to answer this question in any detail; rather we are concerned with exploring the methods, approaches and architecture to build anti-fragile organisations. Hence, our focus is on establishing this anti-fragile concept of the firm and exploring its application. Also, however, we aimed to develop understanding of the mechanisms whereby business fragility is embedded within organisational strategy, structure and systems, people, relationships and culture, as well as products, services, markets, use of information and the technology base. And, of course, we wanted to connect and contrast anti-fragility thinking with conventional approaches. So, it is not unreasonable to expect us to cover the common pitfalls of fragile firms.

Actually, this is a difficult subject on two grounds. Firstly, which are, and are not, fragile organisations? This is far from clear. Fragility occurs because of inadequately expected or planned for stresses on the organisation, associated with its external or internal environment. So, in advance, it is not always possible to identify fragile organisations. That is the reason why stakeholder monitoring is so crucial. Retrospectively, after the unexpected or unplanned for stress, particularly if it does serious damage, it is usually much easier to tell. And yet, it would be very wrong for the author to base this section only on organisations that have failed or come close to failure. Organisational fragility is much more extensively distributed than that; these are just the tip of an iceberg, with a lot more than nine-tenths below the waterline.

Secondly, there is a difficult issue of root causes. Typically in a fragile organisation there are many manifestations of fragility, if they can be seen. For example, could we have seen and predicted BP's operational failure in the Gulf, with all its environmental and financial implications, beforehand? Of course, we could. Trouble is, we could have predicted failure also of a large number of other organisations and, clearly, not all have done so. Two things are in play here. We already talked in Chapter 6 about the fact that we cannot sensibly calculate the cost of organisational fragility a stock-out might lead to, since it will depend on the environmental circumstances – in some circumstances it may kill the organisation, in others it will not. This is the issue of randomness in our model – does the killing blow come along at the right or wrong time? Our causal fragility factors only increase propensity to fail, they are not normally outright killers. Apart from this, though, how do we determine which manifestation of fragility is the fundamental root cause of failure? The realistic answer is that we cannot.

So, on this basis the *ten common pitfalls of fragile organisations* that we consider here are purely the author's construct, based on his experiences, prejudices and previous arguments. Each is partly a description of a fragility issue in itself, and partly an *indicator of underlying fragility*. Hence, each is, or should be, a *call to action*.

They are:

1.   **Not knowing that they are fragile.**
        This is partly a question of organisational cognition – does the organisation as an entity have the level of awareness to recognise its internal condition and the threats in the external and internal

environments? Tied to this is the question whether the precepts of the organisation limit this awareness and effectively prevent the organisation developing such awareness. Many initially strong organisations are established on the basis of powerful beliefs and vision, which over time becomes outdated and causes of fragility. Can the organisation open its collective eyes adequately and quickly enough to see this? Historically, many organisations have not been able to. These organisations are the ones most in need of a *fragility check*, but often the most resisting. *Conversely, anti-fragile organisations are most aware of their own potential fragility.*

2.   **Not being joined up.**
      Collective organisational cognition also implies issues about shared vision, management control, internal communication, deployment of strategy and alignment of objectives. If the organisation is not joined up then its ability to respond to stresses, or the threat of stresses, adequately is likely to be in doubt.

3.   **Knowing, not doing.**
      Knowing that the organisation is fragile but not doing anything about it can be for various reasons. It is possible that those in charge of the organisation have a high risk propensity or have shared their risks over several organisations and 'don't care'. It may be deliberate – *no risk, no gain*. There may be a distracting power struggle. It may not be a priority, or Groupthink may obliterate normal concerns. It is also, of course, partly a cognition issue, about understanding the need and the method to act.

4.   **Doing Risk Management incorrectly.**
      We have already discussed this at some length. ERM goes some of the way to solve this but there are fundamental weaknesses in current Risk Management practices, particularly where they are largely delegated to middle management and become a compliance driven ritual.

5.   **Too much emphasis on money and short-termism.**
      As a *sole* business driver, money is dangerous, as it distorts decision making, culture and operations. Similarly, an exclusive short-term emphasis creates fragility by neglecting big issues.

6. **Bureaucracy and emphasis on control.**
    Disempowered following of rules and procedures, an emphasis on discipline, centralised decision making and worship of hierarchy all mitigate against flexibility and agility.

7. **Badly managing change.**
    Change Management is key to anti-fragility. Badly managing change, therefore, is a clear indicator of underlying problems.

8. **Weak processes or an emphasis on initiatives.**
    Process weakness, whether in the core operations area or in isolated support processes, indicates that the organisation has not yet tackled an underlying fundamental weakness. Conversely, it is possible for process management and improvement techniques, like ISO 9001, TQM, Lean and Six Sigma to become ends in themselves within the organisation. This can fuel complacency and distract attention and resources from pressing fragility issues. It is also possible to increase fragility by applying these methods badly, like hard-wiring Lean systems.

9. **Non-transparent decision making.**
    Decision making is a central management activity, but rarely codified, and often subject to biases and seen as a source of power. Unclear decision-making processes can increase inaction and sluggish responses, and be a great source of fragility.

10. **Naive offshoring and ignoring customers.**
    We have discussed both of these supply chain issues previously. Both are potentially major sources of fragility. Offshoring of both products and services without adequate safeguards has created quality problems, disruptions to supply and customer dissatisfaction. Insufficient attention to customer interfaces has similar effects.

Review of This Book

As we are coming towards the end of this book, we shall now review the contents and discussion to date. To the author's knowledge, this will be only the second book to be published in the world on anti-fragility. It is not yet a mature subject. And yet, most of the ideas that we have discussed in this book are not completely new – anti-fragility has given us a new way of looking at an organisation, a new perspective or lens, but the imperatives in running that organisation are not changed by the concept, just made more explicit.

In Chapter 1 we introduced the anti-fragility concept, based upon Nassim Taleb's seminal book. We have defined terms, explained reasons and looked at the relationship of this new approach with current holistic organisational models and analysis methods. Because of their important resonance with the anti-fragility concept, two of these in particular have reappeared frequently throughout the book. These are Soft Systems Thinking and the EFQM Excellence Model. We ended Chapter 1 with a basic fragility test for readers to apply to their own organisations. At the end of Chapter 7, having engaged with the author's ideas, it is suggested that readers repeat this test. Hopefully this opportunity for reflection has revealed the development of your own thinking. We hope it has developed as that is the primary purpose of this book.

In Chapter 2 we explored anti-fragile strategy, governance and risk, starting from a discussion of the progress that has been made in ERM. Despite this progress, we concluded that all is still not well in the pursuit of anti-fragile organisational governance. We then explored current Risk Management practices in some detail and identified a key deficiency, that it was based on a presumption that you could actually a priori conceive of all of the risks that the organisation faces. We then considered anti-fragile organisational strategy and structures and, considering change strategies, we saw that one based on the EFQM Excellence Model results in superior economic performance. We concluded the chapter by saying that we will often rely on people, rather than systems and processes, to provide robustness and anti-fragility in relation to inherent weaknesses in our organisation, or ones created by unforeseen stress.

Chapter 3 was concerned with developing anti-fragile people and culture, and we started it by discussing why people are both a major exploitable source of anti-fragility and a major source of fragility in themselves. We considered various management approaches and theories of management, and concluded that to develop an anti-fragile organisation we need to avoid thinking based on the Classical Approach to Management and Transactional theory, both on the part of the organisation and of individual employees and managers. We discussed motivation and Maslow's hierarchy of needs, which, like many theories in this area, appears to have a natural affinity with the concept of anti-fragility. An organisation's position in relation to Hofstede's cultural dimensions also clearly relates to its overall fragility, robustness or anti-fragility. We also found, in common with what we subsequently found in other chapters, that the relevant EFQM Excellence Model criteria support much of the requirements for anti-fragility, but are more focused on efficiency and effectiveness. To become anti-fragile an organisation needs to become a Learning Organisation. Finally, internal organisational politics cannot be avoided in considering organisational change towards anti-fragility. The change agent needs to be good at establishing and managing alliances with stakeholders in pursuit of change objectives.

In Chapter 4, we considered making processes and operations anti-fragile. We discussed the meaning of fragility in processes, and that this was more than just the danger of process stop, also including the process operating with no output, or acceptable output, or below specification performance. We postulated a possible U-shaped relationship between process fragility and efficiency. We then looked at various important process improvement methodologies from an anti-fragility perspective covering, in particular, ISO 9001, Lean, Six Sigma and Poka Yoke. Lean methods are inherently fragile but can be used well to make a real contribution to process, operations and organisational anti-fragility. Six Sigma also can be applied in a fragile, robust or anti-fragile way. Poka Yoke Mistake Proofing is inherently robust, and the potential to mistake proof every process in an organisation, in a way that utilises feedback in real time, is an aspirational anti-fragile target operating model.

Use of information and technology, and the impact of innovation, is discussed in Chapter 5. Technologies that start robust or anti-fragile will, over time, become fragile, and currently worldwide technology is causing considerable organisation and system fragility. Hard-wired technology, such as rigid flow-line systems and large inflexible business systems with vendor lock-in, are also fragile. Cloud computing may well offer a solution for the latter, but at the price of trading a decrease in local fragility for an increase in global fragility. The contribution properly conducted Benchmarking can make to organisational anti-fragility is large, but with the development of the Internet there are considerable dangers in trusting analyses based on public domain data sources. Measuring and comparing anti-fragility is inherently more difficult in comparison to measuring efficiency or effectiveness, but it is easier to compare fragility rather than anti-fragility by considering metrics such as lost time, number of process stoppages, breakdowns and so on. We discussed why innovation in the context of disruptive technologies is a cause of fragility and how organisations should protect themselves. Finally, we reviewed the relative rigidity, inflexibility and lumpiness in relation to technology and information management decisions, typically representing heavy investment, long change cycles and major purchase decisions. Thus, wrong decisions are typically costly and time consuming. Human decision making is particularly fragile but the risk of fragility can typically be reduced by careful planned use of group decision making. The pursuit of an anti-fragile decision-making process would require a level of explicit monitoring of, and learning from, the decision-making process that is currently not realistic within most of our organisations.

Chapter 6 concerns the supply chain, environment and CSR. Supply networks and supply chains are fragile because they rely on linkages and relationships which go beyond the boundaries of the organisation, and the hazards facing a supply chain are, in general, both considerably more numerous and more complex than those for operations within an organisation. Good quality information flow is an underlying requirement for anti-fragility in the supply chain; this can be improved by information sharing, aligning planning and control decisions, improving flow efficiency and better forecasting. The discussion of Inventory Management in this chapter illustrated an issue about using the cost of failure, or fragility, as a measure. It is difficult to properly cost the impact of a hazard in creating organisational fragility, as this will be at best an expectation, not reflecting the worst case due to environmental circumstances – cost is therefore not a good proxy for fragility measurement. We also discussed why the information (sub) supply chain is more problematical than the rest of the supply chain within which it is embedded, as typically data is provided by customers themselves and other stakeholders with, at best, only an implicit contract. Our discussion here also covered how the environmental and societal, or CSR, impacts of the supply chain are related to anti-fragility at three levels; they impact on *organisational* fragility; they impact on the fragility of the *environment, society* and the *economy*; and they impact on the fragility of the *organisational environmental management system* itself, and its *CSR equivalent*.

In Chapter 7, we discussed fragility, robustness and anti-fragility related to markets, products and services. Partly because most products and services have a finite lifecycle, and even if they are robust now they are unlikely to stay so indefinitely, anti-fragility of product and service offerings is more appropriately considered on the basis of a product or service portfolio rather than in terms of individual products and services. Utilising the Boston Matrix, we found that *cash cows* are a source of robustness, *dogs* are a source of fragility, *question marks* could be sources of either future fragility or robustness, and *stars* are at least temporarily a source of robustness, but may become a source of fragility over time. Whilst having much in common with that for the private sector, the question of fragility for public sector organisations has distinct and subtle differences. Also, we postulated that many large consumer-facing organisations display rigid fragile customer interfaces. Authority, and the ability to make ad hoc exceptional decisions, or substantially change the system, in these systems are often high up, and often not easily accessible to the front line or customers. Different types or classifications of service have different anti-fragility issues. For example, services based on intangible actions or where people are not the direct recipients of service may contain dormant undiscovered fragility, or undiscovered failure. Professional Service may appear more robust and potentially anti-fragile than Service Shops, Service Factories or Mass Service, however, the overall Professional Service provision may also be the most fragile, as it uses a lot of labour and needs a lot of customisation, so may be under cost and time pressure. Fragility in the service concept potentially causes greater overall fragility to the service than the package of service elements and the service delivery system.

Finally, in this Chapter 8, we have looked at our place in a fragile world. Starting with a discussion of local and global fragility and their interrelationship, we also briefly discussed the fragility of the world and the universe, the accounting and finance systems, and engineering. We considered the implications of this for organisations, government, international institutions and the individual. An important discussion concerned the creation of metrics of anti-fragility. Here, we defined anti-fragility to be measured by the rate of decline of fragility due to exposure to stress. Whilst the denominator of this rate of decline can be taken as stress level, it is more useful to take it as time in order establish easy to measure metrics which can be used to monitor the anti-fragility of the organisation. Using an analogy with velocity, we introduced a number of new useful terms and discussed their relationship: pointwise robustness, ongoing robustness, declining robustness and the anti-fragility acceleration rate. We also discussed how to define an overall organisational fragility, robustness and anti-fragility profile, and the establishment of an organisational summary fragility metric. Prior to this review of the book, we also considered the common pitfalls of fragile organisations, including not knowing that they are fragile.

What We Still Don't Know

The theory of anti-fragility is new, immature and largely untested. However, it links well to the majority of organisational management theory, in the broadest sense. Partly, it has been tested through practical applications through the author's consultancy activities, and those of the small emerging group of anti-fragility practitioners.

There is still much to do, and a pressing need to do it, in order to establish anti-fragility into its appropriate place as the basis for:

- a coherent holistic anti-fragile theory of the firm;

- a unifying framework for improvement, including Lean, Six Sigma, Quality and Productivity;

- a more appropriate optimisation criterion than efficiency.

The need now is for research activity to extend our knowledge in the business field. Anti-fragility is an open, but worthy, field with enormous opportunity to link together, and reinterpret, existing management theory. If you are looking for a research topic, or a PhD dissertation subject, there are many theoretical topics or empirical investigations that you can develop within this rich field. *A field which gives a truer representation of reality than we have had before.*

At the simplest level, academics and students might consider any of the following topics as research opportunities:

1. How does the theory of anti-fragility change each of the main business school disciplines – Strategy, Operations, HR, Finance, Marketing and so on – and the theories and methods within them? There is plenty of room for many academic articles, books and theses in each area.

2. How should anti-fragility help to change the unifying models between these disciplines, like the EFQM Excellence Model?

3. The mathematical and statistical formulation of anti-fragility, also barely touched in this book, offers interesting possibilities for study and promise in terms of describing hitherto hard to model business and other phenomena.

4. What is beyond anti-fragility and how does it work? As we have argued, anti-fragility is a second-order effect. Can we conceive and develop other second-order effects, and third-order ones? What are they?

5. Is there an intrinsic anti-fragile characteristic in people? If so, what is it, and how does it work?

6.   There is a key need to build up a library of anti-fragility organisation-specific case studies to help us all understand better the arguments of this book, and to assist the development of business education in this field. These would make very good MBA or Masters Dissertation subjects.

7.   There is also a need for industry-wide studies to help build momentum, understanding and practice in specific fields, where specific circumstances and conditions apply. Starting cross-industry studies might be in financial services, the oil and gas industry, the airline industry, the NHS, construction and local government.

There are, of course, many more opportunities for research areas. The author would be delighted to hear of your work. He may be reached at: tony@servicesltd.co.uk or tony@theanti-fragilityacademy.co.uk.

Meanwhile, though, anti-fragility is a too useful business and improvement concept to wait for the research. Already there is a practical set of application tools available, many of which we have provided in this book. Please, go out and start using it now. And get in touch with the author if you need help.

Epilogue

Final Thoughts, or Are They?
... Who Are You Going to Tell?

Hopefully, by now you realise that it would be against anti-fragility principles for these to really be my final thoughts. I, and I hope you, will continue to learn and apply that learning in implementing improvement, as we get stressed by the practical challenges of implementation.

So these are not my final thoughts, but I do have a final request. Early in the book, I told you about my epiphany, when at the Hay Book Festival in May 2012 I heard for the first time about anti-fragility. I realised then that this was potentially the most important change in management thinking that I had come across in my 40-year career as a business academic, consultant and trainer. That this could unify and simplify all that I, and many others, have been doing for the last 40 years. That is why I decided to write this book, and that is why I now have a question for you. *Who are you going to tell?*

Anti-fragility is a paradigm shift of enormous dimensions. It will take time to spread and to get established. It is important that this happens, and as quickly as possible, because every day organisations needlessly fail, needlessly wasting resources, human spirit and opportunity. Some can be saved and anti-fragility gives us a language to discuss it. So, *who are you going to tell?* You have read this far (or at least skimmed the book), so you understand a lot and can communicate it to others. If you see anything of the opportunities that I do, then please pass it on by word of mouth within your own community, explain anti-fragility to people ... and let me know.

Tony Bendell,
the village of Orniac in the Lot Valley, France,
August 2013

Bibliography

Ackoff, R. and Emery, F. (1972) *On Purposeful Systems: An Interdisciplinary Analysis of Individual and Social Behavior as a System of Purposeful Events.* Chicago: Aldine-Atherton.

Arggris, C. and Schon, D. (1978) *Organisational Learning: A Theory of Action Perspective.* Reading, MA: Addison Wesley.

Atallo-Hazel-Green, D. (2005) Integrating ERM for Business and Regulatory Value. Deloitte and Touche [Online], http://www.ermsymposium.org/2005/erm2005/A5_bk.pdf (accessed 14 October 2013).

Bendell, A. (2012) Getting it Right: Mitigating Risk by the Development of Anti-Fragility, *Journal of Medical Safety*, Vol. 1, pp. 2–8.

Bendell, A., Boulter, L. and Dahlgaard, J. (2013) Total Quality Beyond North America: A Comparative Analysis of the Performance of the European Excellence Award Winners, *International Journal of Operations and Production Management*, Vol. 33, No. 2, pp. 197–215.

Bendell, A, Kelly, J. and Boulter, L. (1993) *Benchmarking for Competitive Advantage,* 1st Edition, London: Financial Times.

Bendell, A., Kelly, J. and Boulter, L. (1997) *Benchmarking for Competitive Advantage,* 2nd Edition. New Jersey: Barnes and Noble.

Berente, N. (2007) C. West Churchman: Champion of the Systems Approach. [Online], http://filer.case.edu/nxb41/churchman.html (accessed 5 January 2014).

Checkland, P. (2010) *Systems Thinking, Systems Practice.* New York: Springer Science and Business Media, LLC.

Checkland, P. and Haynes, M. (2006) Varieties of Systems Thinking: The Case of Soft Systems Methodology [Online], http://onlinelibrary.wiley.com/doi/10.1002/sdr.4260100207/abstract (accessed 20 September 2013).

Chesbourough, H. (2003) *Open Innovation: The New Imperative for Creating and Profiting from Technology*. Boston: Harvard Business School Publishing.

Chesbrough, W.W. and Appleyard, M.M. (2007) Open Innovation and Strategy, *California Management Review*, Vol. 50, No. 1, pp. 57–76.

Christauskas, C. and Miseviciene, R. (2012) Cloud Computing-Based Accounting for Small and Medium Sized Business, *Engineering Economics*, Vol. 23, No. 1, pp. 14–21.

Churchman, C.W. (1982) *Systems Approach and its Enemies*. New York: Basic Books.

Corporate Leadership Council (2002) High Performance Workforce: A Quantative Anaylsis of the Effectiveness of Performance Management Strategies [Online], http://marble-arch-online-courses. s3.amazonaws.com/CLC_Building_the_High_Performance_ Workforce_A_Quantitative_Analysis_of_the_Effectiveness_of_ Performance_Management_Strategies1.pdf (accessed 5 January 2014).

Darwin, C. (1859) *On the Origin of Species*. London: Wordsworth.

Deloitte (2014) Target Operating Model [Online], http://www.deloitte.com/ view/en_nl/nl/services/consulting/strategy-and-operations/operations-excellence/operational-strategy-and-the-target-operating-model-design/ index.htm (accessed 5 January 2014).

Denison, D., Haaland, S. and Goelzer, P. (2004) Corporate Culture and Organisational Effectiveness: Is Asia Different from the Rest of the World? *Organisational Dynamics*, Vol. 33 No. 1, pp. 98–109 [Online], www. sciencedirect.com (accessed: 14 October 2013).

Dougherty, D. (2008) Bridging Social Constraint and Social Action to Design Organizations for Innovation, *Organization Studies*, Vol. 29, No. 3, pp. 415–434.

EFQM (2013) The EFQM Excellence Model [Online], http:/www.efqm.org/the-efqm-excellence-model (accessed 12 September 2013).

Financial Reporting Council (2012) UK Corporate Governance Code [Online], http://www.frc.org.uk/Our-Work/Codes-Standards/Corporate-governance/UK-Corporate-Governance-Code.aspx (accessed 14 October 2013).

Fischer, M.D. and Ferlie, E. (2013) Resisting Hybridisation between Modes of Clinical Risk Management: Contradiction, Contest, and the Production of Intractable Conflict, *Accounting, Organizations and Society*, Vol. 38, pp. 30–49.

Foster, R. and Kaplins, S. (2001) *Creative Destruction: Why Leading Companies Abruptly Lose Their Markets to New Competitors*. New York: Barnes and Noble.

Gray, C. and Lawson, E. (2000) *Project Management: The Managerial Process*. New York: McGraw Hill.

Hendricks, K. and Singhal, V. (1999) Quality Awards and the Market Value of the Firm: An Empirical Investigation [Online], http://www.wlu.ca/documents/17430/quality_awards_marketvalue.pdf (accessed 20 October 2013).

Hersey, P., Blanchard, K. and Dewey, E. (1996) *Management of Organisational Behaviour: Utilising Human Resources*. New Jersey: Prentice Hall.

Hofstede, G. (1984). *Culture's Consequences: International Differences in Work-Related Values*, 2nd edition. Beverly Hills: SAGE Publications.

Hofstede, G. and Minkov, M. (2010) *Cultures and Organisations: Software of the Mind*, 3rd edition. New York: McGraw Hill.

Holme, R. and Watts, P. (2000) Corporate Social Responsibility: Making Good Business Sense World Council for Sustainable Development [Online], http://www.wbcsd.org/web/publications/csr2000.pdf (accessed: 15 October 2013).

Hubbard, W. (2009) *The Failure of Risk Management: Why it is Broken and How to Fix it*. New Jersey: John Wiley and Sons.

International Organization for Standardization (2008) ISO 9001 2008 [Online], http://www.iso.org/iso/iso_9000 (accessed 9 September 2013).

International Organization for Standardization (2009) *ISO 31000:2009; Risk Management – Principles and Guidelines*. Geneva: International Organization for Standardization.

International Organization for Standardization (2011) *ISO 13053-1: 2011 Quantitative Methods in Process Improvement: Six Sigma, Part 1.* Geneva: International Organization for Standardization.

Joyce, W., Nitin, N. and Robertson, J. (2003) *What Really Works: The 4+2 Business Formula for Sustained Success.* New York: HarperCollins.

Kanda, M. (2012) Can a Company Live Forever? [Online], http://www.bbc.co.uk/news/mobile/business-16611040 (accessed 5 September 2013).

Kotter, J. (2013) The Eight Step Process for Leading Change [Online], http://www.kotterinternational.com/our-principles/changesteps (accessed 5 January 2014).

KPMG (2012) Expectations of Risk Management Outpacing Capabilities–It's Time for Action [Online], http://www.kpmg.com/global/en/issuesandinsights/articlespublications/risk-management-outpacing-capabilities/pages/default.aspx (accessed 14 October 2013).

Lancaster University Management School (2014) Professor Peter Checkland [Online], http://www.lums.lancs.ac.uk/mansci/profiles/peter-checkland/ (accessed 5 January 2014).

LaPorte, T.R. (1996). High Reliability Organizations: Unlikely, Demanding and At Risk. *Journal of Contingencies and Crisis Management*, Vol. 4, pp. 60–71.

Lewin, K. (1951) *Resolving Social Conflicts: Field Theory in Social Science,* Washington: APA.

Lovelock, C.H. (1983) Classifying Services to Gain Strategic Marketing Insights, *The Journal of Marketing*, Vol. 47, No. 3, pp. 9–20.

Meadows, D. (2014) Leverage Points: Places to Intervene in a System [Online], http://www.donellameadows.org/archives/leverage-points-places-to-intervene-in-a-system/ (accessed 5 January 2014).

McKeown, M. (2011) *The Strategy Book: How to Think and Act.* London: Pearson Education.

Meadows, D. (1999) Leverage Points – Places to Intervene in a System [Online], http://www.sustainabilityinstitute.org/pubs/Leverage_Points.pdf (accessed 14 October 2013).

Minzberg, H. (1979) An Emerging Strategy of 'Direct' Research. *Administrative Science Quarterly*, Vol. 24, No. 4, pp. 582–589.

Minzuno, S. Akao, Y. and Yoshizawa, T. (1991) *Quality Function Development: Integrating Customer Requirements into Product Design*. New York: Productivity Press.

Nohria, N., Joyce, W. and Roberson, B. (2003) What Really Works, *Harvard Business Review*, July 2003.

Northhouse, P.G. (2013) *Leadership: Theory and Practice*, 6th edition. Los Angeles: Sage.

Parasuraman, A., Zeithaml, V.A. and Berry, L.L. (1985) A Conceptual Model of Service Quality and its Implications for Future Research, *The Journal of Marketing*, 49, No. 4, Autumn, pp. 41–50.

Parsons, C. (2011) Roads to Ruin: A Study of Major Risk Events. The Cass Business Institute [Online], https://www.cassknowledge.com/research/article/roads-ruin-study-major-risk-events (accessed 14 October 2013).

Peters, T. (2011) A Brief History of the 7-S ('McKinsey 7-S') Model [Online], http://www.tompeters.com/dispatches/012016.php (accessed 5 January 2014).

Peters, T. and Waterman, R.H. Jnr (1982) *In Search of Excellence: Lessons from America's Best Run Companies*. New York: Harper and Row.

Pfeffer, J. (2007) *What Were They Thinking: Unconventional Wisdom about Management*. Boston: Harvard Business School Publishing.

Porter, M. (1979) How Competitive Forces Shape Strategy. *Harvard Business Review* [Online], http://hbr.org/1979/03/how-competitive-forces-shape-strategy/ar/1 (accessed 12 October 2013).

Prahalad, C. and Ramaswamy, V. (2000) *The Future of Competition*. Boston: Harvard Business School Publishing.

Rajeshwari, S. (2012) Decoding the Matrix: Inherent Challenges and Opportunities [Online], http://www.shrmindia.org/hr-buzz/blogs/shrm-india/decoding-matrix-inherent-challenges-and-opportunities (accessed 5 January 2014).

Schmenner, R. (1986) How Can Service Businesses Survive and Prosper? *Sloan Business Review*, Vol. 11, No. 1 [Online], http://sloanreview.mit.edu/article/how-can-service-businesses-survive-and-prosper/ (accessed 5 January 2014).

Schumpeter, J. (1942) *Capitalism, Socialism and Democracy*. London: Allen and Unwin.

Shingo, S. (1986) *Zero Quality Control and the Poka-Yoke System*. London: Productivity Press.

Shostack, L. (1984) Design Services that Deliver, *Harvard Business Review*, Vol. 62, No. 1, pp. 133–139.

Slack, N., Chambers, S. and Johnston, R. (2010) *Operations Management*. London: Prentice Hall.

Slim, W. (1957) Fourth William Queale Lecture, *Australian Army Journal*, September 1957, pp. 5–13.

Spencer, H. (1884) *Principles of Biology*. London: Harrison and Sons.

Taleb, N. (2013) *Antifragile: Things that Gain from Disorder*. London: Penguin.

The Deming Prize (2013) Deming Prize Model [Online], http://deming.org (accessed 19 September 2013).

The EFQM Excellence Model (2012) [Online], http://www.efqm.org/the-efqm-excellence-model (accessed 12 September 2013).

The Foundation for the Malcolm Baldrige National Quality Award (2012) Malcolm Baldrige National Quality Award Model [Online], http://www.nist.gov/baldrige/publications/upload/2011_2012_Business_Nonprofit_Criteria.pdf (accessed 10 September 2013).

The Geert Hofstede Centre (1980) Dr Geert Hofstede Cultural Dimensions [Online], http://geert-hofstede.com/countries.html (accessed 17 September 2013).

Tidd, J. and Bessant, J. (2007) *Innovation and Entrepreneurship*. Chichester: Wiley and Sons.

Toyota Motor Corporation (2014) [Online], http://www.toyota-global.com/company/vision_philosophy/toyota_production_system/jidoka.html (accessed 5 January 2014).

Triarchy Press (2014) Russell Ackoff [Online], http://www.triarchypress.net/russ-ackoff.html (accessed 5 January 2014).

Tuckman, B. (1965) Developmental Sequence in Small Groups, *Psychological Bulletin*, Vol. 63, No. 6, pp. 384–99.

Tushman, M.L. and O Reilly, C.A. III (1996) Ambidextrous Organizations: Managing Evolutionary and Revolutionary Change, *California Management Review*, Vol. 38, No. 4, pp. 8–30.

Womack, J.P., Jones, D.T. and Roos, D. (2007) *The Machine That Changed the World*, New edition. Detroit: Free Press.

Index

For Product Safety Concerns and Information please contact our
EU representative GPSR@taylorandfrancis.com Taylor & Francis
Verlag GmbH, Kaufingerstraße 24, 80331 München, Germany